CyberStrategies

Other VNR Business Technology/Communications Books. . . .

- **Designing TCP/IP Internetworks**
  by Geoff Bennett
- **Cases in Network Implementation: Enterprise Networking**
  by William E. Bracker, Jr. and Ray Sarch
- **Information Proficiency: The Key To The Information Age**
  by Thomas J. Buckholtz
- **Doing More Business on the Internet**
  by Mary J. Cronin
- **Currid's Guide to Business Technology**
  by Cheryl C. Currid
- **Networking Device Drivers**
  by Sanjay Dhawan
- **Routing in Today's Internetworks**
  by Mark Dickie
- **Spinning the Web: How To Provide Information On The Internet**
  by Andrew Ford
- **Digital Signal Processing in Communications**
  by Marvin E. Frerking
- **The Complete Cyberspace Reference and Directory**
  by Gilbert Held
- **Working With NetWare: For Network Supervisors and Users**
  by Gilbert Held
- **Global Expansion In The Information Age: Big Planet, Small World**
  by Thomas J. Howard
- **Online Marketing Handbook: How To Sell, Advertise, Publicize, and Promote Your Products and Services On the Internet and Commercial Online Systems**
  by Daniel S. Janal
- **Digital Telephony and Network Integration, 2nd Edition**
  by Bernhard E. Keiser and Eugene Strange
- **Internet Trainer's Guide**
  by Diane K. Kovacs
- **Low-Cost E-Mail With UUCP: Integrating UNIX, DOS, Windows and MAC**
  by Thomas Wm. Madron
- **The Illustrated Network Book: A Graphic Guide to Understanding Computer Networks**
  by Matthew G. Naugle
- **Making Telecommuting Happen: A Guide for Telemanagers and Telecommuters**
  by Jack M. Nilles
- **JPEG Still Image Data Compression Standard**
  by William B. Pennebaker and Joan L. Mitchell
- **Successful Reengineering: An Implementation Guide To Using Information Technology**
  by Daniel Petrozzo and John C. Stepper
- **Reducing the Cost of LAN Ownership: The Business of Running a Network**
  by Salvatore L. Salamone and Greg Gianforte
- **Using Wireless Communications in Business**
  by Andrew M. Seybold
- **Fax Power: High Leverage Business Communications**
  by Philip C. W. Sih
- **Applications for Distributed Systems and Network Management**
  by Kornel Terplan and Jill Huntington-Lee
- **SNMP Application Developer's Manual**
  by Robert L. Townsend
- **A Network of Objects: How To Lower Your Computing Cost and Improve Your Applications Delivery**
  by Thomas C. Tsai
- **Communications Standard Dictionary, 2nd Edition**
  by Martin H. Weik, DSc.
- **Enterprise Networking for Information Systems Professionals**
  by Norman Witkin

CyberStrategies

How to Build an Internet-Based Information System

Michael L. Carroll

with contributions from W. Scott Downs

VAN NOSTRAND REINHOLD

I(T)P™ A Division of International Thomson Publishing Inc.

New York • Albany • Bonn • Boston • Detroit • London • Madrid • Melbourne
Mexico City • Paris • San Francisco • Singapore • Tokyo • Toronto

I(T)P™ A division of International Thomson Publishing, Inc.
The ITP logo is a trademark under license

Printed in the United States of America

For more information, contact:

Van Nostrand Reinhold
115 Fifth Avenue
New York, NY 10003

International Thomson Publishing GmbH
Königswinterer Strasse 418
53227 Bonn
Germany

International Thomson Publishing Europe
Berkshire House 168-173
High Holborn
London WCIV 7AA
England

International Thomson Publishing Asia
221 Henderson Road #05-10
Henderson Building
Singapore 0315

Thomas Nelson Australia
102 Dodds Street
South Melbourne, 3205
Victoria, Australia

International Thomson Publishing Japan
Hirakawacho Kyowa Building, 3F
2-2-1 Hirakawacho
Chiyoda-ku, 102 Tokyo
Japan

Nelson Canada
1120 Birchmount Road
Scarborough, Ontario
Canada M1K 5G4

International Thomson Editores
Campos Eliseos 385, Piso 7
Col. Polanco
11560 Mexico D.F. Mexico

1 2 3 4 5 6 7 8 9 10 QEBFF 01 00 99 98 97 96 95

Library of Congress Cataloging-in-Publication Data
Carroll, Mike L. (Michael L.)
CyberStrategies: how to build an Internet-Based information system / Mike L. Carroll, W. Scott Downs
p. cm.
Includes index.
ISBN 0-442-01988-2
1. Information technology—Management. 2. Information resources management. 3. Internet (Computer network) 4. Information superhighway—Management. I. Downs, W. Scott II. Title.
HDSO.2.C368 1995
658.4'038—dc20 95-16742
CIP

CONTENTS

PREFACE

Many firms today grapple with a glut of electronic data spawned by substantial stockpiles of incompatible computers. They have Macs and PCs, workstations and minis, mainframes and supercomputers. They have disks, CDs, and tapes in all sizes and shapes, and data in all formats: megabytes, gigabytes, terabytes of data—but all locked and frozen in the incompatible computing systems that gave them birth.

Welcome to the 1990s. Welcome to the Information Age.

Never before has there been so much information to be shared—and so much difficulty in sharing it. Many say that the winners of the 90s will be those who can effectively manage and make rapid use of information. Yet we generate new piles of information at a bewildering rate. We are drowning in a sea of information.

Welcome to the Information Age. Welcome to Infoglut!

This book is about an approach to information sharing and computer interaction that offers some hope to a world drowning in information. It isn't a new approach and we certainly didn't invent it. In fact, although it has gained noticeable public attention in recent years, it has been developing steadily for nearly 30 years. It is the approach that gave rise to the Internet.

This book is not about the Internet itself—it is about an approach to information handling and sharing that is characteristic of the Internet. It is about how you can use this approach internally within your existing corporate information system. It is about building an enterprise-wide, corporate-internal internetwork using Internet tools and methods.

From 1992 until early 1995, while at the Lockheed Corporation (now part of Lockheed Martin), I was privileged to participate in the development of an information system called the Technology Broker System. As its name suggests, this system facilitates the sharing of technology-related information across the corporation. Its purpose was to encourage scientists and engineers to exchange research data and collaborate on technical projects.

The Lockheed experiment got off the ground in 1991, when Dr. Marc Fleischmann, then a young computer scientist at the Lockheed Missiles and Space Company in Palo Alto, California, suggested that some public domain Internet tools called NetNews and WAIS could be used to meet the system's requirements. Few would have guessed at that time that this experimental system would grow within Lockheed to become a microcosm of the Internet. Today, the Technology Broker System is a thriving electronic community with new members and information sources being added every day. It has outgrown its original purpose as an information system for scientists and engineers, and now serves knowledge workers in many functional areas including business development, manufacturing, information services, communications, and legal. With the merger in March 1995 of Lockheed and Martin Marietta to form the Lockheed Martin company, information systems specialists have integrated similar systems on the Martin side with those on the Lockheed side. The new system will span dozens of operating companies and be accessible eventually to over 150,000 Lockheed Martin employees.

Lockheed Martin is not alone in this experiment. Hughes, Rockwell, IBM, AT&T, SAS Institute, and countless others have independently discovered the potential of Internet technologies for building corporate-wide information systems.

This book gathers and shares what we at Lockheed and others elsewhere have learned about building Internet-based information systems, sometimes called Internet clones.

Naturally, I think you have much to gain from using Internet tools and methods in a business environment; otherwise I wouldn't have written this book. I have seen first-hand that Internet tools can foster wide-area communications and open up new opportunities for collaboration among knowledge workers within an extended, virtual enterprise. But I certainly don't pretend that these tools are a panacea for all the ills of a company's information systems. The Internet paradigm is not a silver bullet with which to slay the werewolf of infoglut. On the contrary, I have found that some of the Internet tools and methods are not yet ready for prime time in a business. And, of course, no technology can make up for deficient processes or a poorly trained work force. This book tries to keep the pros and cons of using these tools and methods in proper perspective.

I also do not propose Internet-based information systems as a wholesale replacement for more traditional ones. Internet tools are still in their infancy and in many ways lack the sophistication and robustness needed of mission-critical business information systems. Their developers certainly did not intend for these tools to fulfill the requirements imposed by such mission-critical environments. These tools provide neither the complete functionality nor the robustness required in such environments. Nonetheless, I believe that you can use Internet tools effectively to augment your existing systems in beneficial ways.

In this book, I do not examine each Internet tool in great detail; there are already many good books on the market to guide the user through each keystroke and mouse-click of the more popular Internet tools. *CyberStrategies* is not merely another Internet user's guide. I discuss only briefly the prominent features of various Internet client tools available today; instead, I emphasize how you can use them in a business environment.

I strive in this book to blend the management and technical aspects of building an Internet clone for internal business use. The intended audience are management and information systems professionals who need to gain a big-picture understanding of how to integrate Internet tools in the work place. I have organized the book according to the standard system development methodology. This methodology begins with a consideration of goals and constraints, sometimes referred to as requirements engineering. We view the Internet tools themselves as constraints, since they are the given building blocks for constructing an Internet-based information system. Next we consider the synthesis and evaluation of alternative system architectures. Then we follow with a consideration of the detailed specification and design of the selected architecture and the actual construction of the system. We then round out the discussion with an examination of the major issues involved in operating and maintaining the system.

Next, we examine some of the trends likely to impact the course of future evolution for such systems. Finally, we close with a retrospective consideration of the merits of building an Internet clone and recap some of the major themes developed throughout the book.

In Appendix A, we discuss the client/server paradigm and provide more background on the technologies underlying the Internet. We hope to assist those readers not familiar with the jargon of networking and client/server. Appendix B provides some general guidance on how to plan and execute a pilot project aimed at evaluating Internet technologies in a corporate setting.

ACKNOWLEDGMENTS

Many people played a role in the development of this book, and I would like to publicly acknowledge their contributions. First, I would like to thank my wife Leandra Carroll for putting up with this project which took much longer than originally expected. Second, I want to thank Scott Downs for his valuable contributions to this book. Third, I want to acknowledge my indebtedness to my former employer, the Lockheed Martin Corporation, for having afforded me the opportunity to discover, experiment with, struggle with, and grow in understanding of Internet technologies through involvement with the Technology Broker System. In particular, I wish to acknowledge the generous support of Dr. R. P. Chris Caren, former vice president, science and engineering, Lockheed Corporation. Without the vision and insight of Dr. Caren there would never have been a Technology Broker System. Finally, I wish to thank the people at Van Nostrand Reinhold who patiently held my hand throughout the publishing process. In particular, I am indebted to Neil Levine, Mike Sherry, and Lesley Rock, whose professionalism and encouragement kept me going when the going was rough and there seemed to be no end in sight.

Michael L. Carroll
Upland, California
October 1, 1995

CyberStrategies

Chapter 1

INTRODUCING THE INTERNET AND CORPORATE INTERNET CLONES

The Internet is a hot topic. Hardly a day goes by without the Internet being mentioned in the newspaper, on the radio, or on television. Almost every month a major conference convenes in which librarians, computer professionals, and marketing specialists cram workshops to learn more about the Internet. Even Chief Information Officers of large corporations are busy learning more about the Internet and its business potential. Providers of Internet access and vendors of Internet navigation software seem to be popping up on every street corner. Organizations of all kinds—especially businesses—are rushing to connect to the Internet, and many are already conducting commerce there.

Meanwhile, many businesses are experimenting with Internet tools and techniques within their own corporate information systems. At Lockheed Martin Corp., engineers and information systems specialists have installed over a dozen information servers using public domain software retrieved from the Internet. These servers provide information on aerospace industry news, government contracting, R&D reports, and U.S. Air Force mission need statements. Software engineers use USENET news, the electronic bulletin board scheme of the Internet, to post questions to each other regarding the availability and location of reusable software assets.

At GM Hughes and SAS Institute, much the same is happening. Archives of public domain software and internal newsfeeds are cropping up at many Hughes divisions from California to Maryland. SAS Institute has deployed Internet technologies widely to support information sharing and collaborative software development.

Companies like Lockheed and Hughes are creating Internet clones—microcosmic imitations of the Internet itself within the confines of a secure, corporate-wide internetwork of computers. And they are not alone. Hundreds of companies throughout the world are not only discovering the Internet as a resource for communication and information retrieval, but are also beginning to incorporate the services, methods, and tools of the Internet into their own private information systems.

In order to understand the integration and use of Internet tools and methods in a business, you must first understand what the Internet is and how it works. Therefore, in this introductory chapter we present first an overview of the Internet itself and discuss some of the technical, social, and economic dimensions of the Internet that are of interest to business users. We then proceed to introduce corporate Internet clones, which are enterprise-wide internetworks that follow the Internet paradigm.

1.1 The Internet

The Internet is certainly one of the most talked about computer-related phenomena of the 1990s. Everyone—from CEO to secretary—is connecting to the Internet, and, even if not quite "surfing the net," they are testing the waters with occasional electronic mail. At cocktail parties, young professionals exchange e-mail addresses like business cards. Indeed, if your business card does not already have an e-mail address on it, some may regard you as computer-illiterate.

What is the Internet? Is it a fad? Or does it represent a significant technological development likely to affect the way we communicate and do business? If it isn't a fad, what is its real potential?

1.1.1 What Is It? What Isn't It?

As with anything showing phenomenal growth and economic promise, considerable hype surrounds the Internet. There are many out there who want to make a fast buck off the Internet phenomenon. Some play up the quantity and quality of information available on the Internet and play down the difficulties in discovering it. Perhaps overuse of the term "information superhighway" adds to the confusion.

In this section, we try to look past the hype and take a sober look at some of the business-relevant facts concerning the Internet.

1.1.1.1 A Network of Networks

First of all, the Internet is not really a thing at all; i.e., it is not a single tidy network of similar computers running similar software. No single organization owns or manages the Internet. Indeed, many people find it hard to grasp that no one really owns and no one really manages the Internet. For it is not really a single network at all. The term "Internet" derives from "internetwork" and simply refers to a worldwide collection of computers and networks that have agreed to interconnect and communicate using a common, non-proprietary protocol suite called TCP/IP.[1] In short, the Internet has emerged because the owners of many isolated networks have agreed to interconnect their networks. As a result, these networks are no longer isolated. Although it appears to be a single network, the Internet is actually a vast collection of networks; it is many separate networks cooperating as one.

Although it is correct to say that no one owns the Internet as a whole, each of its pieces has an owner. There are several major networks comprising the "backbone" of the Internet. The NSFNET, for example, is one of the more prominent backbone networks in the United States. Metaphorically, you can view each of the Internet's constituent networks as a small country or fiefdom. Although each of these "countries" has its own independent government, there is no single "world" government. To facilitate the development of technical standards and foster collaborative research, however, several consensus-building organizations like the Internet Society and the Internet Architecture Board have sprung up.

Although it is technically correct to say that the Internet is not a single network, it does have the look and feel of a single network, and people often call it simply "the Net." We will adopt this usage as well. Indeed, the Net, even though not a single physical network, is a single virtual network.

1.1.1.2 The Miracle of TCP/IP

This power of TCP/IP to enable isolated networks to interconnect is, in our opinion, one of the greatest byproducts of the Cold War.[2] We remember Tang orange juice and Teflon touted as important byproducts of the space race. Well, the impact of TCP/IP on humankind far exceeds that of Tang and Teflon. TCP/IP has enabled the creation of a whole new community called cyberspace.

1.1.1.3 Who Pays for the Internet?

Many people still think the U.S. government still subsidizes the Internet for non-profit academic and military research and that the Internet is, therefore, completely off-limits for commercial activities. This is a misconception. It is no longer true that the government subsidizes the NSFNET, formerly the Internet's central backbone network. Some major networks that are part of the Internet are still owned and operated by the government, and it is still inappropriate to use such networks for commercial purposes. These networks have guidelines called ***acceptable use policies***, or ***AUPs***, which limit how you use them.

---

[1] TCP/IP, which stands for Transmission Control Protocol/Internet Protocol, is actually a family of protocols.

[2] The TCP/IP protocol suite was developed under the sponsorship of the U.S. Department of Defense's Advanced Research Projects Agency (ARPA). The original charter was to develop a computer network for command and control capable of surviving a nuclear attack.

The funding for the Internet has shifted, however, from public to private sources. The NSF has phased out its sponsorship and management of the NSFNET. As of April 30, 1995, the NSFNET is officially retired. Each of the major regional networks that formerly connected to the NSFNET backbone has elected to adopt one of the major telecommunications carrier services like MCI, AT&T, and Sprint. They have also agreed to interconnect at ***network access points***, or ***NAPs***. There are several NAPs located at key points around the country.

So the real answer to the question of who pays for the Internet is simple: You do! Those who subsidize the Internet are the thousands of businesses who buy high-speed dedicated links to the Internet through a private Internet access provider and the millions of individual users who pay for dial-up access. The Internet is going commercial.

Thanks to organizations like the Commercial Internet eXchange Association, or CIX Association, it is now possible for commercial Internet access providers to interconnect directly with each other and bypass those portions of the Internet that are still restricted to non-commercial uses. The CIX Association is a non-profit trade association whose members are public data internetwork service providers. Member networks must provide either TCP/IP or OSI network services to the general public. The CIX Association promotes both national and international public data internetworking by providing a neutral forum for the exchange of ideas and the pursuit of experimental projects among suppliers of internetworking services. It facilitates the development of consensus among its members on legislative and policy issues, and encourages technical research and development for the benefit of suppliers and customers of data communications internetworking services.

If your organization seeks a connection to the Internet, contacting a CIX member is a good place to start. CIX member networks exchange commercial data traffic with each other on a peer basis, thus avoiding the restricted, government-subsidized networks.[3] However, not all Internet access providers are members of CIX, nor does lack of membership prevent many such providers from exchanging data traffic. It appears as of July 1995 that, in the long run, CIX will no longer occupy the central position for commercial Internet access which it enjoyed during the early years of Internet commercialization.

1.1.1.4 It's More Than Just a Network

Of course, an internetwork, to be useful, needs more than simple connectivity and standard protocols—it also needs common applications software and shared information resources. This is precisely what the Internet has to offer. Certainly, the recent explosion of interest in the Internet is no accident; the Internet marvel has coincided with the emergence of some

---

[3] For a list of CIX member networks, contact the CIX gopher server at *gopher.cix.org*, or the CIX Web server at *www.cix.org*.

useful application programs that glue the network together into a cohesive whole and give it a remarkable degree of virtual homogeneity. It would be hard to overestimate, for example, the significance in this regard of the World Wide Web and gopher systems. The World Wide Web (or, simply, the Web) links users and resources more profoundly than the simple connectivity of wires and protocols. With the Web's hyperlinks—and with a web browser like *NCSA Mosaic* or *Netscape Navigator*, the Web's most popular, easy-to-use, point-and-click interfaces—you can retrieve information files from around the world almost as easily as files from you own local disk drive; thousands of worldwide computers are now within a few mouse clicks' reach of your own computer. Such collaborative systems of applications are helping to bring the Internet out of the research laboratory and into the marketplace.

Although the Web is now easy to use and shows considerable promise for integrating diverse file access retrieval protocols, the Internet is still a long ways from becoming merely an extension of the user's desktop. The local loop of voice-grade lines in the telephone system still largely limits network bandwidth. On a normal, voice-grade line, the maximum data rate is generally 56 Kbps; while downloading a graphic image file at this rate requires patience, retrieving a short video clip seems to take forever.[4]

1.1.2 The Size and Growth of the Internet

The Internet, already quite large, is growing at a steady rate. Some claim that it already has nearly 25 million users and is growing at almost 10 percent per month. Difficult to verify, these numbers are subject to debate (Lewis 1994).

Figure 1-1 shows a graph of hosts connecting to the Internet, as estimated by Mark Lottor's Zone program.[5] Using an estimate of 10 users per host, you can conclude from this graph that the number of Internet users is appoximately 48 million users.[6]

---

[4] It must be remembered that at NSCA, the developer of Mosaic, high-speed graphics workstations and T-1 communications speeds are quite common and perhaps taken for granted.

[5] Mark Lottor works at Network Wizards. Information on the Zone program can be obtained from the World Wide Web site at *http://www.nw.com.*

[6] Internet demographics are unclear. It is not obvious, for example, that the estimate of 100 users per network is justified.

Regardless of the actual number of users connecting to the Internet, the growth trends are clear. The graph in Figure 1-1 indicates nearly doubles every year!

Even more startling than the growth of the Internet is the growth of that important subset of the Internet known as the World Wide Web, often referred to as WWW, W3, or simply the Web. The Web is a collection of servers—called Web servers—interlinked using a mechanism called ***hyperlinking***. This system yields a virtually integrated library of information, thus making over 12,000 computers and their data files appear to the user as a single information resource.

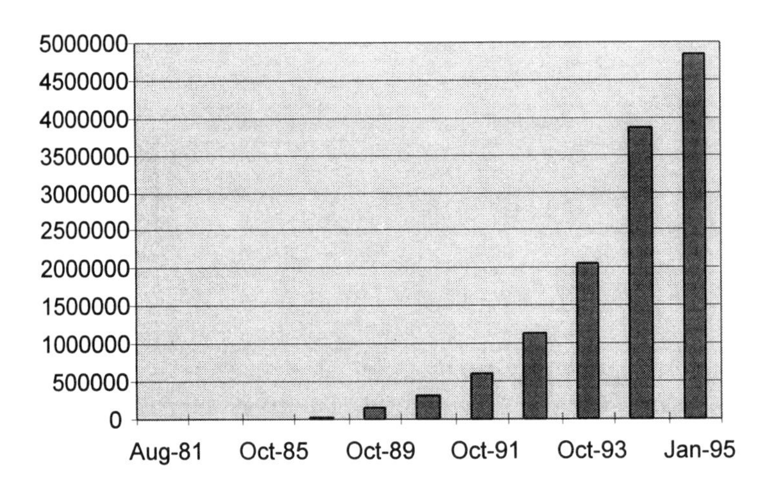

Figure 1-1. Hosts Connecting to the Internet

Figure 1-2 shows a graph of Web growth as captured by Matthew Gray's World Wide Web Wanderer program. The Web owes its tremendous growth to the appearance of *NCSA Mosaic*, the first multimedia, graphical user interface providing easy access to the Web's hyperlinked information resources. *NCSA Mosaic* appeared in the spring of 1993; as the graph in Figure 1-2 shows, the tremendous growth of the Web followed closely on the heels of *NCSA Mosaic*. It is nothing short of astonishing that in only six months time, from June to December 1994, the number of Web servers grew by an order of magnitude!

The World Wide Web and Web browsers like *NCSA Mosaic* are to the information age what Sputnik was to the space age. Suddenly, a whole new frontier has opened up, the frontier of cyberspace—a frontier limited only by the human mind and its ability to imagine. Of course, Internet veterans are quick to point out that the Internet is not really new. It has been incubating and gestating for over 25 years. But with graphical Web browsers, millions of mere mortals suddenly have easy access to this frontier.

With the recent explosive growth of the public, worldwide Internet and the emergence of private Internet clones within corporations, two previously separate worlds are beginning to collide: the academic and the commercial. The age of innocence for the

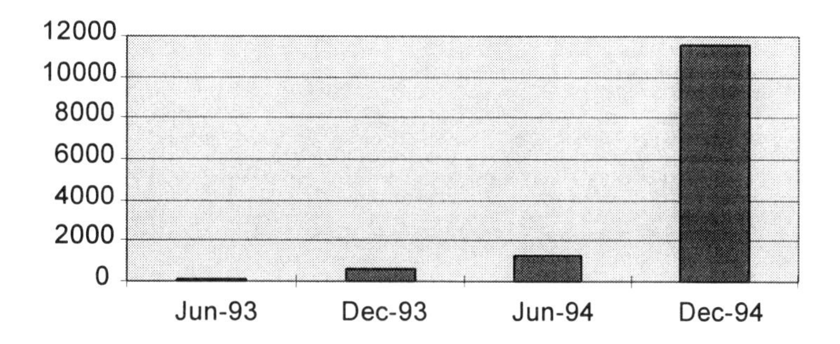

Figure 1-2.* *World Wide Web Growth

Source: Matthew Gray, mkgray@netgen.com

Internet, when it was a sleepy virtual village of researchers, appears to be lost forever. The Internet will never again be the same. Although some lament this loss of original innocence and predict the imminent demise of the Internet (Elmer-Dewitt 1994), others are more optimistic. We think the "collision" of these two worlds, the academic and the commercial, yields a dynamic tension bringing value to both and making the Internet a better place for all. The resulting cross-fertilization will make both domains more robust. Academics will learn something about the economics of information and business people will learn something about openness and collaboration. After all, in the real world, many domains coexist and copenetrate; we should expect the same of cyberspace. And the Internet is the de facto cyberspace.

1.1.3 The Openness of the Internet

The Internet is conspicuous for its "openness." By this we mean that the Internet is an open environment in which users can access many information resources freely without the encumbrance of user authentication. Most host computers on the Internet are open to anyone and do not require special accounts and passwords. They are publicly accessible. Many services do not require a login at all. You simply connect to the appropriate server and access the available information. Other services do require logins, but either have publicly available passwords or will accept any stream of characters as a password.

This does not mean that there is no such thing as user authentication on the Internet. Indeed there is. You can configure some applications so that they require standard user names and passwords. However, since data packets containing your password usually travel to their destination in the clear, someone "out there" on the Internet can intercept, capture and exploit your information.[7] This, too, is an aspect of the Internet's openness. We shall have much more to say on the subject of security in Chapter 5.

Nevertheless, the openness of the Internet is not an impediment to conducting business transactions there. The vast majority of normal business communications do not require explicit user authentication. The normal use of the telephone, for example, does not usually require any such authentication.[8]

Yet another kind of openness prevailing on the Internet is a cultural one. Users are very passionate about freedom of speech and the free exchange of information. Censorship is certainly not welcome. This cultural sense of openness is doubtless also a legacy of the Internet's academic roots.

There is a final connotation of openness, however, that should be of considerable interest to businesses. It has to do with open systems technology. By an open system is generally meant a vendor-independent system, affording some degree of "plug and play" and making it easy for systems to interact and communicate. This connotation of "openness" is indeed positive, and it is this connotation, we think, that is rapidly making the Internet the common denominator of inter-business networking.

---

[7] There are several client/server pairs on the Net today that do use encryption techniques for transactions. Netscape Communications' Netscape Navigator and their Commerce Web server can cooperate using encryption.

[8] It can be safely argued, of course, that our ability to recognize the human voice at the other end constitutes implicit user authentication.

1.1.4 Social Aspects of the Internet

Openness, combined with global connectivity, numerous information resources, and user-friendly applications, has transformed the Internet into a worldwide virtual community. The demographics of this community are complex and rapidly evolving. Millions of people are interacting in new ways, displaying new kinds of social behavior, and forming new kinds of social units. In this section, we explore some of these new social aspects of the Internet community, and we examine their implications for businesses using the Internet and incorporating Internet methods and technologies into their corporate information systems.

1.1.4.1 The Electronic Wild West

Wallich (1994) has likened the Internet to an old west frontier town. Like a frontier town, there is little enforceable law and order.[9] Although the street battles of this town are fought with keyboards instead of real guns, keyboards can wreak plenty of havoc. There are some rowdy, rude, and unruly people roaming the alleys of this cybertown, and merchants wishing to set up shop here need to protect themselves. Newcomers need to be aware of the prevailing mores or they might find themselves chased out of town by a lynching party of several thousand irate townspeople.[10]

Most users of the Internet, however, are civilized and adhere to a code of ethics known as netiquette. There are some taboos, some unofficial dos and don'ts, and some widely accepted processes for establishing new bulletin boards. Each major Internet access provider has a legally binding acceptable use policy.

1.1.4.2 Social Dynamics

Internet-style communications methods such as e-mail and USENET bulletin boards can influence in subtle ways the way people interact. Individuals who previously had little or no contact with each other can suddenly find themselves exchanging e-mail or participating in a bulletin board discussion. These electronic communication services facilitate new kinds of resource discovery and social networking among experts. In this subsection we take a look at some of the subtle influences these tools can have in the workplace.

---

[9] Although each local or regional network providing immediate access to the Internet has its own set of rules and guidelines for its own users, those rules and guidelines do not extend beyond the boundaries of the local network. Other local networks are not bound by those rules.

[10] Canter and Siegel are two Arizona lawyers who experienced first-hand what it is like to be lynched in cybertown. For details, see Elmer-Dewitt (1994).

On the Internet, people converse mainly in two ways—through electronic mail, generally known as e-mail, and USENET news, the distributed, electronic bulletin board system of the Internet. Electronic mail interaction is usually personal—a direct, one-to-one, electronic correspondence between two people; but it can also be a one-to-many broadcast from one user to several.

With one-to-one e-mail, a user sends a message directly to another individual user; with one-to-many e-mail broadcasting, a user sends copies of a single message to multiple recipients. Mailing lists can be either private or public. With a private list, the sender controls and maintains the list of subscribers. With a public list, however, a software tool like *listserv* or *majordomo* manages the subscription process automatically.

USENET news, the primary electronic bulletin board system of the Internet, consists of individual bulletin boards called newsgroups. Newsgroups are sequential collections of messages or notices "posted" by individual users. In Internet jargon, people usually refer to these notices as ***articles***. Newsgroups are dedicated to specific interest areas and are organized hierarchically, much like the file systems on most computers.[11] For example, there is a category of newsgroups called *comp*, which stands for "computer." Within this category, a subcategory called *comp.sys* deals with specific kinds of systems. Finally, at the lowest end of the hierarchy is *comp.sys.mac*, a specific newsgroup hosting discussions of interest to Macintosh computer users.

People in the workplace user seem to use internal e-mail and newsgroups differently than people on the Internet. The traditional users of the Internet often tend to be open in their use of e-mail and bulletin boards. By this, we mean they often say whatever they want and do not worry too much about the repercussions. Business users, however, are generally more cautious about what they say, and some are more reluctant to speak their minds, especially when it is not clear who is listening. This is true of all business communications, not just communication using Internet tools.

You can forward e-mail very easily. The original recipient of the message can easily forward a received message to someone else without notifying the original sender. This is one way e-mail differs from the telephone. Participants in a telephone conversation do not usually record their conversation. But e-mail is a store-and-forward technology that stores messages in electronic files—usually text files. With a few mouse clicks, e-mail recipients can easily forward their messages to others. Often the sender also retains a copy of the original message and can send it to yet another recipient without the original recipients knowing anything about it.

---

[11] On Network News Transport Protocol (NNTP) servers, newsgroups and articles are implemented as a tree of directories and files.

Of course, the same holds true of paper memos. But the slowness of generating and proofreading manually typed paper memos naturally retards the memo delivery process, thus facilitating further deliberation and perhaps better judgment. The old paper process reduced the risk of "knee-jerk" reactions. At the bat of an eye, however, you can whip out e-mail messages and send them to hundreds of recipients. Similarly, you can easily and rapidly forward received messages to others without fully considering the potential impact of their content.

E-mail is certainly not new in the workplace. Most major corporations have had internal e-mail systems for over 10 years. What is new is the connectivity with the outside world and the integration of e-mail with other applications. For example, you can easily convert e-mail messages to newsgroup articles, and vice versa. Thus, you cannot guarantee that even a personal, one-to-one e-mail conversation will remain private. What you send privately to a "friend" today may end up posted to a USENET newsgroup tomorrow.

A good rule of thumb for the use of e-mail in this new, Internet-connected business environment is never to say anything in an e-mail message that you wouldn't want to have shouted from the rooftops. At the very least, you should be keenly aware of who you are writing to and to what degree you can trust their judgment. If you intend the e-mail message to remain private, it is a good idea to explicitly state your intention in the e-mail message, preferably near the top. Even that, however, does not guarantee that the recipient will not forward your message to somebody else.

All this caution may seem silly to the non-business Internet cybernaut. Traditional Internet users are renowned for being unabashed in expressing their opinions in e-mail messages or newsgroup postings. Why all this caution for business users?

There are some good reasons, both private and business-related, for being cautious with e-mail and newsgroup postings. In the open world of the traditional Internet, people expect accountability far less than in the business world. The worst that can happen to you on the Internet is to be labeled a jerk, incur a few flames, or perhaps have your Internet access privileges revoked (this might be horrible enough to a confirmed cybernaut). In a business setting, however, people are constantly forming an opinion of you—and your company—by what you say and do. You can easily achieve the personal reputation within your company for being a loose cannon if you let loose too many half-baked e-mail messages. Far worse, you might make your company liable for the things you say via these electronic media.

Let's explore a little further these last-mentioned liability issues associated with e-mail and newsgroups. Any communication from one of your employees to someone outside tends to give the impression that he or she is acting as a representative of your business. This is certainly true, for example, of correspondence written on company stationary. If one of your employees gives advice that is harmful or leads to injury, the injured party may come after the employee and your business—especially if your company has deep pockets.

On the other hand, it is very easy to forge Internet addresses (Wallich 1994). This may make it impossible to prove in court that an e-mail message was authentic, i.e., not forged. A skillful demonstration of how easy it is to forge e-mail messages might be enough to convince a jury to throw a case out of court. By the same token, an ordinary e-mail message may fail to stand as a legally binding document. To achieve true legal standing, e-mail may have to include encryption and digital signature.[12]

Internal corporate policies on this matter are a good idea. For example, you should require that all users append a ***signature file*** to each e-mail message they compose. Signature files should contain appropriate disclaimers. This might provide a certain amount of protection. Most of the e-mail messages we receive from senders at other corporation have such disclaimers as part of their signatures. Nevertheless, the return address of your e-mail messages will doubtless contain something like *you@your_company.com*, forever associating your company with what you said in the message.

We hope the preceding comments do not cause undue paranoia. There are few court precedents to date providing clear guidance on what company policies ought to be; but caution is advisable if you would avoid having your company set the precedent for what not to do!

The foregoing remarks apply equally well—if not more so—to USENET newsgroup communications. Most USENET newsgroups are deliberately public. There is no telling who will read your postings or how they will interpret your ramblings. An Internet newsgroup is a good place to get quick answers to questions. With the unwritten law of free give and take on the Internet (see Section 1.1.4.4 on information bartering), you can receive advice on almost any subject. But it is just as easy to give away company secrets, and corporate users need to be aware of such risks. Public newsgroups are hardly the forum for members of one company to discuss their latest trade secrets.

The workaround is to build a system of private newsgroups behind a corporate firewall. Such newsgroups are invisible to the general Internet public. In fact, you can configure newsgroups with various access restrictions. You can also monitor and moderate their use. For more details on setting up private USENET newsgroups within a corporate firewall, consult Chapter 5.

Newsgroups represent a new paradigm in intracompany communications. Most internal corporate communications in the past have been one-way, either one-to-one or one-to-many (broadcast). The newsgroup model by contrast is many-to-many. Many people can monitor and participate in the newsgroup discussion. In this way, it resembles a meeting or teleconference. However, unlike these forms of conferencing, newsgroup communication is

---

[12] It should be pointed out that encryption and digital signatures are not yet in widespread use.

not bound by time constraints, and the discussions can slowly evolve over days or weeks. Newsgroups are also less controlled than meetings and teleconferences. Participants drift in and out, and discussions are often open to all passersby or "lurkers," as they are known on the Internet. Once again, we see in newsgroups evidence of openness, whatever its pros and cons.

The newsgroup approach to conferencing is inherently participative. This is certainly one of its strengths, but also perhaps one of its weaknesses. A newsgroup is only good when used. It cannot survive if the only "users" are passive lurkers—those who read the postings but never post anything themselves. This gives rise to what we call the "bootstrap problem," which can affect newly created newsgroups. Users will sometimes visit a newsgroup and look for interesting tidbits of information or illuminating, on-going discussions. In the beginning of a newsgroup's life, however, they might not find any noteworthy items. They might visit the newsgroup only once or twice, but only passively, and conclude that there is nothing of value there, not realizing that it is incumbent upon each visitor to populate the newsgroup with interesting material. We have seen many private corporate newsgroups suffer from this problem.

1.1.4.3 The Internet's Code of Ethics — Netiquette

Much has been written about the Internet's internal code of ethics, often referred to as netiquette (Dern 1994). These conventions, which boil down to common sense and courtesy, deal primarily with interpersonal communications via e-mail and USENET newsgroup postings. They stress respect for others and for the resources that make Internet access possible. Abusive language, for example, is often unwelcome, as are chain letters and mass mailings.

The case of Canter and Siegel demonstrates the consequences of failing to observe the rules of netiquette. Laurence Canter and Martha Siegel are a husband-and-wife law firm in Scottsdale, Arizona. In April 1994, they posted a seemingly innocent advertisement to the USENET news system, offering foreign nationals legal assistance in obtaining permanent U.S. resident status. The problem was not so much what they said but how they said it: Using an automatic mass mailing program, they posted their ad in virtually every USENET newsgroup on the Internet, approximately 6,000 newsgroups at the time. Retaliation by the Internet community was swift and severe.

Within hours of their first postings, Canter and Siegel began receiving electronic hate mail by the thousands. Within days, the deluge of incoming mail swamped their Internet access provider's computers with the incoming mail. Several times the computers came to a halt, unable to handle the extra workload (Elmer-Dewitt 1994).

Such hate mail, known in the jargon as ***flaming***, is quite common on the Internet. In electronic mailing lists and discussion groups like USENET newsgroups, one frequently encounters fairly heated discussions between staunch supporters of opposing views. Usually, the number of people taking part in these lively debates is relatively small, perhaps a dozen or two. But in the case of Canter and Siegel, thousands got into the act. For many a veteran Internet user, a serious transgression of netiquette had occurred.

Businesses seeking to advertise their products and services on the Internet should take note of the Canter and Siegel case. Internet Direct of Phoenix, Arizona, canceled Canter and Siegel's subscription to their service. Clearly, junk mail and unsolicited direct marketing are taboo on the Internet.

Netiquette also concerns respect for resources. Dern (1994) lists some of the resources consumed every time someone travels the Internet information highway:

> It costs money to run the computers and services you access, maintain the archive files, and so on. And it costs money to provide, operate, and maintain the many networks that comprise the Internet and the services needed to make the Internet work—the nameservers that convert network names into numeric identifiers, the routing tables, the administration of on-line mailing lists, the creation of RFC documents, and so on.
>
> When you drive your car, no one sends you a bill for "use of highways," snow plowing, police, traffic lights, etc. The funding for these very necessary services comes through indirect sources: taxes, license fees, more taxes, highway concessions, state and federal funding derived from still more taxes, etc. Similarly, there's rarely a "meter" visibly ticking away at your workstations, any more than at most telephones, roads, televisions, or radios. But every second, keystroke, network bit, CPU cycle, and storage byte is costing someone, somewhere, some money—and someone is paying for it. Even where computers have been fully paid for, and "cycles" are now free, someone has to pay for electricity, the space being occupied, and a share of network connectivity. Consequently, it's important to understand how "big a bill" you can run up using the Internet, which you or your organization may be liable for in one way or another.

Although it's important to be aware of the Internet resources consumed, it is even more important to respect the time of others. Asking frivolous questions in newsgroup postings simply because you are too lazy to look up the answers yourself in a list of ***frequently asked questions***, usually called a ***FAQ***, or in a reference book, is clearly a waste of other's time.

Even if they never answer your query, chances are they will waste time looking at it and muttering something unmentionable under their breath. Besides wasting their time, you have also disturbed their peace of mind. Rather than looking at your postings, they could have spent their time looking at something more valuable. On the Internet, there is already too much information of value to wade through; people don't want to waste time wading through information they don't need.

1.1.4.4 Information Barter

An interesting sort of give and take occurs on the Internet. Apparently, it is an unwritten law of the Internet that users should share information freely. For example, many users are unreserved about giving expert advice to anyone who asks knowing that they will receive like treatment when they ask for information outside their particular specialty. The general unspoken policy seems to be that "if you know the answer to some question, you should give it freely." (This does not apply to FAQs, of course. See the paragraph on FAQs later in this section.) This policy is particularly evident in newsgroups.

Not only do Internet users freely give their advice and opinions, but they also give away at not cost to the recipient vast storehouses of information and software archives built at considerable expense. Many of these archives were built at government, i.e., taxpayer expense, and the public has a certain claim on their use. The story of *NCSA Mosaic* offers a very instructive example. This Web browser was widely hailed as the "killer application" of the Internet. Many say it has done for the Internet what spreadsheet programs did for the PC—transform it from a toy into a real business tool.

NCSA Mosaic is the brainchild of a programming team at the National Center for Supercomputing Applications at the University of Illinois at Champagne-Urbana. Led by Joseph Hardin and Marc Andreesen, this team developed an all-in-one client software program that is able to communicate on the back-end with several popular data server protocols, including the World Wide Web, WAIS, USENET news, FTP, and gopher. When NCSA made Mosaic available to the public over the Internet, the news of its usefulness spread quickly throughout the Internet and requests to download the files via FTP soon swamped NCSA's file servers.

In essence, this is the philosophy of "what goes around comes around." It is interesting how well and for how long this has worked. Some would even say that this philosophy is at the heart of the Internet paradigm and that it is the primary reason for the Internet's growth and success. Some of these same people would also say that the current trend of business use of the Net will destroy this underlying philosophy. We tend to disagree with that assessment.

There are some drawbacks to the Internet's information bartering scheme. First, users are not really committed to continually monitoring newsgroups and looking for queries. There is no Internet, Inc., that employs these experts and requires that they have a real commitment to providing answers. Serendipity seems to be the rule here. If experts happen to be browsing the newsgroup to which you have posted your desperate plea for help, they may stumble across your plea. Chances are, if they know the answer to your question, they will give it. But they may not be interested in your question—especially if they have already answered questions similar to yours many times before in this same newsgroup.

In the case of newsgroups, one way of dealing with this problem is to post compilations of ***frequently asked questions*** (and answers) known as ***FAQ***s. Each FAQ compilation deals with the subject area of a particular newsgroup. Fortunately, many newsgroups have a volunteer who compiles, maintains, and periodically posts the FAQ to the newsgroup. Newcomers to a newsgroup should consult the FAQ posting to avoid the embarrassment of asking basic questions already answered in the newsgroup over and over again.

Another pitfall of this bartering scheme is that the advice you receive is sometimes only worth what you pay for it (i.e., nothing). Generally, you do not know the credentials of the people who respond to your postings. One way to deal with this is to take the discussion "off-line" by corresponding with the respondent directly via e-mail or telephone. You can usually tell by the answers to a few well thought-out questions whether you are dealing with an expert or a would-be expert.

1.1.5 The Internet as a Global Marketplace

The Internet's size and rapid growth make it an obviously attractive marketplace. Advertisers are already using the Net as a new medium for their messages.

The current approach to advertising is a refreshing new model that appears to be consonant with the Internet's culture of user empowerment. It represents a radical departure from the model presupposed in the traditional print and broadcast media. It seems to bypass the need for a "publisher" to be the intermediary required to furnish markets or audiences to advertisers; instead, the advertisers can go directly to the audience, provided they respect the intelligence of the average Internet user and avoid "in-your-face" advertising..

We discussed some of the obstacles to marketing on the Internet in the section on netiquette. Unsolicited electronic junk mail can generate outright hostility. Fortunately, there are more acceptable ways to advertise on the Internet. The World Wide Web—and to a lesser extent the Internet gopher—provides excellent opportunities to empower the end user to browse at will with interactive advertising. Instead of being bombarded by one-way, brain-dead broadcasting, the user can point-and-click her way through cyberspace, in effect creating and controlling her own infomercials.

This form of interactive advertising has engendered a new breed of electronic publisher called an Internet presence provider. These publishers build Web pages on behalf of their clients, giving them a presence on the Internet. At the time of this writing there were over 600 such Internet presence providers listed on the Yahoo server.[13] Some of the more prominent are the Internet Business Center managed by The Internet Group, and MecklerMedia's Internet Mall.

1.2 Corporate Internet Clones — An Overview

What is an "Internet clone?" An Internet clone is a TCP/IP-based wide area network that has the look and feel of the Internet but is in some sense isolated—for security reasons—from the Internet itself. It may be completely separate (i.e., disconnected from the Internet), or it may be connected while allowing only certain kinds of data traffic to flow between itself and the external Internet. Apart from these security considerations, an Internet clone resembles the Internet in the applications software and methods used to share and access information resources. Unlike the Internet, however, it is very private; a private organization owns it and keeps it inaccessible to the public. It is a private, corporate internetwork (though the organization need not be a for-profit corporation), operating in much the same decentralized way as the Internet itself, though varying degrees of value-added network and information management are often imposed on the operation and use of the internetwork.

Internet-based information systems are in some sense microcosmic clones within a corporate environment of the Internet itself. Why should businesses bother to build an Internet clone. Why not just build a unique information system tailored specifically to the needs of the business? Why look to the Internet at all?

Before jumping right into the thick of this debate, we should recognize that this issue does not represent a black and white, either/or dilemma. Many businesses have internal networks that look nothing like the Internet. Having an internal Internet clone does not mean you cannot have other kinds of information systems as well. A full spectrum of possibilities exists for linking up with the Internet, ranging from stand-alone, dial-up access for the corporate librarian to full-blown T-1[14] access from every desktop in the whole corporation. The matter of Internet clones for businesses, then, is not simplistic, and we are not dealing with mutually exclusive alternatives.

The extent to which an Internet clone makes sense for your business depends naturally on your specific business goals, your lines of business, your organization, and your internal corporate information culture. A multinational corporation, for example, with a large

---

[13] See *http://www.yahoo.com/* for one of the most comprehensive and useful electronic directories on the World Wide Web.

[14] T-1 is a designation in the Bell T-carrier system and represents a data communications speed of 1.544 megabits per second (Mbps).

staff in the field, may benefit considerably not only by using Internet tools to augment their business communications systems, but also by using the Internet itself. Given the right kinds of security layers, using the Internet itself for electronic mail may be more cost-effective than leasing a dedicated backbone for the same purpose. A widely dispersed corporation with a heterogeneous computing infrastructure can achieve considerable integration with a TCP/IP-based WAN. The Internet tools and resource services, many of which are available at no cost, can help the dispersed operating units share information more freely.

For some businesses like software vendors, providing customer support services over the Internet makes a lot of sense. For those whose customers may not be accessible through the Internet, the need to connect may be less urgent. Those needing to use the Internet itself will naturally need to have an internal system compatible with the Internet technologies. Internet clones, not surprisingly, provide the highest degree of compatibility with the Internet.

We feel that regardless of your information system, you should be able to communicate with the Internet, because the Internet is fast becoming the de facto information highway of the world. For better or for worse, businesses and individuals are conducting more and more commerce over the Internet. Proprietary networks based on proprietary protocols, on the other hand, are fast becoming islands of information, cut off from the mainstream of information exchange. Although proprietary networks are fine when interaction with the outside world is less important, the trend is nevertheless toward increasing interaction with the outside world. Regardless of its technical strengths and weaknesses, TCP/IP is rapidly becoming the lowest common denominator, the lingua franca, of inter-business computing.

Why is this happening? Because specific private interests develop and control proprietary networking protocols. They are, by definition, not open systems protocols. TCP/IP, on the other hand, is different. Many different people and organizations collaborated over the years to develop TCP/IP. The very nature of TCP/IP represents a compromise or consensus. It does not belong to IBM, it does not belong to DEC. Its fate is independent of any specific company. In the same way, the Internet, built on TCP/IP, will outlive any of its current constituent subnetworks, whether private or public. The Internet is greater than the sum of its parts and will outlive any of its parts. The underlying physical layers of the infrastructure may change. Newer datalink protocols such as Fast Ethernet or by Asynchronous Transfer Mode may supplant Ethernet,[15] but that will be transparent to TCP/IP. The only serious threat to TCP/IP is that it may fall victim to its own success; its rapid growth may soon exhaust the available IP address space; but that is a story for another chapter.

Granted that businesses should have some interface with the Internet, why should they bother with importing Internet tools and methods into their information systems?

---

[15] Ethernet is an electronic computer communications protocol at the OSI datalink layer. For more information, see Appendix A.

The main answer to this question has to do with consistency, simplicity and, ultimately, cost. If businesses use one set of tools to access and process their internally-generated business information and a completely different set to do the same with external information on the Internet, the overhead cost to train workers to be proficient with both sets of tools is certainly higher, perhaps double, what it would be with just one set. It is a waste of mental energy to constantly shift gears depending on the source of the information. It is clearly an advantage to be able to simply point, click, drag, and drop files from one computer to another regardless of where the files reside, whether inside the organization or outside. But if you have to learn and apply a specialized sequence of keystrokes and commands in the one environment and a different sequence in the other, frustration is inevitable.

A seamless and smooth interoperation between different environments is clearly preferable to a disjointed and painstaking readjustment each time you switch environments. This is a good argument for having a consistent set of tools for accessing both internal and external resources. It does not clarify, however, why this consistent set should be precisely those found and used in the public domain on the Internet.

Commercial-grade versions of Internet tools are coming out every day; businesses should look to these tools for long-term, supported solutions. However, companies should also be open at least to experimenting with Internet tools in a limited way, because the Internet is a hothouse of innovation for TCP/IP-based client/server tools. Many commercial software houses base the development of their own tools on the existing functional baseline of Internet tools. They start with Internet tools, make them more friendly, more robust, document them, and support them. Really new, innovative tools like *NCSA Mosaic* seem to show up first on the Internet. This might not remain true for long, however, as commercial software vendors take note of the growth potential of the Internet and begin to pour more development resources into building Internet navigation and server software.

Many business computer users are rightly concerned about the quality of public domain software. Can a program developed voluntarily by graduate students really compare with serious shrinkwrap software sold by Egghead Software? How robust can it be? And where is the support? Who do you call when you run into a bug? The grad students have long since graduated. The support issue is real and we will consider it later. For now, we emphasize that Internet freeware is surprisingly robust, not nearly as "buggy" as you might imagine. Because the Internet is a very large and unforgiving proving ground for new software, it squeezes new software tools through a wringer. If something does not work as promised, the Internet community will know about it—usually within hours of the experience. The rapid spread of bug reports around the Internet—principally by means of the USENET news bulletin system—fuels a collaborative debug process. If a tool shows promise, its developers will soon release a new and improved version. The Internet is thus both a development and beta site for many emerging client/server tools.

New ideas for navigating complex internetworks like the Internet are naturally first tried out on the Internet itself. A corporate information system that mimics the Internet can rapidly integrate and deploy these new technologies as soon as they become available. Companies with proprietary networks frequently have to wait until commercial variants of the Internet tools become available for their specific environments. Internet tools, on the other hand, are here today and are certainly adequate at least for use in a pilot project designed to explore their benefits.

In the last analysis, however, most businesses cannot survive unless they keep their costs down and their operations profitable. To do so, they must make effective use of their information resources, both inside and outside the business. So the question of Internet access and Internet clones for businesses is primarily an economic one: Can a corporation gain a competitive advantage by making use of the Internet and/or building an internal Internet clone?

Obviously, technology that is readily accessible and already well on its way to becoming standard will not give any company a competitive advantage. Although such technology may not guarantee that you win the game, it may be necessary in order to stay in the game. In that sense, integrating your information systems in some fashion with the Internet may be necessary (but not sufficient) to achieve a competitive edge.

In the long run, what will differentiate your company from another will be how you use these standard tools and, more importantly, the value-added applications you build to extract value from your information resources. Internet tools and the Internet will give you access to a wider pool of external resource and help you organize some of your important internal information. By themselves, however, they cannot guarantee any advantage. It is how you use these tools and methods—and how you integrate with them—that will make the difference. Although it may not be a competitive advantage to use these tools, it may well become a competitive disadvantage not to use them.

1.2.1 The Business Potential of the Internet and Internet Clones

We perceive the following advantages to be gained from both the Internet and the use of Internet tools within the enterprise:

- Synergy/Collaboration
- Time and Cost Savings
- Access to Resources

One of the greatest business benefits of the Internet and internal enterprise-wide internetworks is the opportunity they provide for cultivating high-payoff business relationships. Internet tools support a wide variety of communications, from e-mail and bulletin boards to audio and video teleconferencing. They support both point-to-point and workgroup conferencing communications.

When correctly implemented and carefully integrated with existing business information systems and data legacies, Internet tools can speed up the access to important enterprise information, thus saving time and money. Having rapid access to information can shorten product development cycles and time-to-market.

Networks have long been recognized as a means to share resources. One of the primary functions of a local area network in a workgroup, for example, is to allow the group to share a common printer or file servers. Similarly, with a wide area network the whole enterprise can access strategic assets like supercomputers and share their costs.

We defer further discussion of the business potential of the Internet and Internet technologies until Chapter 4, in which we present a discussion of the benefit-to-cost ratio of corporate Internet clones.

1.2.2 Risks

Despite all the praise commonly lavished upon Internet tools, you must realize there are some risks. Most of these risks result from unfamiliar ways of doing things and are quite manageable. Using Internet methods and Internet tools requires a willingness to explore new paradigms, especially in the area of support. In the next few paragraphs, we explore some of these issues.

1.2.2.1 Presumed Functionality

Internet tools are not always what they are cracked up to be. Sometimes expected functions are missing. For instance, although the user authentication features worked in the first Macintosh version of NCSA's Mosaic, they did not work in the first MS-Windows version. Perhaps this was a consequence of priorities. Maybe the developers at NCSA wanted to have user authentication features, but were not as concerned about them as business users would be. This is an important point. Features that may be important to the business community may not, in fact, rank high with the research and education community.

Workarounds are available, however. One workaround, on the client side, is to try another client package. There are usually one or two "competing" client tools out there, especially in the world of Web browsers. For example, some people prefer Web browsers like Netscape or Cello to *NCSA Mosaic*. Another alternative is to seek "customer support" by rolling up one's sleeves and jumping into the discussion groups and mailing lists. Surely not everyone in a company should have to be bothered with this. It makes more sense to have an internal Network Information Center (NIC) staffed with Internet experts who know how to navigate and interact with the relevant newsgroups and mailing lists.

1.2.2.2 Potential for Chaos

Can a corporation afford to let its internal Internet clone grow in the same manner and at the same pace as the Internet? We think the answer to this is "no." We believe there is a decisive strategic role to be played by management in guiding the development and operation of a corporate Internet clonc. Wc bclieve that unplanned and unmanaged data highways are no more immune to chaos than unplanned and unmanaged vehicle highways. On the other hand, we also believe there is something positive about the grassroots, user and consensus-driven approach that characterizes the Internet. The days of autocratic, centralized, master/slave computing are over. But, as the potential for chaos is real, we feel it is important to achieve a proper balance between top-down planning and bottom-up evolution.

By outlining some of the potential sources of chaos in an Internet-based, corporate information system, we hope to underscore in this section the need for management to take a proactive role in balancing the forces latent in these systems.

1.2.2.3 Information Overload

The buzzwords "infoglut" and "information overload" are already well-entrenched in today's vocabulary. Everywhere we look, we see evidence of what these terms mean: in the stacks of paper in our in-baskets at work; in the 500 channels selectable on our TV sets; in the junk mail in our mailboxes at home; in the seemingly endless list of unanswered messages in our e-mail folders. The more we strive to get away from paper documents by using computers, the more we seem to churn them out by using printers attached to our computers! Enabled by computers, we can now generate information much faster than we can consume it.

The Internet is sometimes characterized as a vast information dump. It is certainly one of the largest collections of distributed information repositories. Keeping up with its rapidly growing and ever-changing information storehouses is practically impossible.

Corporate Internet clones show the same tendency toward information explosion. It is easy for users to dump information, regardless of value, into e-mail, newsgroups, WAIS sources, gopher directories, or WWW HyperText Markup Language[16] (HTML) files. In the halcyon days of mainframe computing, this was not a problem, because the mainframe was under central control. Each user received a fixed quota of disk space and her files were not generally open to other users. Now, however, electronic publishing to the corporate internetwork is no longer centrally controlled, and every UNIX workstation and unused PC can become a server.

---

[16] The HyperText Markup Language is the document presentation language used on the World Wide Web. For more about HTML, see Chapters 2 and 3.

The result is a labyrinth of interconnected servers and information sources causing the information seeker to waste valuable time searching for a few precious nuggets of information.

The utility of information to an end user is directly proportional to the inherent value of its content but inversely proportional to the time it takes to find and assimilate it.

1.2.2.4 Net Surfing

A shared concern among business people who contemplate connecting their businesses to the Internet is that information resources of the Internet will become an opportunity for their employees to waste time wandering aimlessly around the network, guided only by their curiosity. Often referred to as "net surfing," this activity seems to based on the principle that "time flies when you're having fun," and, no doubt, exploring the Internet is fun. Unfortunately, those having fun on the Internet may not realize that time is flying—time paid for by their employer!

This situation needs to be handled like any other involving the personal use of business assets. The employees need to be made aware of company policies, given appropriate ethics training, and trained to navigate the internetworks in an efficient and effective manner; and their use of the Internet should be monitored. An excessive number of visits to newsgroups that obviously have nothing to do with the employee's job description is cause to counsel the employee. Such monitoring can be automated, of course, and it is easy to fashion script files that will monitor and report patterns of use.

1.2.2.5 Security Risks

For businesses connecting to the Internet, security risks are naturally high-priority concern. We mentioned previously that the Internet at times appears to be a fairly untidy place. The world of corporate information management is traditionally just the opposite. All data files are buttoned down, secure behind a username and password. There are many good reasons for this. A company has many stakeholders who depend on the viability of the business. In a publicly owned corporation, for example, stockholders entrust their money to the executive officers of the corporation. Bankers have lent money to the firm. Employees depend on the profitability of the firm for their livelihoods. A corporation is accountable to these stakeholders for all its assets—including its information assets. Mission-critical information underlying the firm's competitiveness should not be given away via anonymous FTP. It must be protected. Trade secrets that may ensure the firm's viability in the future should not be given away.

It is not surprising, therefore, that businesses are very cautious when it comes to connecting to the Internet. Their caution also extends, we have found, to the Internet clone. Internet clones are modeled on the same kind of openness that characterizes the Internet.

Usernames and passwords are reserved for special situations, and even these do not always provide the protection they seem to offer.[17]

In this section we take a closer look at openness within the Internet clone and its implications for security. We are not dealing, however, with openness in the sense of the open systems paradigm of client/server computing. That kind of openness is concerned more with the information technologies themselves and how they interoperate. Here we are concerned more with openness in terms of information culture.

1.2.2.5.1 New Paradigms: The Pros and Cons of Openness

Openness certainly has its advantages. First, the user can access many information resources quickly without having to remember a long list of unique passwords. Second, open systems have reduced administrative burdens. The systems administrators do not have to maintain user accounts and password files.

But openness has a downside. It places a greater burden on data file owners. Data owner must think twice before releasing information to an Internet clone, since they will not know who will be viewing the data. In the mainframe environment, where everyone has a password, the burden of controlling who looks at the data is shared to some extent with the system administrator. Further, the data owner usually has some control over the file access privileges, i.e., the read/write/execute attributes of the file. He can usually restrict access to groups of users using, if not the same computer system, at least a fairly homogeneous group of interconnected computers. But with Internet technologies the data owner no longer has much control. Certainly, data serving mechanisms like FTP can be configured to disallow access to all but a select group of IP addresses, but these are easily circumvented. Spoofing IP addresses is very easy to do.

On the other hand, it can be argued that the Internet-style environment is deliberately open. In other words, you simply do not make data available unless it is meant to be seen by many eyes. Within the corporation, systems of firewalls can be set up to filter IP addresses, but again, spoofing is sometimes possible. However, more sophisticated routers can be set up to check not only IP layer addresses, but also Ethernet (or Datalink) layer addresses, thus providing an extra measure of protection. There will be more on this in Chapter 5.

1.2.2.5.2 Role of Central Authority in an Internet Clone

How does the decentralized, distributed nature of the Internet square with the hierarchical, controlled environment of most businesses? The answer depends on your perspective. To the dyed-in-the-wool Internet techie, the new, decentralized paradigms of cyberspace are a welcome, liberating force undermining (hopefully for the better) the traditional autocratic

---

[17] TELNET password packets, for example, are generally transmitted in the clear, meaning that their contents are not scrambled by encryption.

structures of the corporate world. To the tenured corporate MIS manager, however, the Internet represents nothing but chaos—in spades. Our position is to take a conservative middle course between these two extremes, recognizing the value each side has to offer. We like the idea of synthesizing a new corporate information culture, taking the best of both worlds. Therefore, we feel there is most certainly a role for central authority in managing the Internet clone, in preventing it from becoming chaotic; but we also wish to emphasize the value and take advantage of the flexibility, openness, and scalability of the distributed paradigm.

Regardless of how the client/server architecture and the Internet philosophy differ in detail from more traditional approaches, it seems that the underlying principles of system management should remain the same. This is the topic of the next few paragraphs.

The principles of good system management apply regardless of the specific nature of the information system architecture. What differs is how you embed these principles in the policies and procedures governing the day-to-day operations of your system. For example, the common-sense principles of configuration management remain the same whether or not you have a centralized or decentralized computing system: You should always know what hardware and software assets you possess and what state of configuration they are in. You simply cannot grow a system (or contract it) unless you know what components belong to the system. This is especially true if your system evolves into a nest of bugs (bugs are not just limited to software—they often result in the networked environment from an unforeseen interplay between hardware and software). Once bugs manifest themselves in a system, they are difficult to remove unless you have a record, or trail, of how the system configuration has evolved. The evolutionary path can then be used to back out the latest changes that might have spawned the bugs.

Another common-sense principle of system management is that you should always back up your most valuable enterprise data. In the distributed system, this probably means empowering the end user to participate in the backup process. This does not mean that the end user is simply told to backup his or her data without being given the appropriate tools, training, and procedures to accomplish the task. "Empowerment" doesn't mean simply making the end user the "stuckee."

Finally, it has always made good system management sense to monitor the performance and utilization patterns of your network. An enterprise is a living organism subject to change, responding to both internal and external pressures. The suite of information tools employed by the enterprise will exhibit the same patterns of ebb and flow in their use as the enterprise itself. These patterns need to be monitored in order to reconfigure or fine-tune the system to match the user's changing needs. Naturally, the more automation and intelligence that can be embedded into such monitoring tasks the better.

We will have more to say on this subject in a later chapter when we discuss the day-to-day operation of the Internet-based information system. For now, it suffices to emphasize that there is nothing fundamentally new about Internet-based systems as regards system management. What is different is a redistribution of functionality and the presence of many more players in the running of the system: the IT-empowered end users.

1.2.2.6 Overcoming the Risks

Despite the risks involved in building an Internet clone, there are rational means for minimizing them. Indeed, risk management is not foreign to the building of any kind of system. Rather than address some of the typical methods of risk management here, however, we prefer to point straight to some of the approaches we believe can help mitigate risk in the specific area of building Internet clones within the corporate environment.

We believe there are two main areas for helping to ensure the success of the Internet project. The first involves paying close attention to the needs of the intended users (what a novel idea!), and the second concerns the size and type of the project itself—we recommend that the novice corporate builder of Internet clones embrace the pilot project approach. Accordingly, in this final section we consider the following two topics:

- Humanware
- The Pilot Project Approach

1.2.2.6.1 Humanware: Programming the Humans for Computer and Network Literacy

We firmly believe in embracing a human-centered approach to all information technologies, not just those associated with the Internet. We know all too well the temptation that besets info techies: The technology, which is supposed to be a means to an end, suddenly becomes an end in itself. We have seen information specialists build whiz-bang World Wide Web servers and WAIS databases and not bother to supply end users with the infrastructure and client software tools needed to access the servers! Unfortunately, end users are left to fend for themselves in obtaining, installing, and learning to use the client side of the Internet tool suites. Although it is a great idea to "empower" users, they are not really empowered unless they have the tools and the knowledge that empowerment requires.

In this context we are concerned not only with computer literacy, but network literacy. Users, to be empowered, need to know something about how to navigate networks, to find resources, to download and install software, etc. Clearly, not everybody in the organization needs to know this to the same degree, but the majority of business users, in our opinion, should have basic network survival skills.

Given the premise that most users need some level of network literacy, how much literacy do they need and how should they acquire it? Here are some of your options:

- Self-teaching materials
- On-line help
- Formal training
- Some combination of the above, or
- None of the above

Self-teaching materials are, we feel, only marginally effective. First, they require either time taken away from the job or the sacrifice of the worker's own personal time. Neither of these alternatives is very attractive. The former results in lost productivity, while the latter results in disgruntled employees. Another reason self-teaching materials are undesirable is because users will devote varying amounts of time to self-study, resulting in a disparity of knowledge and skills.

The second approach, using on-line help, is attractive because it is very context-sensitive; the user only resorts to it when he or she really needs it. This results in better appreciation for and retention of the lessons learned. However, there are some deficiencies in this approach, too. In the case of canned, on-line help, some users may feel intimidated by the help facility, not knowing where to start. Of course, this can be alleviated by the careful design of the help files.

Another species of on-line help that is in some ways superior to canned help involves the use of the USENET news tool as a collaborative help utility. Users that are stuck can query the appropriate newsgroup for advice. Enterprises can add value to this process by assigning "gurus" the tasks of monitoring the internal newsgroups and chiming in with advice whenever its required. Other perusers of the newsgroup can also add their comments. In this way, a collaborative help utility is created. We find that this approach, combined with canned on-line help can provide an effective on-line help facility.

One feature provided by the collaborative USENET news approach, a feature that is missing from the canned approach, is the social dimension. Users not only learn how to operate their client software and navigate their networks, but they also become acquainted with one another. They learn about each other's strengths and weaknesses and receive the satisfaction of not only being helped but also providing help to others. This sort of mutual support can help forge ties between members of the organization. This fosters a sense of "belongingness" and ownership of the system and can also help ensure the success of the fledgling project.

Formal training, though expensive, can be very useful in providing a basic educational foundation for network users. Many users do not appreciate the basic principles of file management and network interaction. However, formal training is not only expensive, it has the same drawback as self-teaching—it takes people away from their work or their free time. Sometimes this is necessary. But we do not recommend that you rely on it exclusively.

Obviously, some mix of the above approach to training, with emphasis on on-line help (both canned and collaborative) is desirable. The appropriate mix depends on the needs of your intended users and the resources (both funds and skills) at your disposal.

The final alternative—that of providing no training support—is one we do not recommend. Yet it is surprising how many organizations opt for this alternative. Some enterprise cultures seem to embrace a philosophy of rugged individualism leaving everyone to fend for him or herself. They are very stingy when it comes to training budgets. In these organizations, training is viewed as an expense—a sort of necessary evil—rather than an investment. We prefer to endorse and promote a culture that is proud to call itself a learning organization, one in which all the knowledge workers are linked not only via information technology, but also in the vision of helping each other journey into a fast-changing future. Unfortunately, however, there are many organizations in which departmental jealousies and "not-invented here" syndrome seem to be the operative values. Such embedded cultural attitudes always tend to slow down the learning process, because users are afraid to expose their ignorance, or the knowledgeable won't share their knowledge for fear that someone else may end up more knowledgeable than they. They suffer from what the famous psychologist Maslow termed "deficiency motivation" syndrome. No amount of information technology can dismantle that kind of culture overnight. However, some of the communication and collaboration paradigms that have evolved with the Internet may help spread the spirit of collaboration even in enterprise cultures traditionally hostile to such spirit. There is reason for hope, therefore, and we encourage those Internet clone builders who may find themselves surrounded by a culture inimical to the spirit of collaboration not to give up.

1.2.2.6.2 The Pilot Project Approach

The rate at which the business environment is changing today makes obsolete the slow, three-year strategic plan approach to fully architecting the information system solution. The pace of change necessitates the use of methods like rapid prototyping for quickly assessing the value of new information technologies. That is why we will stress again and again in this book the importance of executing a small, cost-effective pilot project to explore Internet technologies. These technologies are emerging at such a rapid pace that it is hard to keep up with them, and it is also difficult to tell from the outset which technologies will have a favorable impact on your enterprise. That is another reason why these technologies are attractive: They present the opportunity to "try before you fly, and fly before you buy." Since they are so inexpensive, they can be assembled, integrated and tested prior to making major funding commitments, and your information technologists can get a hands-on jump up on the TCP/IP client/server learning curve prior to full-scale implementation.

Davenport (1993, 1994) has noted the deficiencies of the traditional approach to developing information architecture. Writing for the Harvard Business Review (Davenport

1994), he notes: "Given today's rate of business change, even if an enterprise model is finished in a year or two, it's likely to be outdated."

The Internet clone, built according to the pilot project approach, affords information professionals the opportunity to build an embryonic system that can scale up as it evolves into a more viable system solution. The open systems philosophy of plug-and-play, inherent in Internet technologies, offers a modular, scaleable approach to system design. The system can evolve in whatever direction—up, down, sideways—in response to current business needs. In this way, information systems managers do not need to possess a crystal ball and play a guessing game with the future. The future is created along with the information system.

While the pilot project approach has the aforementioned advantages, it is not without its own disadvantages. Since it "starts small, but thinks big," it can easily take on a grassroots, bottom-up flavor that can easily evolve in directions that are interesting to those fascinated by the technology, but not necessarily aligned with the business objectives of the enterprise. This theme recurs throughout the course of this book. It can hardly be stressed enough that the pilot project must be guided and kept focused on serving the goals of the enterprise.

Chapter 2

THE CURRENT STATE OF INTERNET TECHNOLOGIES

2.1 An Overview of Some Important Constraints

After formulating your system goals and objectives, you need to understand the limitations of an Internet-based information system. This is the second step in the process of developing a long-term strategy for electronic commerce and information sharing. Naturally, this strategy—especially the system goals and objectives—must be directly linked to your prioritized business goals and specific, measurable business objectives. Regardless of goals, however, constraints must be considered in order to ensure your envisioned system is indeed feasible. This will minimize the number of negative surprises you'll encounter as you build and deploy your system.

Constraints are the business and technical realities limiting your number of design options. Unlike goals, constraints are not desirable for their own sakes; they are facts of life placing limitations on what you can do. For example, if everyone were honest and had respect for other people's property, there would be no need for security. If your company had not already made a significant investment in network infrastructure, you would not have to worry about making maximal use of your existing network resources. Your business probably did not just spring up overnight with an endless supply of cash with which to finance a brand new system. You have legacies. You have limitations. You have limited budget and resources at your disposal. In short, you have constraints.

Besides considering these physical and financial constraints, you must also consider the limitations of the Internet information technologies themselves. Implementing these technologies from the ground up requires a great deal of experimentation—in effect, traveling the same path as many others before you. Rather than repeating the mistakes of others, you are well advised to plan your system from the top down by making a conceptual roadmap that leverages the lessons others have learned. That is what this book is all about. We have experienced some of these pitfalls ourselves and know the value of up-front planning. By understanding system limitations you will minimize the risk of having to restructure later, and you will enable your system designers to make the best possible decisions.

In this chapter and the next, we focus on the constraints imposed by some of the Internet tools. Although we leave the details on how to use these tools to the many good books currently available on the subject, we do provide a brief description of each tool. We look at the advantages of each tool and summarize its limitations for use in a business context. Finally, we describe some of the more common commercial tools and examine some of the broader constraints associated with an integrated, internetworked system.

2.2 The Internet Tools

The power of the Internet lies not only in its vast collection of physical networks spanning the world, but in the software tools that, through development collaborative efforts, have yielded simple and robust information-sharing capabilities. Having evolved in an academic and research environment free from commercial pressures, these tools provide open access to information for personal enrichment, research, and collaborative work. Today, the focus of these tools has shifted dramatically from the needs of academia to that of commerce. Internet tools and methods are helping to steer the course of evolution of internal business information systems.

Internet technologies are constantly migrating from the technologist's laboratory to the business computer user's desktop. Revision after revision and improvement upon improvement have fueled internetwork expansion and have opened the door to information resources around the globe. Virtually anyone with a computer, modem, and telephone can participate in this rich and ever-changing environment.

Many of the limitations we describe in this chapter are currently being addressed by standards committees and are subject to rapid new developments in technology. The Internet—and its associated internetworking technologies and tools—are evolving so fast that it is difficult to say which innovations will prevail. One thing, however, is fairly certain—you can use today's tools to implement your own cyberstrategy for information sharing. Whether you are reengineering your internal information infrastructure or developing a strategy for accessing external Internet resources, you will probably find that Internet tools can be adapted to a variety of situations.

What are the Internet tools? How are they used? How do they fit into a corporate Internet clone? In this section we look at E-Mail, USENET, FTP, WAIS, Gopher, and the World Wide Web system. Each of these tools plays a unique role in a business information infrastructure, and they each offer advantages over traditional, centralized systems—both in terms of flexibility and ease of use.

2.2.1 Electronic Mail, Asynchronous Communication

Application:	E-mail, E-mail reflectors
Protocol:	SMTP (Simple Mail Transfer Protocol)
Specification:	RFC 821[1]
Origin:	The TCP/IP protocol suite
Location:	Packaged with most TCP/IP products

2.2.1.1 SMTP Overview

Electronic mail in some form is so ubiquitous within corporations today that it hardly needs any elaboration. It is clearly recognized as a vital means of in-house communication. Recent developments in inter-business e-mail communications, however, are being shaped by the Internet implementation of e-mail and are therefore relevant to our discussion of Internet tools.

Today, when people talk about Internet e-mail, they probably mean SMTP, the Simple Mail Transfer Protocol. SMTP is a means of transporting electronic messages between local and remote users connected by a TCP/IP internetwork. Although there are many commercial e-mail protocols in wide use for LANs (e.g., cc:Mail, Microsoft Mail, etc.), SMTP is widely regarded as the de facto standard for e-mail systems. Just as TCP/IP has become the de facto standard protocol suite for interconnecting different types of local networks, so SMTP has become the de facto standard mail application protocol to handle messages transferred from one kind of LAN system to another.

Like most Internet applications protocols, SMTP is built on the client/server model. There are three pieces to the SMTP model. The first piece is a client program that helps the end user create e-mail messages. Called the ***mail user agent*** (***MUA***) because it provides an interface to the user, this program passes newly created messages to a server program called the ***mail transfer agent*** (***MTA***). The MTA determines whether the message recipient is a user on the local server machine or on a remote machine connected via an internetwork. If the recipient is local, the MTA hands off the message to a third agent called a ***mail delivery agent*** (***MDA***), which stuffs the message into a file that serves as the recipient's mailbox. Otherwise, if the recipient is a user on a remote machine connected to the local one by an internetwork, the MTA on the local server—acting now as a client—handshakes with another MTA on the

[1] RFCs (Requests for Comments) can be downloaded from *ftp://nic.ddn.mil/rfc/rfcXXXX.txt* (RFC 0821, for example, could be retrieved from *ftp://nic.ddn.mil/rfc/rfc0821.txt*).

remote machine. This remote MTA then passes the message to its own MDA for final delivery.

There are many MUAs available on many different platforms. Examples are *elm* (see Figure 2-1 for a picture of the *elm* mailer client MUA), *pine, mail, mush,* and *mh* on UNIX systems, and *Microsoft Mail*, *cc:Mail*, *Pegasus*, and *Popmail* on PC systems. Macintoshes users frequently use a client package called *Eudora*. There are also many MTAs. The most common ones on UNIX machines are *sendmail* and *smail*.

MUA functionality varies across applications. Features like attachments, document conversions, and e-mail receipts belong to the MUA; they are not directly addressed by the SMTP standard. Each MUA may implement additional features beyond the basic transfer of text messages.

It should be pointed out that with SMTP messages the sender and recipient do not have to be humans. On the Internet, it is quite common to implement ***mailbots*** of various kinds to originate or receive e-mail messages. For example, an e-mail message sent to *info@csz.com* could in fact be delivered to a program that automatically responds by sending a canned e-mail message back to the original sender. The MTA on a host machine at csz.com could be configured to make sure that all in-bound messages headed for "user" *info* are to be fed in fact as input to the program that generates the canned message.

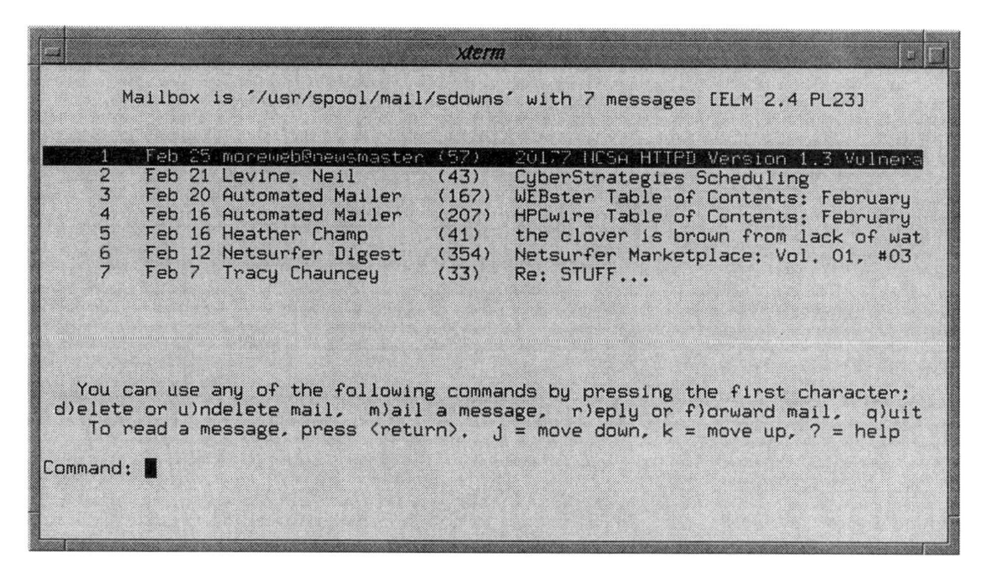

Figure 2-1. *The* Elm *Mailer—Version 2.4*

Since the basic SMTP standard only deals with the transport of ASCII text messages, binary data types like graphics, audio and video files must be encoded as ASCII prior to transmission. ASCII encoding is simply the conversion of binary data into printable plain text (7-bit ASCII). To e-mail a binary file, the sender must encode it, include it in an ordinary ASCII text message, and send it via SMTP to the recipient, who will have to decode it back into its original binary form. In order for this to work, however, the sender's and the recipient's encoding/decoding tools must be compatible, i.e., they must be capable of generating and accepting a common format for encoding and decoding non-ASCII files.

UNIX systems, for example, provide the *uuencode* to convert binary files to ASCII and *uudecode* to translate ASCII files back into binary format. The ***uu*** prefix stands for "UNIX-to-UNIX."

Manual encoding and decoding using command line syntax is generally inconvenient for the today's average computer user. When the encoding and decoding are integrated with the MUA, however, the process is less painful. With a few clicks of the mouse, the user can include a binary file into an ordinary e-mail message and send it on its way. Including a non-ASCII file with these tools is usually no more difficult than specifying an attachment.

MUAs that support Multipurpose Internet Mail Extensions (MIME) further simplify the process of transporting non-text data types like mode word processing, spreadsheet, and graphics files in native binary format. In addition to encoding and decoding facilities, MUAs with MIME support often come pre-configured with a few default ***viewers*** for certain widely-used data types. Auxiliary applications launched by the MUA, viewers read a binary data file in its native mode and display it to the user in formatted, human-readable form. Some MUAs are also pre-configured to recognize certain file extensions as standard MIME types. For example, some MUAs recognize that the file extension ".doc" indicates a MS Word document and that MS Word should be launched as a viewer. Similarly, some can recognize an attached MPEG video file, automatically decode it, and play it using a predefined MPEG player as a viewer.

MIME, which is defined in RFCs 1521 and 1522, simplifies the process of encoding and decoding and provides a standard method for applications to handle various data types. MIME content types include video, sound, and graphics, and can be transported using existing mail protocols. Because MIME does not affect the underlying MTA, it can be readily implemented without major changes to the configuration of your mail server.

2.2.1.1.1 Post Office Protocol—POP

On most multi-user, multi-tasking systems like UNIX, the MUA and the MTA run on the same machine, although under different processes. The Post Office Protocol, or POP, developed by the microcomputer support staff at the University of Minnesota, physically separates the MUA from the MTA in classical client/server fashion.[2] The MUA becomes a local client, the MTA a remote server. While the MTA continues to communicate with other MTAs using SMTP, the client communicates with its designated MTA using POP.[3] Thus POP and SMTP are two distinct protocols.

POP provides a method for e-mail storage and retrieval for clients that infrequently connect to an internetwork or are mobile. Using POP is analogous to having a box at your local post office. Mail will continue to be delivered and you can pick it up at your own convenience. It doesn't matter if you move from one end of town to the other. Your mail will still wait for you at the post office.

The user's e-mail address carries the hostname of the POP server, not the client. This means that the user must also possess a regular login account on the server machine. This is not really an extra burden, however, since the login process is performed automatically by the client software and is therefore transparent to the user.

For more information on Popmail, contact the microcomputer support staff at the University of Minnesota, at the e-mail address *popmail@boombox.micro.umn.edu.*

2.2.1.1.2 Electronic Mail Reflectors

Electronic mail reflectors expand the capabilities of e-mail by providing distribution list management and group communication facilities. When a user sends an e-mail message to a reflector, the reflector sends a copy of the message to all users who have previously "subscribed" to a list maintained by the reflector. In this way, you can achieve broadcast—i.e., one-to-many—communications. An on-going group discussion can take place. The mail reflector automates the process of subscribing and unsubscribing to mailing lists.

Mail reflectors can also act as e-mail file or information servers. For example, by sending an e-mail message addressed to *info@csz.com*, our reflector will automatically send you an ASCII text file containing information about our company CyberStrategies. Such e-mail file servers are not limited to text files. Their underlying script files can just as easily attach a binary file as a MIME type. More sophisticated reflectors can parse data items specified in the subject header of the incoming e-mail message and return different files depending on the values of the data items. For example, Tabor-Griffin Communications, an electronic publisher, uses an e-mail reflector to publish WEBster, a bi-weekly e-zine

---

[2] Technically, a client/server interaction does not require physical separation. Two processes on a single UNIX machine, for example, can interact as client and server. But the typical or classical client/server approach is often thought to involve two distinct machines connected by a network.

[3] Actually, on most UNIX systems providing both SMTP and POP server functions, the SMTP and POP servers are two separate programs, usually *sendmail* and *pop3d.*

dedicated to following the happenings on the World Wide Web. A subscriber to WEBster scans the table of contents and selects articles of interest by placing their number in the subject header of an e-mail message back to Tabor-Griffin. The WEBster mail reflector then sends the full text of each specified article in separate messages back to the user, usually within seconds.

The two most popular tools for automating e-mail reflector functions are *listserv,* developed by Anastasios Kotsikonas, and *majordomo*, a Perl application developed by Brent Chapman. For more information on *listserv*, check the FTP archive at Boston University: *cs-ftp.bu.edu/pub/listserv*. Information on *majordomo* can be obtained from Greatcircle's FTP site: *greatcircle.com/pub/majordomo*.

2.2.1.1.3 Electronic Data Interchange—EDI

Similar to electronic mail is electronic data interchange, or EDI, which is a method of exchanging standardized business documents directly between computers. EDI eliminates not only the need to exchange paper documents, but also the slow and costly process of shipping, receiving and handling those documents. Transmitting paper documents often requires the manual re-entry of data back into a computer at its final destination. EDI helps eliminate these time-consuming and costly intermediate steps by allowing the computers at the sending and receiving sites to exchange data directly.

Electronic Data Interchange, already a widely implemented means of transferring critical business information, is making its debut on the Internet. The Internet Engineering Task Force (IETF) has established a working group to develop solutions to the problems associated with EDI information security and privacy in pubic networks. The transport of undisturbed EDI protocols over mechanisms like e-mail, for example, are being developed as an extension to existing EDI transports.

Why is the subject of EDI relevant to the corporate Internet clone? By having access to EDI data, users can track the progress of purchases and plan their activities accordingly. Once EDI machines are compatible with the Internet, they will also be compatible with the internal Internet clone. Thus, clone users will be able to access EDI databases (assuming there are no cultural or enterprise-political obstacles to hinder this). This may appear as a threat to some traditional purchasing organizations. By giving every desktop direct access to external supplier information, some of the internal purhasing department overhead can be bypassed, freeing purchasing personnel for more important purchasing-related decisions. The purchasing department would no longer have to be an information broker between external suppliers and internal users of supplier information.

Some examples of typical standardized documents exchanged using EDI are purchase orders, invoices, credit memos, shipment advises, receiving notices, and requests for quotation. The American National Standards Institute, or ANSI, has chartered the Accredited Standards Committee (ASC) X12 to develop EDI standards. Certain industry segments have further refined and added to the list of standards proposed by the ASC X12. One very important type of EDI is called Electronic Funds Transfer, or EFT, and is used heavily by the banking industry.

EDI over the Internet is attractive because of the potential for interoperability and the elimination of some of the expenses associated with dial-up telecommunications. With the Internet, a local dial-up call can put your machine in contact with any other Internet-connected machine. This eliminates the need for a long-distance call to the receiving computer. For example, a purchase order from a company in New York to a company in Singapore could be sent using traditional EDI via a very expensive dial-up call to the computer in Singapore. With the Internet, the same connection could be accomplished by first dialing up a local Internet access provider and then using that connection to communicate directly—at no extra cost—with a similar computer associated with the company in Singapore. The computer in Singapore would simply have to periodically dial-up its local Internet access provider and check for the arrival of any EDI documents. And if the two companies have direct, dedicated access to the Internet, they can eliminate the dial-up steps all together and simply communicate directly at any time, 24 hours a day, 7 days a week.

A more traditional approach to this is to use an EDI service provider who maintains a third party proprietary network. Third party networks provide their customers with an electronic mailbox. Customers upload their documents to the mailbox, and the network service provider distributes the documents to the mailboxes of the intended recipients. This method of distribution avoids the many point-to-point communications that would otherwise be necessary in a direct EDI exchange between trading partners. This approach, however, is more expensive than the previously described Internet-based scenario.

This does not mean that the Internet will replace the Value Added Networks (VANs) provided by third parties. It may mean, however, that the Internet will become an affordable infrastructure medium for these VANs to use when exchanging data with each other and their client companies. In fact, it is reasonable to expect the appearance of new VANs that rely almost exclusively on the Internet. These Internet-based VANs may provide cost-effective and competitive alternatives to the traditional VANs that have overhead expenses wrapped up in proprietary network costs and gateways between other VANs. Naturally, these newer VANs will have to offer their customers the same traditional services like encryption, authentication, business document translation, installation, and training. Further, the Internet may eliminate the need for maintaining numerous gateways between the different proprietary VANs (although for the time being, Internet-based VANs will have to continue interoperating with proprietary VANs).

Although currently limited, Internet-based EDI is growing rapidly. Those companies using or planning to use EDI heavily, should give careful consideration to how the Internet will influence the direction and cost-effectiveness of EDI VANs. Companies should be on the lookout for start-up companies (and some forward-thinking traditional ones) that will operate EDI VANs on the Internet. They should also consider implementing Internet-based EDI software internally in their own Internet clones. Many large corporations, for example, conduct considerable commerce between sister divisions. Using Internet-based EDI software can eliminate going to a third party for this service (which often carries a variable usage cost), and can also avoid the cost and configuration management overhead associated with maintaining many point-to-point links.

2.2.1.2 Potential

E-mail is one of the fastest growing interpersonal business communications tools of the 90s. Its simplicity combined with the Internet's worldwide infrastructure, makes it possible for over 25 million users to send messages back and forth. For systems without native SMTP capabilities, gateway software can provide SMTP mail translation services—thereby expanding e-mail's reach to non-internetworked systems. An important feature of SMTP e-mail, therefore, is that it has the potential to be the lingua franca uniting heterogeneous networks and systems.

Among Internet tools, e-mail is a basic workhorse. Many other TCP/IP applications depend on or are designed to interoperate with e-mail. Many Web servers and browsers, for example, allow users to feedback information to information providers by providing an SMTP e-mail interface. Similarly, most USENET news systems provide a way for users to post articles by e-mail. Indeed, the preferred way to respond to a news posting—when the answer to a query is not in the general interest of everybody using the newsgroup—is to reply by e-mail. Gopher also relies on e-mail as one of its ways to forward information to users.

There are also many gateways between e-mail and other applications. The Internet FAX server method of transforming a long-distance e-mail message into a local FAX transmission is a prime example. Thus, e-mail is an essential building block for the entire Internet clone.

Despite the glamour and appeal of other Internet tools, e-mail by itself suffices to justify the building of an Internet-based information system. The communications capabilities provided by e-mail are rivaled probably only by the telephone. Whether you are sending a reminder to a co-worker around the corner or getting information on a new product line from a supplier halfway around the world, e-mail provides an effective communications tool for both businesses and individuals.

E-mail supports communications not only between individuals but also among groups. Group mailing lists and e-mail reflectors can be used to distribute reports and discuss topics of common concern. For workgroup communications, e-mail can save both time and paper.

For the most part, e-mail is easy, affordable, and reliable. It's easy when used with one of the many fine MUAs. It's affordable because you usually pay a flat rate for your internal and external links regardless of how many IP packets traverse those links. In other words, most businesses do not have to pay by the e-mail message. It's reliable because of the redundancy built into the protocol—e-mail continues to attempt delivery even if a particular network segment is down (within a nominal time period—usually three days). When you consider that an e-mail message to anywhere in the world is delivered just minutes after it was transmitted, you begin to appreciate the benefits of desktop-to-desktop connectivity.

Since e-mail is one of the most common e-mail protocols, it makes sense to develop a business strategy that includes this functionality. And since SMTP is the common denominator among e-mail protocols, we strongly recommend that organizations adopt SMTP as their corporate-wide standard.

2.2.1.3 Limitations

Although SMTP provides a standard mechanism for the transport of e-mail, it does not mandate specific MUA features. There are many implementations of internetwork e-mailers which have very similar features. Still, many other MUAs provide capabilities that may only be useful if both the sender and recipient have identical mailers. Without strict compliance to a standard like MIME, transport of data types other than text may be difficult for end users.

Privacy is another area in which most MUAs are still lacking. Encryption is the primary approach to e-mail privacy, but one generally has to augment the MUA with a separate program using RSA-style security (*pgp*—Pretty Good Privacy—is a typical example). Although encryption techniques can guarantee a secure pathway between sender and recipient, they are still subject to some of the problems associated with general MUA inconsistencies. Without a common and widely accepted method of encryption, a message encoded using one package may not necessarily be decoded by another. Until a clear standard for encryption emerges, secure e-mail transactions on a large scale will not be possible.

Digital signatures and encryption are largely unproved for official communications. Contracts, for example, must still be signed with ink on paper before most banks will approve a financial transaction. Until it becomes clear that electronic transactions using digital signatures are legally binding, electronic business transactions of a sensitive nature will be confined to EDI with established business partners. With the explosion in the development use of security protocols to enhance World Wide Web transactions, however, we expect rapid progress in the areas of digital signatures and encryption.

E-mail also suffers from problems due to the difficulty in diagnosing delivery problems and finding addresses. Undelivered mail error messages often leave users in a quandary about where to turn. The best bet for resolving undeliverable mail messages is to contact a local e-mail administrator or your company's SMTP postmaster (*postmaster@domain_name*). As for finding addresses, the X.500 standard for directory services is far from being widely implemented. For the most part, we will have to find addresses the old fashioned way—by asking the recipient. Within the corporation, however, policies and procedures can require that all new e-mail accounts be registered with a few central directory servers.

2.2.2 Bulletin Boards, Asynchronous Conferencing

Application Name:	USENET News, NetNews
Protocol:	NNTP (Network News Transfer Protocol)
Specification:	RFCs 850 and 977
Origin:	USENET was originally developed for UNIX systems in 1979
Location:	*ftp.uu.net*

2.2.2.1 Overview

From Chapter 1, you already have a pretty good idea about what USENET news is and what it can do for you. In this section, we'll take another look at USENET and provide some insight into the USENET news server capabilities as well as this tool's use as an internal bulletin board system.

USENET can be thought of as comprised of newsgroups, the people who use them, and the computers they reside on. You can think of USENET as an electronic bulletin board that people use to communicate. They use it to ask for help and to discuss a seemingly endless variety of topics. On the Internet there are more than 20,000 newsgroups covering a vast range of special interests from hobbies such as wine-making to highly technical subjects like artificial intelligence. An overview of some of the many Internet newsgroups can be found in Ed Krol's *The Whole Internet User's Guide & Catalog.*

USENET client applications—called ***newsreaders***—allow users to read, post, subscribe, unsubscribe, and kill postings. Depending on the application, news postings may be listed chronologically or sorted into threads tracing a discussion from a single original posting. The *Netscape Navigator* by Netscape Communications, for example, sorts news postings and follow-ups into coherent, logical threads of information. In this way, a user need not scan through a chronological listing to find the answer to a posted question—all replies are embedded under the original topic.

USENET, often referred to as Network News or simply NetNews, presents an unusual set of challenges for the first time user. For those using NetNews on the Internet, users are expected to observe ***network etiquette*** (***netiquette***)—loosely based on the original Accepted Use Policies of the network provider. Netiquette, although not fully understood by many users (see the lawyer incident—Chapter 1), is important because, unlike e-mail messages between individuals, users need to have a greater appreciation for the wide variety of attitudes found in a large and diverse audience.

Many things are considered inappropriate for the USENET system. The blatant use of commercial appeals, for example, often results in ***flames*** (a virtual flogging) for those responsible for the posting.

Users of the USENET system will discover that e-mail is the preferred method of transferring responses. Reposts and follow-ups are often used to contradict or support an

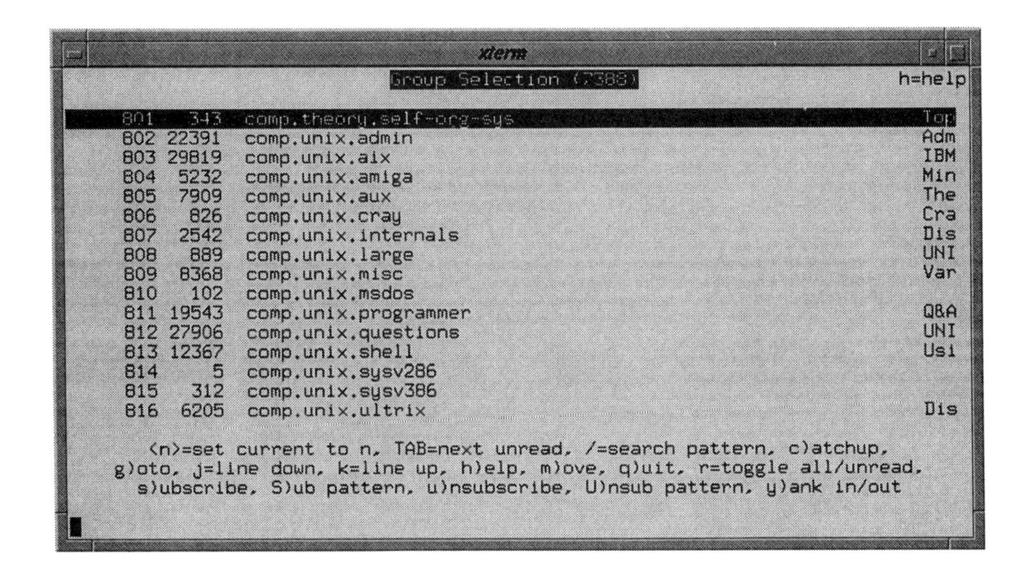

Figure 2-2. *The TIN Newsreader—Version 1.2 by Iain Lea*

established point for the benefit of newsgroup subscribers. In general, though, responses for help requests and other information are transmitted directly to the author of a posting via e-mail.

Like many software programs available on the Internet, news clients and servers come in several different shapes and sizes. Internet providers offering shell accounts often provide a choice of several different network news clients that might include *Netscape Navigator*, *tin*, *rn*, or *xrn*. The *tin* newsreader is shown in *Figure 2-2*.

To help users sort through the overwhelming amount of USENET information, newsreaders offer capabilities to subscribe and unsubscribe to newsgroups. This helps reduce the infoglut and provides a way to build a more focused collection of meaningful, work-related newsgroups. Subscribing and unsubscribing are the processes by which users can select and deselect from an alphabetical listing of available newsgroups. In subsequent sessions users are presented with their subscription list and may either add new groups or delete those they no longer use.

For UNIX systems, the reference implementation of NNTP as defined in RFC 977 can be found at the following FTP site maintained by Academ Consulting Services in Houston, Texas: *ftp.academ.com*. An alternative news server is the InterNetNews, or INN server written by Rich Salz. The INN server software can be found at *ftp.uu.net*. Information regarding the philosophy and protocols underlying USENET, its set-up procedures, as well as USENET terminology and conventions can be found in the FTP archives at MIT located on *rtfm.mit.edu*. Finally, it is a good idea to browse the resources given by *http://www.academ.com/academ/nntp.html*, maintained by Academ Consulting Services, as this is a good starting point for many different USENET-related information sources. Another good source of such information can be found at Sunsite's Web page located at *http://sunsite.unc.edu/usenet-b/home.html*.

USENET servers provide a number of features like restricted access, monitoring, and limited propagation. These features can be tailored to meet the needs of each environment. In a corporate setting these features allow the creation of internal newsgroups whose articles will not be propagated outside the corporate firewall.

Newsfeeds from commercial and public sources provide an almost constant stream of information to and from businesses using the USENET system. With more than 20,000 newsgroups on the Internet today, it's not hard to see how internal processing requirements can be quickly overwhelmed (particularly in terms of disk space). Commercial newsfeeds are often the first choice of businesses who need to provide a local news server for their users. In most cases, commercial feeds provide greater reliability than public feeds, and if you have problems you won't have to track down a graduate student at some college to help you out.

2.2.2.2 Potential

NetNews offers the business user access to current information sources and assistance from other users across the enterprise or around the world. It can be used to resolve problems, answer questions, and raise awareness.

NetNews also provides an opportunity for internal information distribution, dissemination, and feedback. Internal newsgroups may be created alongside public groups for the purpose of discussing internal concerns or topics of interest. These groups can be set up on internal servers so that they do not propagate beyond the corporate perimeter.

Another application of internal USENET newsgroups is to provide centralized help desk services. Routine questions can be answered by FAQs, effectively reducing the overhead required to answer each individual's questions personally over the phone.

Newsgroups also provide an opportunity to preserve corporate memory. Ongoing discussions can be archived and provide a trail of decisions and resolutions reached at virtual, asynchronous meetings. These archives can also be indexed for storage as WAIS sources.

2.2.2.3 Limitations

Providing a complete USENET service on an internal server can be expensive both in terms of system management and system resources. A complete USENET newsfeed from the Internet is estimated at over 5.4 gigabytes per month. Disk space may be conserved by purging old information more frequently or eliminating unimportant newsgroups, but both of those activities increase the need for system management.

A full newsfeed can eat up much of the bandwidth of a dial-up connection. It can take up to 15 hours per day with a 14.4 modem. If your organization requires a newsfeed to and from the outside world, you should first consider obtaining dedicated Internet access with much higher bandwidth.

A number of companies offer commercial newsfeeds for a fee. Netcom is one such provider. Public access USENET feeds are also available. A list of host names of public newsfeeds can be retrieved from Phoenix Data Systems of Houston, Texas via *http://www.phoenix.net/config/news.html*. As with all things provided free, you cannot expect much in the way of support or reliability. This is an inherent limitation of public newsfeeds.

Another limitation of establishing internal newsgroups is the labor overhead required to ensure that they are used for work-related purposes, that policies—e.g., to encourage a coherent newsgroup naming scheme—are in place, disseminated, and enforced, and that they are properly moderated when it is appropriate to do so.

Newsgroup naming conventions are especially important when newsgroups originating within the organization reside alongside those originating outside in the public domain. Unless you provide some value-added programming on the server side to clearly mark newsgroup postings as confidential, it is generally only through some kind of naming convention that you can indicate to your internal users which newsgroups are private and which are public.

2.2.3 FTP— File Transfer Protocol

Application Name:	FTP (File Transfer Protocol)
Protocol:	FTP
Specification:	RFC 959
Origin:	The TCP/IP protocol suite
Location:	Packaged with most TCP/IP products

2.2.3.1 Overview

The File Transfer Protocol, or FTP, defines how files can be transferred from a remote computer to a local one and vice versa. It supports the transfer of both ASCII and binary data files. FTP has been implemented on many different platforms, the first being the 4.2 BSD version of UNIX. The UNIX client program is called *ftp*, which stands for *file transfer program*. FTP servers on UNIX usually run the *ftpd*, or *FTP daemon*, program.

The traditional user interface for FTP is a command line interface. While this makes it fairly straightforward to implement batch processing scripts, most GUI users shy away from such arcane command-driven interfaces. Fortunately, there are a number of GUI versions of FTP client programs that make it very easy to transfer files at the click of a mouse button. NetManage's Chameleon, for example, includes both FTP client and server programs with a familiar MS-Windows interface. Similar products are provided by FTP Software, Inc., and Quarterdeck. There are also public domain versions of FTP programs to be found *ftp.ncsa.uiuc.edu*. On Macintoshes, the most common public domain FTP client is called *fetch*.

The FTP server software (also referred to as *ftpd*—the *FTP Daemon*—on UNIX platforms) is enabled by default on most UNIX machines and on many other systems running the TCP/IP networking protocols. A user who has an account and password on a remote machine running an FTP server can use FTP to transfer files to and from his or her local machine to the remote machine, provided, of course, that the local machine has FTP client software.

In addition, FTP servers may also provide an anonymous login capability that permits access to a public information directory. ***Anonymous FTP*** provides the same functionality as other FTP file transfers with one major distinction—the user is locked into a captive directory structure from which he or she may upload, download, or simply browse files.

The anonymous FTP logon process, by convention, requires a user to enter the username *anonymous* (or simply *ftp*) at the username prompt. By default, the password to the anonymous account can be any non-empty character string. Many servers on the Internet, however, require the user to enter a full e-mail address for further accountability. The FTP server does not verify, however, that the submitted e-mail address is genuine.

Setting up anonymous FTP servers requires additional configuration steps—special attention should be paid to security over the course of this process. Refer to the ftp configuration manual for your system or see the information at *http://ftp.cert.org* on configuring secure FTP servers.

Anonymous FTP servers usually contain a separate, protected directory structure that is available for public use. On UNIX systems, access to these directories is generally restricted by normal system file protection mechanisms based on user and group.

Archie is a TELNET-based method of searching for files in public FTP archives around the world. Users may use TELNET to log into one of the many Archie servers on the Internet and search for the locations of publicly available files.

2.2.3.2 Potential

With anonymous FTP businesses can establish public data repositories that are accessible by systems throughout an internetwork. External data repositories may be used to distribute non-sensitive information to customers, suppliers, and the general public. Internal servers can be used as a central archive for documentation, software, utilities and patches, and any other data that needs to be easily accessible. Anonymous FTP is also useful as a central transfer point for the exchange of non-sensitive information.

The ability to script FTP commands within the UNIX shell makes it the preferred way to automate file transfers between systems. Shell scripts can be used to effect off-peak period transfers of large files.

2.2.3.3 Limitations

An inherent limitation of FTP is the inability to transfer a file directly between two users on remote systems without disclosing a password. For example, if USERA and USERB want to exchange a file directly over the net using FTP, either USERA must give his password to USERB or USERB must give his password to USERA.

The natural alternative to this problem is a two-step process whereby USERA drops the file on an anonymous FTP server and USERB picks it up at a later time. The problem with this scenario is that the file is exposed while it is on the anonymous FTP server (i.e. it may be copied, deleted, or replaced by other users on the network).

2.2.4 WAIS—Wide Area Information Server

Application Name:	WAIS (Wide Area Information Server)
Protocol:	Z39.50
Specification:	ANSI Z39.50
Origin:	Thinking Machines, Inc.
Location:	*ftp://ftp.cnidr.org/pub/NIDR.tools/zdist/*

2.2.4.1 Overview

WAIS (***Wide Area Information Server***)[4] is a full-text information indexing and retrieval system. With WAIS you can transform your legacy documents into a searchable database. Ideal for organizing and imposing structure on otherwise unstructured data, WAIS can make your information repositories available to all users on your internal wide area internetwork. Hence the name, Wide Area Information Server.

WAIS consists of three main software components: the indexer, the server, and the client. The indexer, called *waisindex* on UNIX systems, preprocesses your legacy documents and creates several files used by *waisserver*, the WAIS server. The client software runs on the end user's desktop and is known by various names, depending on the platform, operating system, and developer of the client. For example, a popular WAIS client for MS-Windows developed by Tim Gosslin at the USGS is called *WinWAIS* (see Figure 2-3). The most frequently used Macintosh client for WAIS is called *WAIStation*. For X-Windows, the client name is *xwais*.

The typical process for using WAIS to retrieve documents consists of three steps. In the first step, you identify the WAIS databases you wish to search and submit some search terms to the server using your WAIS client. The server then returns a list of headlines which describe (hopefully) the contents of each associated document known to the server. In the second step, you identify the headlines of documents that look promising and then request the server to send you the full-text documents themselves. In the final step of your search, you use the documents themselves to refine and guide further searches for more pertinent

[4] WAIS is a trademark of WAIS, Inc., a division of America On-Line in Menlo Park, CA that offers a commercial version of the WAIS server software. A freeware version, formerly called *freeWAIS*, now goes by the name *Zdist* or *Zserver*. The use of the letter Z reflects the fact that the underlying protocol is Z39.50, which is used by all WAIS-like servers. The Clearinghouse for Networked Information Discovery and Retrieval (CNIDR) is currently responsible for maintaining the Zserver software.

information. This last method of refining your search is known as the method of ***relevance feedback***.

WAIS servers can also be accessed via the World Wide Web. Many Web pages use the ***Common Gateway Interface (CGI)*** to forward WAIS search queries to a WAIS server running either on the same machine or some other machine connected via TCP/IP. The CGI approach has the advantage of allowing the user to employ his or her favorite Web browser without having to switch to a separate, standalone, specialized WAIS client. Most Web

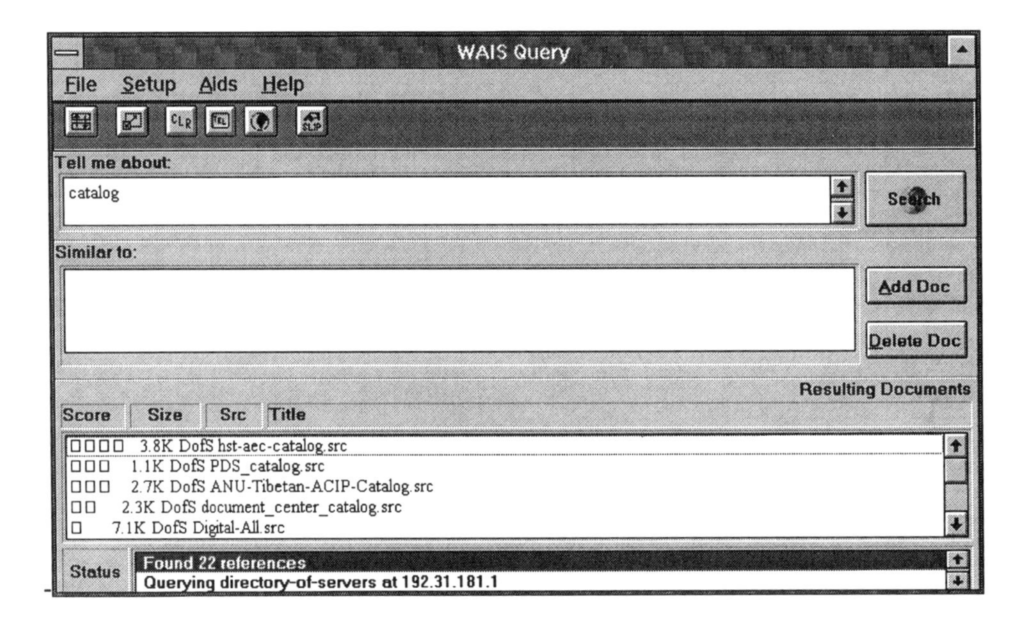

Figure 2-3. *WinWAIS Version 2.1 by Tim Goslin*

browsers, however, do not provide full WAIS client functionality. For example, few browsers implement the relevance feedback feature.

WAIS was developed jointly by Thinking Machines Corp., Apple, Dow Jones & Co. Inc., and KPMG Peat Marwick. According to Brewster Kahle, who led the development at Thinking Machines, the purpose of WAIS is "to bring the library to end users' desks and make it possible for people to access large quantities of text in a user-friendly manner."[5] WAIS is indeed user-friendly in the sense that complex searches can be performed without the user having to formulate queries in a specialized query language. Searches are usually initiated by the user entering a few words that might occur in the database documents and then refined by relevance feedback technique. As mentioned above, this technique allows the user to specify certain retrieved documents as models to be used by the *waisserver* program in finding related documents.

The success of WAIS is also due in part to its flexibility in indexing. It readily accepts several different data formats—including SMTP e-mail message and NNTP news article formats—without special pre-formatting or manipulation. Unsupported formats of structured data usually require only minor formatting changes before they can be indexed. In the UNIX environment, this can easily be accomplished with shell scripts.

Indexing is the process of building a collection of index files that facilitate the search process. Unlike a relational database, WAIS trades searching flexibility for raw performance. Since data are usually indexed off-line, retrievals are optimized—the need to build an "index" in memory is eliminated. The following box shows a typical command line example for executing *waisindex*:

```
Example of indexing:
/wais/bin/waisindex -export -contents -d phone -t one_line phonedir.txt
```

In this example, *waisindex* produces a WAIS database in which each individual line of the company phone directory (contained in the file *phonedir.txt*), is treated as a database record, known in WAIS parlance as a WAIS document. This is the significance of the *-t one_line* command line option. If this switch is absent, *waisindex* will treat the entire file as a single document. The *-export* option tells *waisindex* to include hostname and port number in the *.src* file. This information helps WAIS clients to locate the sources across the network. The *-contents* options tells it to go ahead and index the actual contents of the phone directory file. In some situations, where you are indexing an *.gif* file, for example, you need to tell *waisindex* not to index the contents. WAIS cannot directly index binary files. It can only process text. Finally, the *-d phone* option informs *waisindex* of the name you wish to assign to the database that will be created.

There are many more options that can be used to control the WAIS indexing process. You can obtain detailed information on each of these options by entering the *waisindex* command without feeding it any arguments. It will return with a listing of what arguments and options it uses.

A WAIS source is a collection of documents. These documents are often related in some way, though this is not a requirement. Sources are defined by Source Descriptor Files,

[5] Brewster Kahle, as quoted in Dern (1992).

which are created by *waisindex* and are given the suffix *.src*. In order to access a WAIS source on a remote server, you must have the *.src* files on your client machine. They are maintained, however, on your server like any other document and can be retrieved, therefore, just like any other document. A special file, sometimes called *directory-of-servers.src* or *info.src,* is conventionally used as a descriptor for a WAIS source containing other *.src* files as documents. By first searching this source using a search string like "source," you can retrieve a listing of all the WAIS sources resident on your WAIS server.

A WAIS document, in its simplest form, is an indexed text file. As the basic entity retrieved by WAIS, it consists of a headline and a body. The headline is defined at the time of indexing as some unique characteristic of the information being presented—this may be the first line of the document, the filename, or any number of other options. During a search, if WAIS finds a match for your keyword in the index of a document, it retrieves the document headline. Your client software then displays a list of all the headlines and allows the user to retrieve the full document associated with any of the displayed headlines. Documents are associated with index "types" thereby permitting the storage and retrieval of a variety of information types. Text, graphics, sounds, and even video may be processed within the WAIS environment.

WAIS ranks the information it retrieves by assigning each item a score, which is based on the number of occurrences in the document of the keywords you used. A higher score means that the information retrieved more closely matches the query.

WAIS can search multiple information sources in one search. By selecting more than one data source, you can issue queries that will span multiple info-bases. For example, you might have research and development reports going back several years. If your reports for 1995 were indexed into WAIS source described by *rd_1995.src*, those for 1994 by *rd_1994.src*, and so on, you could include each of these *.src* files in your search space. With one single search session, WAIS will look at each of these sources and return the headlines of all documents containing your search terms. You would not have to perform separate searches on each source.

Relevance feedback allows you to use the results of previous searches to further refine the search. In essence, this technique tells the WAIS server to redo the search using the indexes of one or more retrieved documents as a collection of search terms. In this way, you do not have to know what the search terms are; you are simply telling WAIS to find more documents similar to the ones it has already found and identified by you as models to follow.

It is also possible to perform WAIS searches via e-mail using a server called *WAISmail*. The WAISmail server receives SMTP e-mail messages in which search commands are embedded in the body of the message. The WAISmail server parses the body of the message, translates its commands into normal WAIS search parameters, and passes these to the WAIS server. After receiving headlines back from the WAIS server, the WAISmail server then creates an e-mail message containing the headlines in the body and sends this message back to you. You can then examine these headlines and instruct the WAISmail server to retrieve from the WAIS server any documents you so desire.

2.2.4.2 Potential

WAIS provides a simple method for converting a variety of predefined data types into searchable databases. With a little script programming to create some glueware, you can also transform legacy documents into searchable text. When integrated on the back end of Web servers, WAIS can be a powerful addition to your infobase. To convert an existing document (especially a lengthy one) into HTML for direct browsing via the Web may be too labor-intensive. To save time, you can index the document into WAIS, dividing the whole document into logical sections (e.g., chapters are perfect for this). These sections then become individual WAIS documents in the searchable WAIS database.

Some potentially useful applications of WAIS are the following:

- Electronic Newsfeeds
- Interoffice Memos
- Weekly Activity Reports
- Resumes
- Policy and Procedure Manuals
- Company Phone Books
- E-Mail Directories
- E-Mail Archives
- USENET Newsgroup Archives
- Electronic Mailing List Archives
- Company Newsletters

2.2.4.3 Limitations

One limitation of WAIS is the problem of bootstrapping new users. Not only must WAIS client software be loaded on the new user's desktop, but the user also has to be instructed on how to download the *.src* files. Also, limitations on the length of a filename on some systems (like MS-DOS and MS-Windows) render the names of the source descriptor files rather cryptic, leaving the user to wonder if he or she should download these files at all.

Another inherent limitation of WAIS is that each WAIS source is a standalone information repository without any intrinsic links to other sources. Although WAIS can search multiple WAIS sources, the user must direct it to do so by telling it explicitly which sources to search. A directory of servers can get around this problem to some extent. But WAIS lacks the intrinsic sort of coupling exhibited by the World Wide Web.

To use WinWAIS, you have to know the names of the sources you want to search. Also, you have to seed your WAIS client with the list of available sources, and you have to manually maintain this list, unless you have a directory of servers for your internetwork.

A directory of servers is a WAIS source at a central location that indexes all of the *.src* files within your corporate clone. New users' clients should be seeded with a *.src* that points to this central source. Provided that the administrators and maintainers of WAIS sources around the corporation have been diligent about putting enough descriptive information into their *.src* files, this central directory of servers source will be searchable in a meaningful way. Your users can then use this source as a place from which to download other *.src* files. Naturally, to maintain a directory of servers requires considerable commitment and consistency among WAIS administrators acoss your enterprise.

On the Internet there is a directory of servers maintained at Thinking Machines Corporation. The hostname of this server is *quake.think.com*. In fact, the option *-register* used by *waisindex* causes a copy of your *.src* file to be mailed automatically to the directory of servers at Thinking Machines. You only need to use this option, however, if your WAIS source is going to be made public and is accessible to the Internet community outside your firewall. There is no point in advertising your WAIS source if it isn't really available!

One way around these difficulties is to use the World Wide Web as the front end interface to WAIS. With a WWW to WAIS interface,[6] you can hide from the end user the details of where the WAIS source resides. On the other hand, you may have to do some HTML forms creation and/or script programming in order to capture some of the search guiding power—like relevance feedback—usually present in WAIS browsers but generally absent from the simplest HTML interfaces to WAIS.

The WAIS relevance feedback facility does not always live up to user expectations. In many cases, it simply fails to deliver any meaningful information results at all. In our experience, it may even be more appropriate to call it "irrelevance feedback!" The use of stoplists, however, may be of some assistance here.

Stoplists help you exclude from your WAIS indexes words that do not impart much meaning to your documents. These are typically words that occur so frequently as to be meaningless. In older versions of WAIS, this feature was not available. With more recent versions, however, common words like 'a', 'the', and 'this' can be filtered out by a stoplist. If you do not filter out such words, they may weigh heavily in determining which documents are "relevant" to the ones you've selected as search models.

---

[6] For more information on interfacing WWW and WAIS, see the Web server at Enterprise Integration Technologies: *http://www.eit.com/*.

In the long run, WAIS functionality may become absorbed by some of the more sophisticated client/server database engines. ORACLE, for example, already has developed full-text indexing capability and incorporated it into some of their relational database programs. They have also added the capability to generate HTML output from a search.

2.2.5 The Internet Gopher

Application Name:	The Internet Gopher
Protocol:	Gopher Protocol
Specification:	RFC 1436
Origin:	University of Minnesota
Location:	*ftp://boombox.micro.umn.edu/pub/gopher*

2.2.5.1 Overview

Gopher is a popular method of browsing and downloading information resources. These resources are interlinked via a system of text-oriented menus and pointers.

Gopher provides a menu-driven interface (see Figure 2-4) with which users can search up and down trees of information and directories as well as through indexed databases. Gopher can access local and remote WAIS sources as well as information residing on FTP servers.

The Internet Gopher was developed at the University of Minnesota (whose mascot is a gopher). The client interface is popular especially in environments that use a large number of character-oriented terminals. The Gopher client is available across many different operating systems including: MVS/XA, NeXTstep, OS/2, VMS, VM/CMS, MS Windows, and Xwindows.

Also, because the installed base of Gopher-served information on the Internet is still quite extensive, Gopher remains popular. Gopherspace—i.e., the sum total of all information accessible via Gopher—is quite vast.

Gopher may provide access to information resources outside of gopherspace through the Gopher Gateway (*go4gw*). Written in the Perl scripting language, the Gopher Gateway permits users to access to other information tools like Archie, Finger, NetNews, and Whois.

Veronica is perhaps the ultimate reference utility for finding information in Gopherspace. The Veronica server at the University of Nevada[7] currently boasts a database

---

[7] *gopher://veronica.scs.unr.edu*

of 15 million items gleaned from more than 5000 Gopher servers around the world. The database is created by an agent that traverses the structure of known Gopher servers and builds searchable archives that users may query.

Using Veronica is as simple as entering a keyword or phrase in the title you are looking for. Veronica provides links directly to the information sources resulting from the query. Another keyword search engine for gopherspace is a tool called Jughead. It, too, returns custom-built Gopher menus based on the keywords you submit.

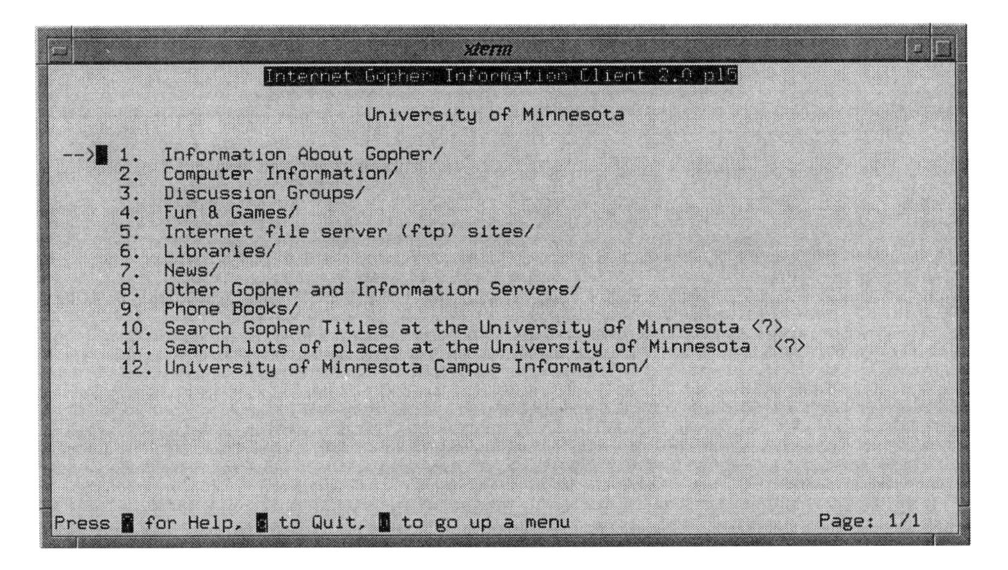

Figure 2-4. *The Internet Gopher—Version 2.0*

2.2.5.2 Potential

Gopher provides an excellent method for migrating legacy business resources to an open environment. Information legacies present a unique problem for budget-strapped organizations striving to improve their information-dissemination processes. Gopher provides a fast and inexpensive way of overcoming these issues. The use of gopher servers on larger back-end machines can help to bring useful information to the desktop systems like PCs and workstations without affecting terminal-based access from devices like IBM 3270's and DEC VT100s. By helping to integrate legacy systems with new technologies, Gopher can provide a smooth migration path for companies that have a substantial investment in historical data.

Gopher continues to be a popular means of sharing information on the Internet even in light of more versatile applications like *NCSA Mosaic*. Its simple menuing scheme is well suited to sites without higher-level graphics capabilities—i.e., those using IBM 3270 or DEC VT100 terminals. Because Gopher is so widely distributed, for some computing systems it makes sense to use Gopher when you need to reach a large audience using the terminals or terminal emulation as the lowest common denominator across all user interfaces.

Gopher continues to be a viable method of making information available despite other more convenient and attractive means of retrieving information. Gopher is relatively easy to install and configure and can be used widely in internetworked businesses that have not made the transition to graphical workstation devices.

2.2.5.3 Limitations

Although useful in migrating legacy data resources, Gopher itself is rapidly becoming a legacy as other forms of information distribution like the World Wide Web begin to occupy center stage on the Internet. Gopher is outpaced by client interfaces like *NCSA Mosaic* and *Netscape Navigator* that provide access not only to gopher information bases but a host of other information protocols as well. Although useful in helping to bridge the past, Gopher appears to have a limited future.

Gopher is going the way of the dinosaurs because its primary function was to provide an easy-to-use, menu-driven user interface and it is now surpassed in that function by Web browsers. In its day, Gopher offered a significant improvement over the command line interface of older file retrieval tools like FTP. As a protocol, gopher will be around for years, but the number of new gopher sites that will appear on the Internet in the years to come will be dwarfed by the number Web sites.

In the next section, we begin to explore the incredible phenomenon of the World Wide Web, the information system that is rapidly outpacing all others on the Internet in terms of growth and variety of information resources.

2.2.6 WWW (World Wide Web) and *NCSA Mosaic*

Application Name:	The World Wide Web
Protocol:	HTTP (HyperText Transfer Protocol)
Specification:	IETF Working Draft
Origin:	CERN (Conseil Europeen pour la Recherché Nucleaire—known in the U.S. as the European Particle Physics Laboratory)
Location:	*ftp://info.cern.ch/pub/www/*
	ftp://ftp.ncsa.uiuc.edu/NCSA Mosaic

2.2.6.1 Overview

The World Wide Web, together with multimedia Web browsers like *NCSA Mosaic* and *Netscape Navigator*, is almost solely responsible for the current Internet craze. By combining the elements of many Internet tools into a single user interface, *NCSA Mosaic* especially has ignited the final stage of the rocket that will propel Internet information usage into orbit. As of March 1995, World Wide Web traffic on the Internet has finally exceeded that of FTP, the long-standing primary consumer of Internet bandwidth.

Because of its transforming influence on the Internet, we devote the entire next chapter to exploring the World Wide Web and its browsers. Here in this section we will merely provide a brief overview of the World Wide Web and *NCSA Mosaic*.

GUI Web browsers like *NCSA Mosaic* (see Figure 2-5) and *Netscape Navigator* are unique among Internet tools. They have ushered in a new era in Internet navigation by making access to global information resources only a "click" away. Their exceptional features and robust interface make them especially useful for businesses and individuals alike.

NCSA Mosaic and its descendants simplify access to multiple information resources. Not only are World Wide Web pages available to such multimedia browsers, but also NetNews, Gopher, FTP, and even local information archives can be reached using these tools. And it doesn't stop there. The easily extensible Common Gateway Interface (CGI) allows other server-side tools and utilities to be seamlessly integrated into the WWW framework. A Web browser can act as a database front end for commercial products like standard client/server relational databases like ORACLE, Sybase, Informix, and DB2.

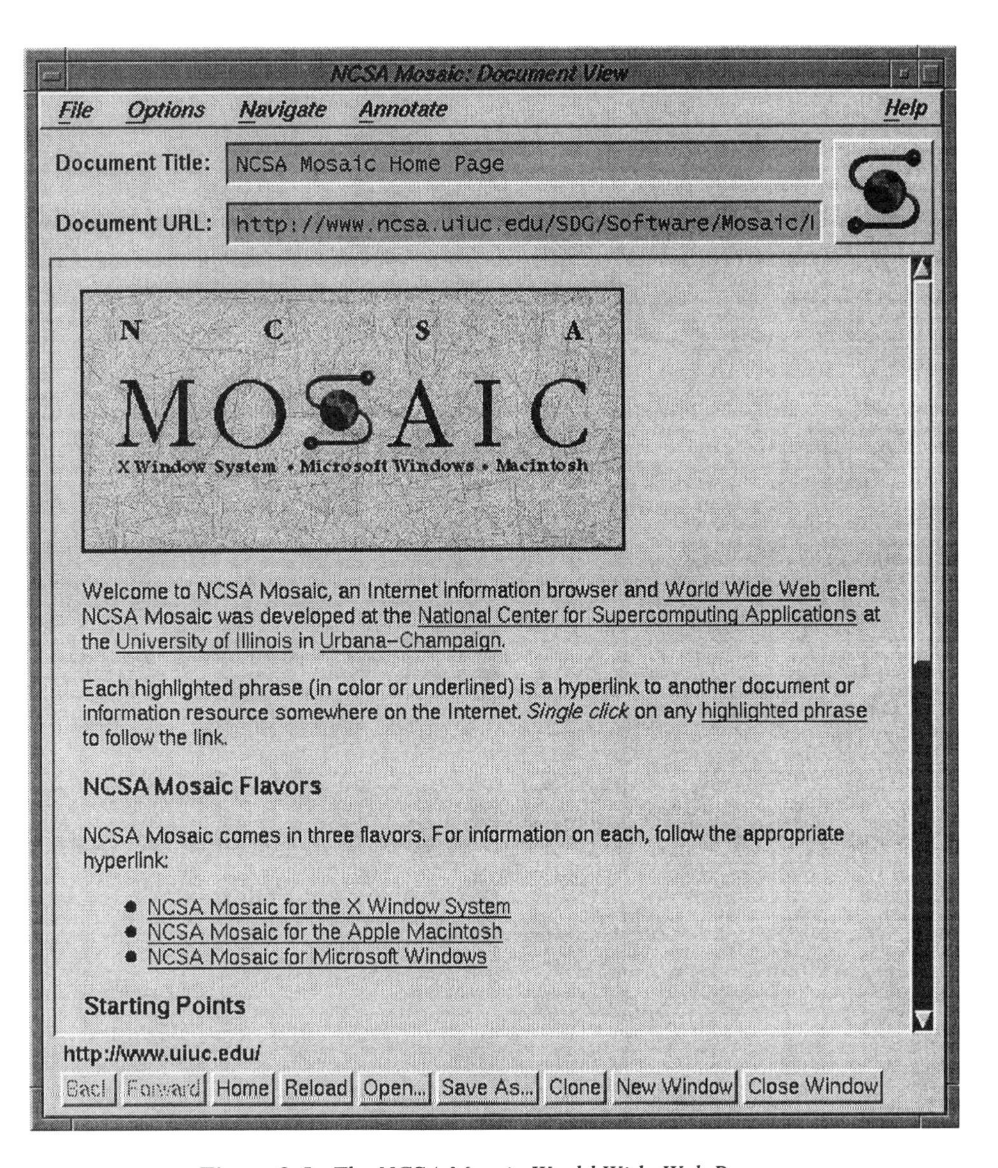

Figure 2-5. *The NCSA Mosaic World Wide Web Browser*

Information sources accessible via Web browsers may be as varied as images, video clips, sounds, and hypertext. Linked together by hyperlinks, these virtual documents are sometimes referred to as hyperdocuments or hypermedia.

NCSA Mosaic and its cousins can also perform authentication, either on a host-by-host basis or user-by-user basis. User authentication can be achieved with the addition of secured directories that are only accessible by specified users. Authentication options include the use of PGP or RIPEM digital signatures or simply by requiring a username and password.

Web browsers build their displays by interpreting text streams composed in HyperText Markup Language, or HTML.

Many browsers like *NCSA Mosaic* provide on-line forms capabilities. This means that they can present the user with fill-out boxes, check boxes, pull-down list boxes, and radio buttons, making user input of data very convenient. With on-line forms, you can provide professional quality front-end processing for a range of applications. From databases to simple queries and lookups, the forms capability in *NCSA Mosaic* and other browsers offers unique and easy to program features.

What's the difference between hypertext and hypermedia? Kevin Hughes (1994) of Enterprise Integration Technologies makes this distinction:

> Hypermedia is hypertext with a difference—hypermedia documents contain links not only to other pieces of text, but also to other forms of media—sounds, images, and movies. Images themselves can be selected to link to sounds or documents. Hypermedia simply combines hypertext and multimedia.

By far the most widely used medium besides text on the World Wide Web is that of graphic images. Most often these images are included in-line. This means that the Web browser sees the reference to the graphics files embedded in the HTML stream and automatically downloads the images for display.

2.2.6.2 Potential

The potential for using World Wide Web technology within the corporate Internet clone appears to be unlimited. Since most GUI Web browsers can function as a front end to just about any kind of application, they offer a fast and easy method for making legacy data resources available in a client/server environment. Since Web servers on the back end can be integrated with just about any application, the chain for linking complex legacy programs is complete. It simplifies access to network information services by providing a simple and consistent application across many computer platforms. The extensibility of the corporate

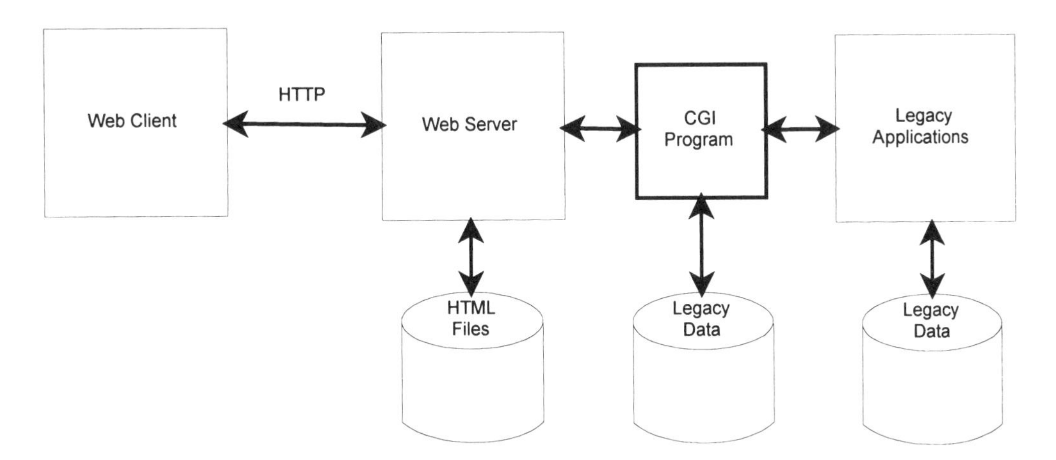

Figure 2-6. *Integrating Legacy Data into a Corporate Web Using the CGI*

Web is illustrated schematically in Figure 2-6.

2.2.6.3 Limitations

Because hypermedia can involve large files of graphics, video, or audio data, bandwidth-limited environments can see long delays in downloading hypermedia documents. This is particularly evident with 14.4 Kbps dial-up connections. If you are planning to provide corporate information to the external World Wide Web, you should bear in mind that many persons in your potential audience are accessing the Internet via such dial-up links. Including several hundred kilobytes of in-line graphics in your home page may be interpreted by users as corporate arrogance or insensitivity.

The Common Gateway Interface has some limitations as well. CGI is limited to data passed on a command line or through the standard input and output. Standard input is data that would normally come from an ASCII keyboard, while standard output data would normally be sent to a terminal for display. Although particularly well suited to UNIX program, many of which are designed to handle data input from the standard input, it may not be well suited to programs running in other environments.

2.2.7 Miscellaneous Internet Tools

This subsection discusses briefly a few other elementary TCP/IP tools you'll need to use in order to build your corporate piece of the Internet. These tools are primarily intended for the system and network manager rather than the typical end user. Additional information on Internet tools can be found in the excellent summary located at John December's Internet Tools Web site:

http://www.rpi.edu/Internet/Guides/decemj/itools/top.html

2.2.7.1 PING

Ping is a program used to determine whether or not a remote computer on your network is on-line and active. It is a basic network troubleshooting tool used to determine if two hosts can exchange IP packets. It works by sending out a series of Internet Control Message Protocol echo request messages. Upon receipt of each echo request message, the remote machine responds back to the originating host with an echo reply message. Besides verifying the status of the remote computer, the sender's *ping* program also computes and displays the elapsed time for the complete round trip of the echo messages. *Ping* is included in nearly every distribution of the UNIX operating system. Most TCP/IP software packages for other operating systems also include a version of *ping.*

2.2.7.2 TRACEROUTE

Traceroute is a TCP/IP network analysis tool that traces the route taken by IP packets across your network. It displays the addresses of all intervening routers along the path to a given remote host. If one of your routers (or somebody else's) is down, you'll know it either from the fact that your packets never reach their destination (in which case *ping* suffices), or they take an alternate route to the one they ordinarily take.

Traceroute makes clever use of the time-to-live field in IP packets. The value of this field is decremented by one at each hop (usually a router) along the way to the destination host. By deliberately setting the time-to-live field to 1, *traceroute* can force the router one hop away to send an error message (a time exceeded message) back to the sending host. This informs *traceroute* that the destination host is more than one hop away. It also tells *traceroute* the name and IP address of the router that is one hop away.

Next, *traceroute* sends a message destined for the remote host but with the value of the time-to-live field set to 2. This enables *traceroute* to determine which router is 2 hops away. *Traceroute* continues in this fashion until the final destination is reached. In this way, the user of *traceroute* can determine the exact route taken by packets from the local host to the remote host and thus gain an understanding of the intervening network topology.

2.2.7.3 NSLOOKUP

Another workhorse of the TCP/IP tool suite is a program called *nslookup*. You can think of this as meaning "nameserver lookup." You can use *nslookup* to translate domain names to IP addresses and vice versa. *Nslookup* examines records in the database maintained by your network's Domain Name System nameserver. It is usually included in standard TCP/IP software tool suites.

2.2.7.4 FINGER

Finger is used to determine if a specific user is logged on to a remote machine on your network. It requires that the remote host be running a server such as the *fingerd* daemon on UNIX systems. It also supplies information about when users last read their e-mail. You can use this program as a security monitoring tool to see who is leaving their terminal sessions unattended.

Chapter 3

THE WORLD WIDE WEB

3.1 The Potential of the World Wide Web

In the previous chapter we touched upon some of the Internet software tools most commonly used by businesses to develop their internal Internet clones. Although we have already introduced the World Wide Web as a subset of Internet tools, the potential importance of the Web for both business communications and internal information dissemination warrants devoting an entire chapter to further exploration.

The rapid advances taking place in the open systems arena today are dramatically affecting the ways that enterprises conduct business. The mainstream movement toward client/server applications transcends the barriers of proprietary computing by bringing open information architectures directly to the desktop. Thanks to industry-wide standards, information previously locked away or isolated by incompatible networks and operating systems can be delivered to multiple platforms using a common network infrastructure. These developments have opened the door to collaborative computing efforts that allow expertise to be defined virtually instead of geographically. Harnessing the power of this interaction can lead to decreased product development times, reduced effort for problem solving, and better customer support and end-user awareness. The premier example of this collaborative development is the astonishing phenomenon of the World Wide Web.

The World Wide Web empowers users to be both information consumers and providers across a wide area. Nearly anyone can have easy-to-use client software, i.e., a Web browser on his or her desktop, and nearly anyone can provide information via a server on his or her desktop. With Web server software like *WinHTTP* from NCSA and easy-to-use HTML authoring software like *HotMetal* from SoftQuad, even a single lowly desktop MS-Windows 486 can become a server of information to an entire corporation, indeed to the whole world via the Internet. Although these Web authoring tools are not yet commonplace, they are rapidly proliferating, and some of the more popular word processing programs like MS-Word and WordPerfect now provide features for saving documents in HTML format. This places HTML authoring capability within reach of ordinary word processing users.

The Web's natural and simple approach to linking otherwise isolated information sources has made it one of the fastest growing client/server systems in the world. In terms of information quantity and sheer numbers of cooperating computers, the Web is arguably the world's largest client/server system. With over 30,000 Web servers on the public Internet and thousands more locked away behind firewalls within corporate Internet clones, estimates of Web growth reach as high as 500 gigabytes per month!

The vast potential of the Web excites the imagination. Everyday new information resources are added, existing servers improve their information content and expand their services, and new ideas are applied to inter- and intra-company communications. As the Internet topology grows to encompass more and more commercial and private networks, this expanding technology will bring greater numbers of businesses and individuals into cyberspace. Those at the forefront of this information revolution are poised to capitalize on a wealth of opportunities that will expand the boundaries of electronic commerce.

The potential for corporate Web expansion goes way beyond the simple addition of new static information resources. Due to the ability of Web servers to interface on the back end with other programs and processes, the potential for making dynamic information available across the corporation is virtually unlimited. Animation and dynamic refresh of displayed data are two examples of back-end, dynamic coupling between Web servers and other programs. Commercial database engines like Oracle and DB2 can now wrap their output in streams of HyperText Markup Language, yielding Web pages with limitless quanitities of information built on-the-fly. The vast corporate warehouses of relational data are now available to corporate users thanks to such back-end programming interfaces and easy-to-use navigation tools like the *NCSA Mosaic* and *Netscape Navigator*.

At Hewlett-Packard, for example, nearly 100,000 employees can launch *Netscape Navigator* from their desktops and access the company's corporate-wide servers. Prior to their installation of Netscape browsers and servers, HP's information managers had to disseminate information daily to file servers on 300 separate LANs. Because of the wide area orientation of TCP/IP and the Netscape client/server architecture, however, these managers now need only to disseminate information to six servers. In addition, HP employees now have access to the thousands of servers on the external World Wide Web.[1]

3.2 The Wonders of the Web

Why all the interest in the World Wide Web? Why are the information resources on the Web growing at a monthly rate of 500 gigabytes, roughly the information equivalent of adding 500 new sets of the *Encyclopedia Britannica* each month?

---

[1] See Kline (1995).

We think the explanation is fivefold, owing to:

1. the ***distributed*** nature of the Internet and the Web;
2. the ***simplicity*** and ***ease-of-use*** of Web browsers like *NCSA Mosaic* and *Netscape Navigator*;
3. the ***multimedia*** and ***multiprotocol*** character of the Web;
4. the ease with which you can offer information on-line and ***integrate*** it via hyperlinks with other WWW repositories; and
5. the ***extensibility*** of Web servers via back-end gateways.

The distributed nature of the Internet and the Web allows parallel development of information repositories. With more than 30,000 Web servers already in place around the world and scores being added independently every day, it is no wonder that the Web is growing so rapidly.

Naturally, there would not be so many Web servers today were it not for the fact that the information they serve is very easily accessed by users of Web browsers. We have already alluded several times to the fact that *NCSA Mosaic* is the killer application that has spurred the World Wide Web revolution. Easy-to-use browsers like *NCSA Mosaic* have created a market pull or demand for more information. Like its forerunner Gopher, the Web has spawned a huge mass market for information.

Another feature of the Web, attractive to consumers of information, is the wide range of media formats accessible via the Web. Text, graphics, sound, video, and animation are all easily accessible via Web browsers. Further, the Web is multiprotocol. Its system of ***URL***s (***Uniform Resource Locators***) offers a uniform method of accessing not only its native ***HTTP*** (***HyperText Transfer Protocol***) applications but also others like Gopher, NNTP, and FTP.

Using hyperlinks, Webmasters can easily extend their Web repositories by integrating it with others. This gives the Web the look and feel of a single virtual (and huge) information library. Not only can you interlink Web documents on different servers, you can also use the ***Common Gateway Interface*** (***CGI***), to integrate your Web server with other, non-Web programs running on the same or different platforms. You do this on the back end in a fashion transparent to users on the front end. A Web server can launch any local software, whether interpreted script or compiled program (as long as it can generate streams of HTML output), and pass the program's HTML output back to the Web browser client. This provides the WWW with considerable extensibility.

3.2.1 History of the WWW

In 1989, Tim Berners-Lee began working on what is now called the W3 initiative. His work at CERN (an international particle physics laboratory in Geneva, Switzerland) fostered collaboration among researchers across the European continent. He designed his system to use hypertext links across an internetwork to build a Web of information resources. As volunteers from all over the Internet joined the W3 project, it advanced rapidly.

According to Hobbes' Internet Timeline, the first World Wide Web application was officially released by CERN in 1992. Tim Berners-Lee, the developer of WWW, had been working for several years to develop the Web's basic data model and implement its basic features. As early as 1989, he envisioned a model different from that of Gopher, WAIS, or FTP. He realized that an object-oriented approach to a hypermedia system would provide wider access to information than other systems available at the time. Consequently, the World Wide Web can incorporate information from a wide variety of systems and protocols—WAIS, Gopher, FTP, NNTP, and local file systems.

The first implementation of a WWW client was developed for the NeXT operating system.

The first graphical WWW browser was *NCSA Mosaic*. It first ran on UNIX workstations running X-Windows and soon thereafter was ported to personal computers like the Macintosh and IBM compatibles running MS-Windows. Released by the National Center for Supercomputing Applications (NCSA) at the University of Illinois in June of 1993, this browser suddenly made the Web accessible to ordinary Internet users using low-end machines. Almost overnight, it created a mass market for Internet information. Few realized at that time how much Web energy this application would unleash. Representing a major turning point in Internet ease of use, *NCSA Mosaic* was the catalyst needed to activate the unlimited potential of the World Wide Web. No longer were the information caverns of the world closed to the average person. Now anyone with a computer, a mouse, a modem, and an Internet connection could "surf the net" in search of information treasures for business or pleasure.

3.2.2 How the Web Works

Many people fail to realize that once you have downloaded a hypermedia document from a Web server, you are no longer connected to that server. The connection stays open only as long as required for the download. Once downloaded, your browser software stores the document locally on your own computer. This section explains this and other operational aspects of the Web.

3.2.2.1 Conceptual Overview

Conceptually, the World Wide Web is both a collection of interlinked information sources and a method of navigating the "space" spanned by these hyperlinks and other Web extension mechanisms like the Common Gateway Interface. Although these sources may have many different storage formats and follow different applications protocols, they share a common user interface on the Web. The WWW currently supports Gopher, anonymous FTP, USENET News (NNTP), local files systems, and a host of other information resources through the Common Gateway Interface (CGI). The CGI permits Web information providers to code their own interfaces to databases and other types of data repositories.

Many people originally tended to identify the World Wide Web with *NCSA Mosaic*, the original killer application that made the Web easily accessible and an overnight sensation. But does the browser exhaust the Web? Isn't Gopher part of the Web? How about FTP? Although each of these things is part of the Web, none of them exhausts the Web in its entirety. *NCSA Mosaic* is merely the original freeware client program for viewing the contents of the Web. It is only one of several windows through which you can view the Web's resources. And Gopher, though it has been integrated into and is thus accessible via the Web, is an independent client/server information system. The same holds for FTP. To understand the Web as a whole, however, you must realize that it is actually an abstraction encompassing many internetworked information resources and services. It is a client/server system—perhaps the largest in the world—composed of many client/server subsystems. (For a general overview of the client/server paradigm, see Appendix A.)

The Web is becoming more broadly defined as the group of information services (and their underlying, enabling protocols) that make up this new information revolution. The Web will continue to grow as it absorbs new application protocols. The term "Web" is catchy and in spite of its vague definition, it's easy to picture a spider's web interconnected at a variety of points. In mathematical terms, the Web is an abstract directed graph. Each hyperlink, for example, connects two servers, but the link has a direction or sense. We speak of a hyperlink ***from*** Server A ***to*** Server B.

Gopher, anonymous FTP, and NNTP, because they are accessible via the system of Uniform Resource Locators (URLs) and have standardized port numbers (to be discussed below), are now included in the Internet's Web of information. Like most Internet information systems, WWW is based on the client/server model for computing. In the most general case, WWW client programs link to HTTP servers. Other applications protocols that may be supported by a particular client include FTP, Gopher, and NNTP. Information distributed via the Web may not require any special formatting at all—plain text is acceptable. To make a data file available via the Web, you only need to deposit it on an anonymous FTP server.

Although there are no hard and fast rules about what Web clients or servers should or should not be able to do, at a minimum they usually feature the ability to communicate via the HyperText Transport Protocol (HTTP). This protocol, together with the ingenious system of Uniform Resource Locators (URLs) devised by Tim Berners-Lee, gives the Web its essential and uniquely cohesive character. The HTTP and URL conventions are the glue—the interface specification—that makes the World Wide Web both world wide and web-like.

HTTP specifies how a browser should go about requesting data from a Web server. The most frequently used request mechanism is called the GET method. It simply tells the Web server to retrieve the file on the Web server specified as an argument to the GET command. The arguments passed to the server via a GET request are most often the path names used to uniquely identify files stored on the server. The path names are taken from the URLs specified in the hyperlinks.

3.2.2.2 Uniform Resource Locators (URLs)

URLs, or Uniform Resource Locators, provide a consistent naming structure for information resources and applications found on the Internet. Just as a DOS directory path indicates the location of a file on a single PC, so a URL indicates a file on a computer on an internetworked system of computers. In essence, it turns literally thousands of computers into an extension of your own computer! URLs make the WWW possible by providing a consistently implemented and widely accepted method of locating information on an internetwork. The URL takes the directory path concept one step further to accommodate an internetworked system.

URLs contain four basic parts: the protocol, the system name, the port number, and the directory path. This is illustrated in the following schema:

protocol://system_name:port_number/directory_path

The following are some of the legal values for *protocol*:

- *file*
- *news*
- *gopher*
- *http*
- *ftp*
- *telnet*

The *system name* is generally a fully qualified host and domain name such as *sushi.widget.com.*

Perhaps you've noticed in surfing the Web that some URLs have a number near the end. For example, you may have seen the number 8001 in a moderately long URL such as *http://www.sushi.widget.com:8001*. This is called the *port number*, which is optional and contains the TCP port number of the protocol server on the remote system. The default port numbers are used if this field is left blank. The following port numbers are the default values for the most common Web protocols:

- 80 for HTTP
- 70 for Gopher
- 23 for FTP
- 21 for Telnet

These ports have come to be known as "well-known" ports for their corresponding protocols. A client and server pair can agree to use virtually any port number. WWW clients understand many different protocols. By using a single client application, users need only learn one set of rules for accessing many different information sources. The advantages are clear—a single application interface can increase the availability of information by making it easier to access. The disadvantages are less obvious—since a single application interface must work with many different protocols, there is a reduced probability that all of a protocol's features will be fully implemented. For example, although most Web clients will perform FTP transactions, some work only with anonymous FTP servers—they have no provision for FTP connections to an account with a user name other than anonymous.

The *directory path* contains the location of the file on the remote system relative to the server root directory. Besides the directory name, this path includes the filename and extension. The file extension is not important to how the browser handles the data, but by convention, HTML files have the extension *.html* on UNIX machines and *.htm* on PCs.

To illustrate the above schema in real life, consider the following full-blown URL for a file on our Web server at our company CyberStrategies:

http://www.csz.com:80/inland/html/iebw.html.

This URL is decoded as follows:

- *http://* indicates the HTTP access protocol
- *www.csz.com* is the hostname of our Web server
- *80* is the port number, which ordinarily would not be specified in the URL since it is the default
- */inland/html/iebw.html* says that the file *iebw.html* is located in the subdirectory *html* which, in turn, is located in the inland subdirectory.

3.2.2.3 HyperText Transfer Protocol (HTTP)

Information on the Web can be distributed in many ways. The most prominent and well known protocol for this distribution is the ***HyperText Transfer Protocol***, or ***HTTP***. This protocol determines the commands, requests, and responses that are exchanged between Web clients (i.e., browsers) and servers. Web clients send requests for information to Web servers, which respond by sending the contents of files indicated by the URL selected by the user.

It is important to realize that a single transaction between a Web client and server pair usually lasts only a few seconds. After the user selects a hyperlink from the page he or she is currently viewing, the browser establishes a connection with the server indicated by the URL associated with the hyperlink, and then receives from the server the requested information. After that download, the connection with the server is terminated. It is not like logging into a computer, in which case some of the computer's process resources are allocated to the user upon login. The HTTP connection is terminated as soon as the transaction is complete, thus releasing the server's process resources for other users on the internetwork. This feature has both pros and cons. On the positive side, it allows the user to view the downloaded information without consuming valuable shared CPU resources on the remote server. On the negative side, however, it means that the server expends extra computing overhead to open and close each connection, adding delays in the transaction. Future versions of HTTP may provide for keeping some connections open

How does the Web client know which URL to use? The HTML file previously fetched by the browser contains special ***tags*** that identify hyperlinks to other URLs. The browser, by convention, displays the name associated with the hyperlink but not the specified URL. This information is kept behind the scenes, though some browsers will display the URL in a small window at the bottom of the screen whenever the user points the cursor at the displayed hyperlink. By clicking the mouse while the cursor is pointing at the hyperlink, the user instructs the browser to fetch the indicated resource from the (possibly new) remote host, and the cycle begins all over again.

3.2.2.4 HyperText Markup Language (HTML)

HTML, or ***HyperText Markup Language***, is a non-proprietary document tagging language based on the International Standard ISO 8879-1986—***Standard Generalized Markup Language*** (***SGML***). It consists mostly of pairs of tags which inform the browser how to display the data transmitted between the tags. For example, one such tag is *<em>*, which tells the browser to emphasize (usually using italics) the following text. This tag turns on the browser's emphasizing font. The corresponding end tag, *</em>*, turns it off. What the browser sees, then, is a stream of tags, text, and references to other files (often graphics files or hyperlinks to other HTML files) which it interprets according to the HTML syntax and presents to the user in accordance with the formatting specified by the tags. Tags are thus primarily formatting and file-fetching directives to be executed by the browser.

3.2.2.5 The Web Client

As the World Wide Web is based on the client/server computing paradigm, we turn now to a discussion of the client side of the equation. The Web client is most commonly referred to as the Web browser.

3.2.2.5.1 Interactive Features

Several interactive features make the WWW unique. The CGI (Common Gateway Interface), image maps, forms, authentication, and animation add unique appeal and extensibility to WWW. Taken as a whole, these features make up an environment robust enough to support a very complex information system, yet also humble enough to satisfy the ease-of-use concerns of the novice user. The Web is thus a rich, multipurpose environment.

User authentication and security is one of the fastest growing areas of functionality for Web tools. Many versions of the NCSA, CERN, and Netscape servers incorporate username/password security with encrypted transmission. Progress in this area has already given rise to considerable electronic commerce on the net. As these security features become more widespread, we may see the current phase of explosive growth in the use of the Internet sustained for several years.

Another interactive capability of the Web is offered by forms processing. In this case, the browser presents to the user a screen of blank forms boxes, toggle boxes, and text areas to be filled in by the user. In this way, database queries, user surveys, and customer feedback can be gathered and processed by the Web server itself and processed by other programs linked via the Common Gateway Interface.

Image maps are static graphic images that have been divided into selectable areas each with its own associated event. These selectable areas are called active subregions. For example, if you had a graphic image of two people standing side by side, the image could be mapped so that more information about either individual could be accessed by clicking in a predefined region (usually the area of their picture mapped onto their pictures). Image maps are pictures that have been logically mapped to hyperlinks. When a point within an image map is selected with a mouse click, the coordinate position on the image is passed through a process that defines the hyperlink to be invoked.

Although image maps can help organize access to information in an intuitive fashion, they do involve graphic images which take longer to download than ordinary text-based hyperlinks. They add aesthetic appeal, but you have to weigh the benefit of that appeal against the user's time you are consuming in the process of downloading the images. Is the bang worth the buck? This may not be a serious issue in internal networks with adequate bandwidth. But if you are serving information to external users, you need to bear in mind that many of them will be using low speed dial-up connections.

3.2.2.5.2 Web Browsers

There are many Web browsers available today. Some are freeware, some are shareware, and some are commercial. Most are graphical, in that they offer full multimedia presentation capabilities, but some are designed to work only with a character-based terminal. In this section, we mention only a few in each category. As we do not intend this to be a user's manual, we will not discuss the pros and cons of each of these browsers; instead, we will indicate where you can go to get more information about each of these browsers. In fact, a great place to begin searching for browsers is:

http://www.yahoo.com/Computers/World_Wide_Web/Browsers/.

Noncommercial Web Browsers. A few of the noncommercial, graphical Web browsers—and the URLs of several sources from which you can obtain them—are contained in the following list:

- Cello—*ftp.law.cornell.edu*
- *NCSA Mosaic—ftp.ncsa.uiuc.edu*
- WinWeb—*ftp.einet.net*

CERN, the birthplace of the Web, offers a simple text-only browser called WWW. Info can be obtained via FTP at *info.cern.ch*, in directory /pub/www. Lynx, another

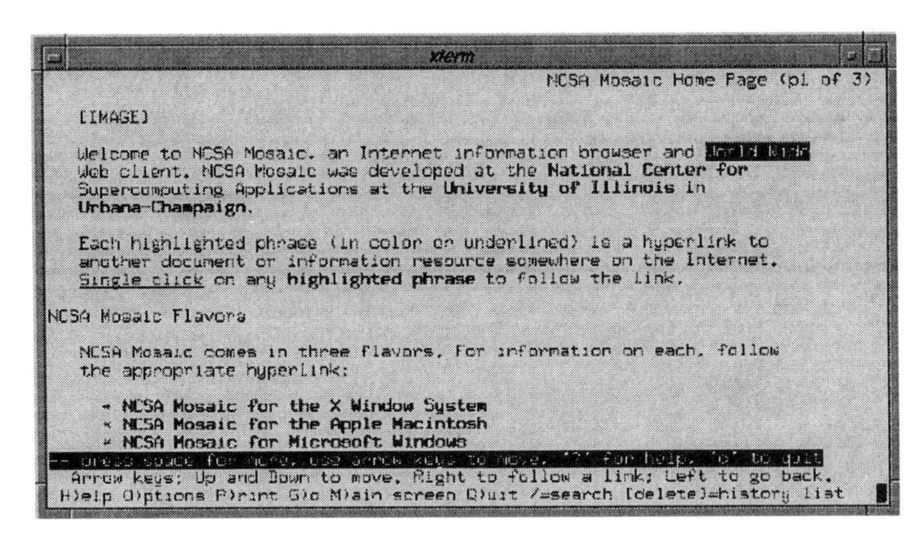

Figure 3-1. *Example of a Web Page as Presented by LYNX, a Character-Based Browser*

character-based browser can be obtained from *ftp2.cc.ukans.edu*, in directory /pub/WWW/lynx. An example of a Lynx screen display is shown in Figure 3-1.

If you don't yet have a browser and need to bootstrap your internal Web, a good place to start your search for a Web browser is the FTP server at NCSA (*ftp.ncsa.uiuc.edu)*. All you need to bootstrap yourself in this case is FTP. In the directory /Mosaic you will find subdirectories for the various distributions of *NCSA Mosaic*. The site contains *NCSA Mosaic* browsers for Macintosh, Windows, and X.

Commercial Web Browsers. In the following paragraphs we discuss some of the more popular commercial Web browsers.

The *Netscape Navigator* boasts some of the most impressive features of any commercial WWW browser. Not only have Netscape's software developers aggressively pushed the much needed extensions to HTML, but they have sought out and developed new technologies that allow information to be securely passed between a client and server. The Netscape browser is, according to most estimates, the most widely used browser on the Internet. One survey ranks the percentage of Web users using the *Netscape Navigator* at nearly 70 percent.[2]

Available for MS Windows, Apple Macintosh, and X-Windows systems, the *Netscape Navigator* supports the following features:

- Support for the NNTP protocol, including a newsreader with sort and posting capabilities
- Multiple, simultaneous, and progressive image loading
- Continuous document streaming
- Local caching
- Native image decompression
- Local printing and saving of both HTML and image files
- Dynamic refresh of data (both client pull and server push)
- Animation
- Tables

Several commercialized variants of *NCSA Mosaic* have appeared in the marketplace. The licensing agent for *NCSA Mosaic* is a company called Spyglass. They have produced their own version of *NCSA Mosaic* and have entered into an agreement with Microsoft to help

[2] See Ed Kubaitis's excellent survey of browser usage located on the University of Illinois Web server at *htttp://www.cen.uiuc.edu/~ejk/bryl.html.*

develop the Web browser offered to customers of Microsoft's Windows 95 operating system and users of the Microsoft Network.

Another popular Web browser based on the NCSA standard is *AIR Mosaic* from Spry, Inc.

Naturally, the salient feature of all these commercial browsers is that they come with documentation and are fully supported. Usually, evaluation copies can be downloaded from the Internet at no cost and used for a limited time. For details, see the README files accompanying these software packages. For information on how to obtain the *Netscape Navigator*, consult Netscape's home page at *http://www.netscape.com/home/welcome.html*. AIR Mosaic can be obtained from Spry's FTP server at *ftp.spry.com*.

What is best for you depends on your situation. If you are only experimenting with Internet technologies, then we advise you to start with *NCSA Mosaic* (read carefully the licensing agreement!) and check out some of the evaluation copies of various commercial browsers before you commit to purchasing thousands of licenses.

3.2.2.6 The Web Server

The Web server, also known as the HTTP server, is the hub of activity for WWW transactions. It is the engine that manages the local complex of Web pages and provides hyperlinks to other servers and back-end programs. Each Web server in a corporate Web is a major node usually containing related information.

The most common Web servers UNIX use the nomenclature *httpd*, the *d* standing for ***daemon***. A daemon is UNIX parlance for a memory-resident program that waits to service connection request originating from networks connected to the server machine. Most of the original Web servers were in fact designed to run on multitasking UNIX servers and workstations. However, Web servers for other platforms, including MS-Windows, Macintosh, and OS/2, are now quite common. *WinHTTPD*, for example, is a Web server that runs under the MS-Windows environment. It was written by Rob McCool while employed at NCSA.

As of this writing, there are two free *httpd* servers available on the net: the NCSA server and the CERN server. There are many variants of these for various UNIX platforms, but most of these are derived from either the NCSA or the CERN server. NCSA binaries for several server platforms are available at the NCSA FTP site: *ftp.ncsa.uiuc.edu*. Precompiled versions of the CERN WWW server and client software products are available via FTP from *ftp.w3.org* in the /pub/www/bin directory.

A good place to begin shopping for either commercial or public domain servers is *http://www.yahoo.com/Computers/World_Wide_Web/HTTP/Servers/*.

Commercial servers offer enhanced security and electronic commerce features. The Netsite server from Netscape Communications is probably one of the most advanced in the area of security and is already in widespread use.

One of the most powerful features of the Web is that information providers are not constrained by the server they choose—information may be provided to the Web via custom programs or scripts accessible by the server on the back end.

HTTP is merely another protocol in a long line of Internet protocols layered on TCP/IP. Like the WAIS, Gopher, or NNTP protocols, the power lies not in how the data is transferred but in what can be done with it. By extending the Web server via a back-end interface such as the CGI, other HTML-generating programs or scripts can be effectively integrated into the Web server. We have already discussed this with regard to the forms interface. The CGI permits information providers the flexibility of customizing the data retrieval mechanisms that go on behind the scenes. It provides a method for handing off information from the Web server to another job for processing.

For example, an HTML form can be used to take query information. That information is then passed over the net to a server that hands the information off to a script or other application via the CGI. The resulting information may then be passed back to the server in raw HTML format, and finally by the server to the client information for display.

Quite often, back-end programs are written in interpreted script languages such as awk and perl, though C programs compiled for optimal speed are becoming more common.

On the server side, back-end processing can provide access to databases or knowledge bases. Information may be parsed "on the fly" to provide users with hyperlinked lists that are the results of a query. This opens the door to "dynamic" pages that are tailored to recipients' needs based on information they provide either before or during an operation. HTTP server can provide secure access to screens via a built-in username and password scheme or through encryption techniques.

The Oracle corporation now provides an HTML interface to the World Wide Web similar to the CGI. In this implementation, Oracle database management functions are separated completely from the retrieval mechanisms like the World Wide Web. Similarly, IBM now provides a DB2 gateway. These database engines can now generate HTML formatted output to SQL queries. Figure 3-2 shows a schematic block diagram of a typical Web server interface with an SQL database.

With the integration of database products and WWW servers, information management and distribution is raised to a new level. The Oracle and IBM approaches present new opportunities to deliver information to desktop systems across an enterprise network. Information providers who have already organized their data within databases structures may use these commercial utilities or develop their own using *NCSA Mosaic*'s CGI and tool sets like GSQL. This development facilitates the integration of legacy systems with the WWW methodology within the corporate Internet clone.

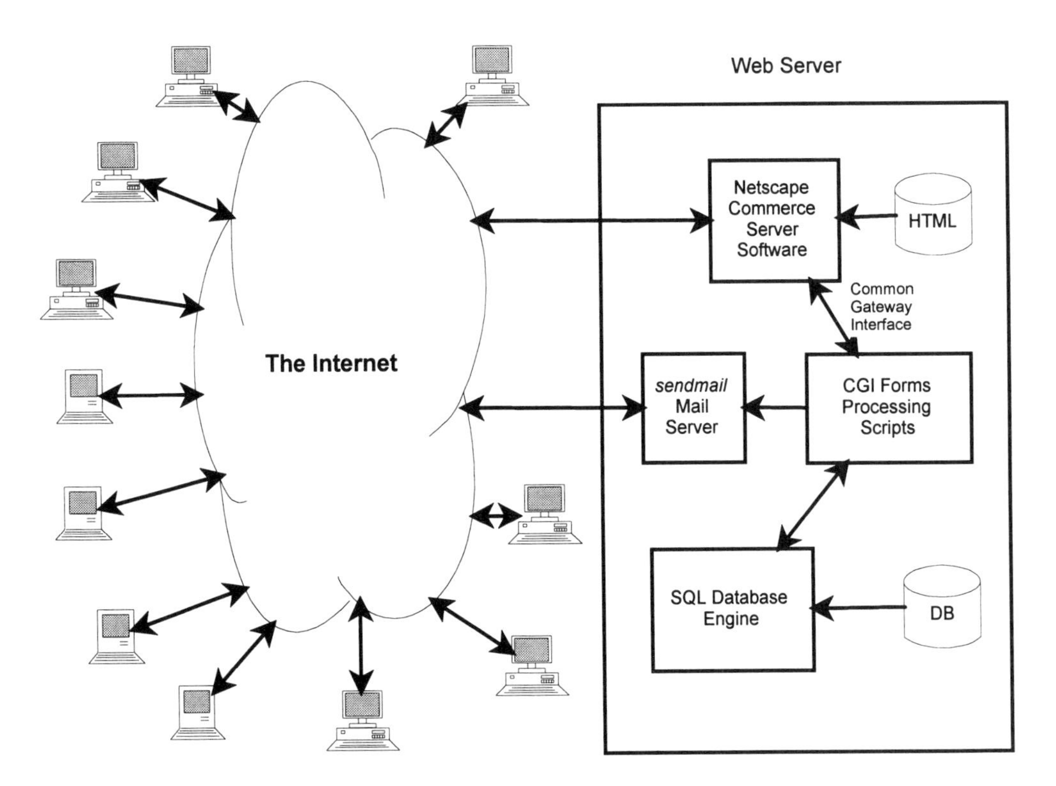

Figure 3-2. *Database Integration with a Web Server*

3.2.3 WWW Authoring Basics

Crucial to developing a corporate internal Web is an understanding of how to build Web pages in the HyperText Markup Language (HTML). In this section we provide the rudiments

```
<HTML>

<HEAD>
<TITLE>Example HTML Document</TITLE>
<H1>Header 1</H1>
<H2>Header 2</H2>
<H3>Header 3</H3>
<HR>
</HEAD>
<BODY>
<IMG SRC="me.gif" ALT="[A Picture of Scott Downs]">
<P>Now is the time for all good men to come to the aid of their country.</P>
<UL>
<LI> List Item 1</LI>
<LI> List Item 2</LI>
<UL>
<LI> Embedded Item 1</LI>
<LI> Embedded Item 2</LI>
</UL>
</UL>
<A HREF="http://www.csz.com">The CyberStrategies Home Page</A>
</BODY>
</HTML>
```

Figure 3-3. *A Simple HTML File*

necessary to get you started. There are many good books on HTML authoring and also many excellent on-line Web sites and resources dedicated to the art of Web page construction. Our brief introduction merely aims to point out that there is really no mystery behind the syntax of HTML and that facility in developing Web pages can be gained without an excessively long or steep learning curve. Moreover, there are many good Web authoring tools—many available on-line—that hide the details of HTML from the author.

3.2.3.1 Developing a Web Page

In Figure 3-3 you'll find a stream of HTML tags and intervening text, all of which might be contained in a typical HTML file. The page that results is shown in Figure 3-4.

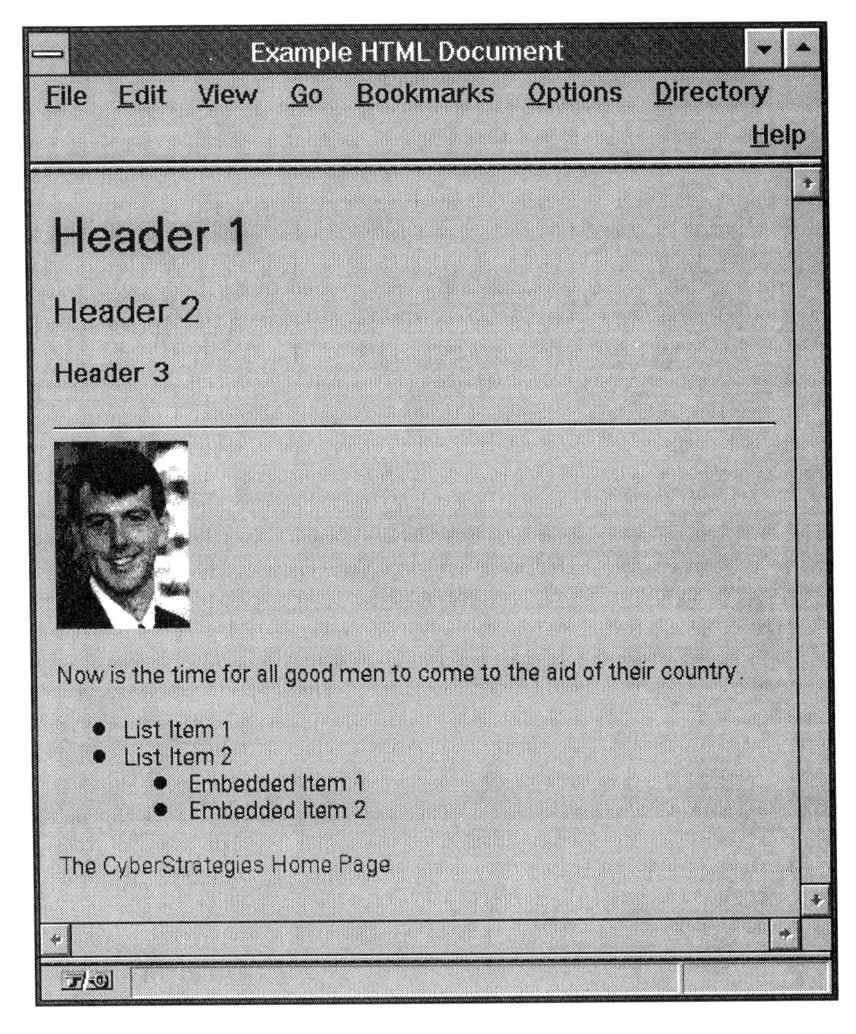

Figure 3-4. *The Resulting Web Page Generated by the HTML in Figure 3-3*

3.2.3.2 *Image Mapping*

Although it is beyond the scope of this book to explain the details of image mapping, the basic idea behind it is simple. The HTML syntax allows you to specify the coordinates corresponding to the vertices of a polygon within a graphic image. When the user points the cursor at a point within the specified polygon and clicks the mouse, the server interprets the selection as a reference to another HTML file (or as a jump within the same file). In this way, icons and graphics can be used as hyperlinks instead of ordinary highlighted text.

3.2.3.3 *CGI Tools*

Most distributions of the Web server software include sample CGI scripts. There are also extensive libraries of Perl and other back-end scripts available on the net. Rather than re-invent the wheel, you should spend the time to become familiar with these archives. See the NCSA or CERN FTP servers—or one of several newsgroups related to the Web or Perl—for more information on where to find such libraries.

3.2.3.4 *Building Effective Web Pages*

Novak and Markiewicz (1995) make several important points about the design of a WWW page. Analyzing their server statistics, they found that the determining factor for a user's selection of a menu item was its position on the screen. "In one month nearly 1000 users looked at the first entry, 100 looked at the second entry, and none looked at the eighth. This showed that users dislike scrolling through windows screens to read information."

They also noticed that reducing the size of their images increased system performance. "By drawing rather than scanning the images, the images' size was reduced sometimes by as much as 60 percent—and the time to download any one page was significantly lessened."

It is also important to keep the number of graphic images presented on any page to a bare minimum. For instance, many users will not wait for ten images to download. Some browsers handle this situation better than others, however. Netscape's Navigator, for example, employs progressive image loading that will first load and display text for you to read while progressively loading and building the graphic files in the background without disturbing your perusal. You should be even more concerned about size and number of graphic files when it comes to delivering Web pages to an audience external to your enterprise. Many users of the Internet are attached to their local service providers via a relatively low-speed dial-up line. The loading of graphic images over a low-speed line may seem interminable.

We are familiar with at least one application where an *NCSA Mosaic* front end integrated with a touch-screen interface is being used to automate manufacturing operations. The overall maintenance and upkeep of the application is greatly simplified with the WEB-like interface. Users are prompted for information to be scanned either from a magnetic or bar code reader. They may then select options by touching the appropriate button on the screen.

3.3 Who's Using the Web and Why?

Today, the World Wide Web is more than just a proving ground for new ideas and technologies. Individuals, governments, and businesses are using the Internet's information infrastructure to communicate and interact in ways unimagined only a few years ago. The commercial domain represents the fastest growing sector of the Internet. Everything from on-line catalogs and IRS tax forms to the AT&T 800 directory is availabile directly from desktops around the world.

3.3.1 Individuals

The World Wide Web has catalyzed the personal use of the Internet. The simplicity of the *NCSA Mosaic* class of browsers puts access to a world of information into the hands of the unsophisticated computer users. The Web offers individual users opportunities for recreation, shopping, education, and telecommuting. Using Serial Line Internet Protocol (SLIP), Point-to-Point Protocol (PPP), or The Internet Adapter (TIA), individuals can enjoy the full graphical features of Web browsers over an ordinary phone line. Individuals are surfing the Web across the world for the price of a local phone call and their local Internet access charge.

3.3.2 Businesses

Here are some reasons why corporations are using Web technology:

- Internal Information Sharing
  - ◊ Departmental Information Publishing
  - ◊ Bulletin Board Services
  - ◊ Weekly Activity or Status Reports
  - ◊ Memo Archives
  - ◊ Calendaring
  - ◊ Project Documentation
  - ◊ Directory Services

- External Information Sharing
    - ◊ Product Catalogs
    - ◊ Direct Marketing Materials
    - ◊ Product Announcements
    - ◊ Public Relations and Press Releases
    - ◊ Direct Sales
    - ◊ Customer Support Services

The Web technology is as powerful inside a business as it is outside. Behind a firewall, the corporate culture is fostered and cultivated by a complex organism of dynamic links connecting multiple disciplines of experts who need to communicate effectively in order to form cohesive teams. Engineers must make their drawings and data available to production specialists. Managers must keep tabs on production status and schedules.

In the past, knowledge workers relied primarily on the company library, various directories, and other knowledge workers to locate critical information. Today, they can also turn to their corporate internal Web as an information resource.

Business communications on the Web fall into three categories:

- Business to User/Consumer
- Business to Business
- Business Internal

To appreciate the tremendous growth in the first category, you need to understand the current demographic trends of the Internet in general and the Web in particular.

Internet demographics point to a fairly well-educated and affluent group—a target market of potential buyers for a variety of sophisticated goods and services. The Web's ease-of-use, however, thanks to browsers like *NCSA Mosaic* and *Netscape Navigator*, is beginning to open the Internet door to even unsophisticated computer users. A home computer with a high-speed modem and a user-friendly browser can put WWW information within easy reach of a potentially large segment of the population.

Of the 3,522 respondents to the *2nd WWW User Survey*,[3] 44 percent were between the ages of twenty-six and thirty. Over 90 percent were male, and 87 percent were Caucasian.

---

[3] The GVU Center's 2nd WWW User Survey was conducted by James E. Pitkow and Margaret M. Recker for thirty-eight days during October and November 1994.

In the two largest occupation groups, 27 percent of respondents described themselves as working in a technical field and 26 percent described themselves as students.

Attuned to the Web's demographic trends, businesses both small and large are using the Web to communicate with and be more responsive to prospective customers and business partners. Many use Web forms to gather critical marketing information from or provide "infotainment" (see discussion below) for prospective customers.

Sales opportunities for businesses abound on the Web. Product and service descriptions directed at prospective consumers can, thanks to the use of hyperlinks, expand to ever-increasing levels of detail. The key to this kind of marketing is realizing that the user is empowered and in control. Control over the amount of detail, inherent integrity and accuracy of content, and a minimum of hype are some of the features that entice Internet users to view your marketing materials on the Web.

This paradigm shift in marketing—away from one-way, in-your-face advertising toward user/viewer empowerment—can hardly be overemphasized. On the Internet there is no such thing as a "captive audience." The Web viewer is only a hyperlink and a mouse click away from "changing the channel." Everyone on the Web is a channel surfer. If they don't like your material, they will jump to somewhere else.

If you think of each Web page as a television channel, then each embedded hyperlink is like an invitation to change the channel! Can you imagine today's television broadcasters actually making it easy for you to change the channel?

To keep the viewer interested, the Web publisher/broadcaster must provide information of intrinsic value to the viewer, something that will motivate him or her to continue down the path of related hyperlinks to the product or service being marketed. Some use the word "infotainment" to describe this kind of marketing. Since the viewer is in control and the remote control (i.e., the mouse) is in his or her hand, the information provided must be informative and/or entertaining, i.e., of utility to the viewer.

Electronic Data Interchange, or EDI, has already made its debut on the Web. A company called First Virtual already provides an e-cash (electronic cash) method of managing remittance. The user first establishes an account with First Virtual. E-cash transactions are recorded by First Virtual and the appropriate debits and credits are handled accordingly. In this way, there is no need for a credit card number to traverse the Net. Even if someone were clever enough to intercept someone's First Virtual e-cash account number, it would be useless outside the Internet cybermalls that honor it. Credit card numbers, on the other hand, are useful in nearly every kind of monetary transaction. Of course, as the cybermalls continue their relentless expansion, this point may become moot. By then, however, encryption will come to the rescue and render credit card transactions over the Net completely secure. This will pose great gain for business-to-business transactions as well.

Business-to-business communications are also on the rise as business buyers are attracted to the range of products and services marketed on the Web. The potential for establishing explicit and exclusive Web communications between trading partners and strategic allies is still largely untapped.

The WWW has the potential to play an important role in the Internet customer/supplier value chain. The ease with which information can be both provided and disseminated together with the continued development of privacy mechanisms makes this system one of the most promising aspects of commerce on a world-wide public network. Already, many businesses are recognizing the business prospects of the Internet. Publishing houses (Time Warner, O'Reilly & Associates, Ziff-Davis, and others), computer vendors, advertising agencies, and market research firms are all tapping into the net to increase profits. The Internet is rapidly becoming a place where businesses conduct business.

Collaboration with business partners, associates, and customers over long distances has always been a complicated matter. The Internet won't eliminate business travel (too many business processes require face-to-face meetings), but it will provide a forum improving communications so that face-to-face negotiations and commerce can be more focused and productive. Although better methods of communication may help eliminate potential problems and thereby reduce long distance commutes, we don't expect this to have a major impact for some time. For example, e-mail and private newsgroups help to flush out problems—issues committed to writing usually require more thought than rough verbal communication. Sometimes written communication can help clarify issues before they get to a stage of being problematic. The converse, too, may be true in this situation—putting pen to paper (i.e., thinking through an issue) may reveal additional problems or oversights. In any event, better communication channels will yield better results (whether problems are discovered or resolved, they will be more apparent and therefore easier to address).

Commerce on the Web and sales of Web-related products is becoming a business in itself—the demand for better and more flexible tools (encryption, enhanced functionality, etc.) will create an entirely new market segment. One only has to look at the growth and status of on-line service providers to see the emergence of a new business sector. Even companies like AOL, Compuserve, and Prodigy are getting into the Internet act. The growth in this industry sector should demonstrate the viability and increasing demand for on-line services.

3.3.2.1 Making Information Available to the External Internet

Web technologies are useful to businesses both in terms of enabling them to establish an interactive presence on the Internet and disseminating information internally. In this final section we discuss the prospect of using this technology to make enterprise information available to the external Internet, to publish internal departmental information, and to gather "point-of-access" information, whether from external or internal sources.

Making information available on the net is a step-by-step process that can fit into the budget structure of even small businesses. Whether you pay a company to establish an Internet presence for you or whether you decide to go it alone, you should know what steps are involved.

The first step consists in deciding whether or not to go it alone. If you plan to establish a presence for your enterprise on the external World Wide Web and do not have much in-house expertise on client/server computing, then you may want to consider having an outside Internet presence provider do the work for you. The effort and cost involved here can be quite minimal, especially when compared with traditional publications and broadcasting media. For example, a typical three-line text ad in a traditional local Yellow Pages can run you about $30/month. On the other hand, a full-page electronic brochure containing both text and graphics may cost as little as $15/month. In other words, for half the cost you can publish many times more information. Moreover, the coverage of the local Yellow Pages is limited to one city and a few surrounding communities, whereas the Internet covers the world and reaches an audience of about 25 million and growing. However, there is usually an upfront set-up charge for designing HTML pages, scanning in graphics, and integrating your pages with those out on the Web. In this respect, the Web page certainly differs from the three-line text ad in the Yellow Pages. But that is to be expected given the quantity and variety of information to be presented.

Although there are many Internet Presence Providers to choose from, you should also carefully consider the Internet marketing services your provider will offer. Some providers do little more for their customers than build Web pages and link those pages to their own home pages. This means that the people visiting your site will be mostly those who are primarily interested in your presence provider's site! You will get much more mileage out of your site if your presence provider also attracts Web audiences to your site. They can do this in a variety of ways, including registration of your pages with prominent directory servers like Yahoo and negotiating on your behalf the purchase of sponsorship hyperlinks from frequently visited commercial Web sites to yours. Your presence provider should not only know about the Internet and its technologies, but also know how to market your pages.

Many Internet access providers also provide Web presence services. However, many of them are primarily interested in selling connections to the Internet to thousands of dial-up customers. They have little interest in and few resources dedicated to helping businesses expand their presence and market their products and services on the Internet. In most cases you are better off going with a full-service presence provider whose chief focus is to create audiences for your site.

The set-up cost for going it alone are even greater if you do not already have the infrastructure and know-how required to run a Web server. Again, many Internet presence providers can also be of help here, providing you with turn-key solutions to get your business connected to the Net and teach you how to build Web pages.

But if you already have some in-house expertise in client/server computing and networking, you are in a much better position to go it alone. All you'll need to do is learn how to get connected to the Net, how to set up and run a Web server, and finally how to build and maintain Web pages. You should contact your local Internet access provider about getting connected. Your in-house gurus can probably figure out how to download the required software from NCSA and how to install the server. If your gurus are UNIX gurus, so much the better. However, you should strive to involve both the technical people and the marketing or advertising people in this effort. Technical people may have the know-how to deliver information to the Internet community but not know what to deliver. You need both content and delivery people.

To construct Web pages there are already many conversion programs available for translating documents from some of the more common word processing formats into HTML. Contact the vendor of your word processing software for details on how to locate and download the appropriate filter for your situation. Many vendors are beginning to announce features to save documents directly into HTML.

There are also several specialized HTML word processors such as HotMetal from SoftQuad and the freeware HTML Assistant. Some are WYSIWYG, while others simply provide shortcuts for inserting HTML tags into your text.

Interleaf now offers a tool called Cyberleaf to produce sophisticated HTML documents. Interleaf has long been known as a provider of premier document development and management tools designed especially for producing long documents.

Some of the documents you can produce with HTML and publish on the Web are:

- Catalogs
- Advertising
- Public Relations Material

3.3.2.2 Gathering "Point-of-Access" Information

The term "point-of-access" information is a take-off on "point-of-sale." It refers to any information gathered regarding the user and his or her access of information on your Web server. The logging facilities of most Web servers capture the IP address of the user, the filenames of the pages accessed, and the date and time of access. This information can be imported into a relational database for sorting, analyzing, reporting, and plotting. It is extremely useful, whether to study the information access behavior of corporate-internal users or the demographics and access preferences of external customers.

The built-in logging features of most Web servers provide valuable feedback to the system administrators, network administrators, and content providers regarding user access and interest areas. System administrators can use access statistics to determine if their system is under- or overloaded. Similarly, network administrators can use these statistics and those from network monitoring devices to determine if the pipes leading the various servers are adequate. In some cases it may make sense to relocate and redistribute Web pages to different servers in order to spread the load more evenly. Finally, content providers can learn from user access data whether or not their presentations are effective and of interest to those accessing them. They can learn which techniques work and which do not.

Statistics provide a basis for trend analysis—this permits systems to be scaled to accommodate large user or customer populations. Many webmasters actually plot a curve showing growth (or decline) in access to their pages and display the plot directly on their pages.

3.3.2.3 Opportunities for Proactive/Anticipative Customer Support Services

In recent years, software and system support services have benefited considerably from the increasing interconnectivity of internetworked environments both inside and outside the enterprise. Only a few years ago, trouble calls were routed to internal support organizations which would then proceed to duplicate a specific event. Once a problem was identified, an internal support specialist might spend hours working with a vendor's support services. This might involve reading memory and core dump information over the phone and faxing error related information to vendors. After some period of time, a patch or system fix was usually prescribed and the system vendor would then process the necessary requests for a tape shipment. After a couple of days the tape would arrive, the patch would be applied and system operation would continue as usual (until the next problem arose).

Today, many computer vendors put their problem report databases on-line for customers to view. In many cases it is not even necessary to contact a telephone support representative. Patches may be downloaded directly from a vendor's site over the Internet and applied usually within a couple of hours. In this instance, support turn-around times have been reduced from days to hours.

Internal support personnel should take a cue from their vendors and use Internet technologies to shorten their own internal time-to-repair.

3.3.2.4 Business Internal Uses of Web Technology

Business internal communication using WWW technology presents a tremendous opportunity. Not overly plagued by security concerns—since their corporate networks are already protected from the Internet-at-large by extensive firewall systems—many businesses have established elaborate internal webs of information on their internal TCP/IP internetworks. The fall 1994 WWW Conference in Chicago sponsored a series of talks and workshops on the subject of corporate internal use of the Web. Featured there were companies like AT&T, SAS Institute, The Analytic Sciences Corporation (TASC) and American Management Systems.

Chris Prah and Diane DiGiovanni of TASC have captured the business motivations for using the Web internally in their electronic paper entitled "Mosaic as a Corporate Data Collector and Dispenser:"

> While the power of Mosaic as an Internet data retriever is apparent, it is also a convenient and intuitive mechanism for local data distribution and collection with a corporate environment. Private corporate information can be protected and distributed to users possessing the appropriate rights, whereas nonprivate information can be distributed to everyone. As such, Mosaic-client/server systems that provide and collect internal corporate data as well as providing WWW access can be easily built and securely deployed.[4]

Companies like AT&T, Lockheed Martin, and IBM have built extensive internal Webs of corporate information. They are using WWW technology to improve internal communications and empower knowledge workers with information. Knowledge workers at AT&T, for example, are using the Web to access distributed databases and reduce costs of achieving ISO9000 certification of AT&T's document control process. They have also used the internal Web to disseminate information about the corporations directions and initiatives. They see the Web as a way to help reduce the time to market for new products.[5]

Of major interest to corporations is the prospect of making vast amounts of legacy data available over the Web without incurring the usual high cost for conversion from legacy formats to HTML. Supported by Bell Communications Research and Rutgers University, Leon Shklar, Kshitij Shah, and Chumki Basu have designed a new language for integrating legacy data in a cost effective way. Called InfoHarness Repository Definition Language (IRDL), this language promises to simplify the process of generating the information required to specify the type, representation, and physical location of data.[6]

Departmental information publishing using Web techniques gives local departments the opportunity to communicate news and information to the rest of the corporation. Departments can use this approach to publish information about their organizational structure,

---

[4] Paper delivered by Chris Prah and Dianne Giovanni at the Second WWW conference, October 1994. It can be found on the Web at h*ttp://www.ncsa.uiuc.edu* in file located at *SDG/IT94/Proceedings/CorInfSys/prah/prah.html.*

[5] Paper delivered by William Holland at the Second WWW conference, October 1994. This paper be found at NCSA's Web site *http://www.ncsa.uiuc.edu* in the file located at */SDG/IT94/Proceedings/CorInfSys/holland/mospap.html.*

[6] From a paper delivered by Leon Shklar, Kshitij Shah, and Chumki Basu at the Third WWW conference, April 1995. The Web site hosting this paper is *http://www.igd.fhg.de* in the file located at *www/www95/papers/78/irdl.html.*

their rules and regulations, their operating procedures, their calendar of events, their project status reports, and so on. This application of Web technologies is limited only by your imagination.

Another feature of value to departmental publishers involves the logging of user access information. Departments can use this feedback as the basis for continuous process improvement. With CGI scripting, internal customer comments and complaints can be stored and routed via e-mail to the appropriate people.

3.3.3 Federal, State, and Local Governments

The role of government and its acknowledgment and support of an emerging information superhighway have helped propel Internet technologies forward. Today, the U.S. federal government has an extensive Web infrastructure that provides information to people around the U.S. and throughout the world.

Governments at all levels (local, state, and federal) are finding new ways of streamlining basic tasks like licensing, filing returns, and perhaps someday even voting (i.e., improving participation in the governmental process).

3.3.3.1 Federal Government

It's hard to ignore the role the U.S. federal government has played and continues to play in the development and use of the Internet and Internet technologies. The long legacy of research support through the Department of Defense's Advanced Research Projects Agency (ARPA) gave birth to the TCP/IP protocol suite and the ARPANET, the precursor to the Internet. The U.S. government has continued its support of the Internet through the National Science Foundation (NSF), the High Performance Computing and Communications (HPCC) program, and the initiative to promote the construction of a National Information Infrastructure (NII).

The federal government has also become an extensive user and supplier of information resources via the Internet. Today there are hundreds of government information repositories on-line and accessible via Gopher and the World Wide Web.

The Library of Congress THOMAS system (*http://thomas.loc.gov*), for example, contains the full text of legislation, resolutions, e-mail addresses for congressional members, and even the full text of the congressional record. The House of Representatives maintains a Web server (*http://www.house.gov*) that provides up-to-date information on schedules, visitor information, the legislative process, and other political and educational items.

Today, you can even browse a server containing information about the White House (*http://www.whitehouse.gov*), the First Family, and the National Performance Review.

Departments	Agencies
Department of Agriculture	Environmental Protection Agency
Department of Commerce	Federal Communications Commission
Department of Defense	General Services Administration
Department of the Air Force	National Aeronautics and Space Administration
Department of the Army	National Science Foundation
Department of the Navy	Securities and Exchange Commission
Department of Education	Small Business Administration
Department of Energy	Social Security Administration
Department of Health and Human Services	United States Postal Service
Department of Housing and Urban Development	
Department of the Interior	
Department of Justice	
Department of Labor	
Department of State	
Department of Transportation	
Department of Treasury	
Department of Veterans Affairs	

Table 3-1. *US Federal Departments and Agencies with Web Sites*

Almost every branch of the federal government uses these technologies today to make it easier for businesses and individuals to find government information. Table 3-1 contains a list of some of the other government departments and agencies that maintain information on the World Wide Web.

3.3.3.2 State and Local Governments

Today, even states and local governments are providing information over the Internet. The information resources provided by state governments has been simplified through the use of on-line information bases designed to ease both the administrative burden of providing information and the perceived inaccessibility by businesses and individuals.

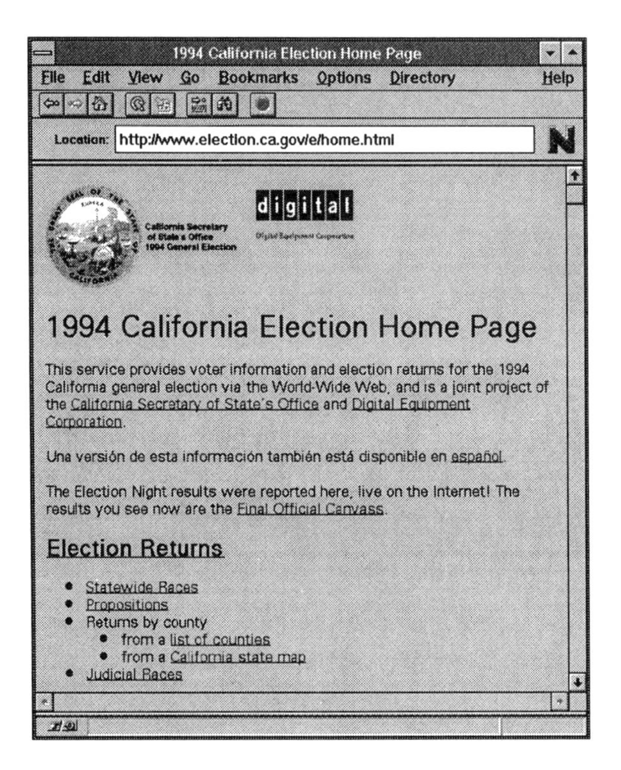

Figure 3-5. *The 1994 California Election Home Page*

California—especially the famed Silicon Valley—seems to be the center of gravity for much of the activity on the Internet and the World Wide Web. Systems like the 1994 California General Election Server (the first of its kind) demonstrate the potential for Internet services within a state-wide political system. Information on candidates, races, and outcomes were provided by a server at *http://www.election.ca.gov/* (see Figure 3-5).

Many cities are also establishing a presence on the Web. Nowhere is this more apparent than in the state and local governments of California. As you can see in Figure 3-6, the city of Palo Alto's Web site is a source of civic information—services, events, and other information is available to help both newcomers and long time residents.

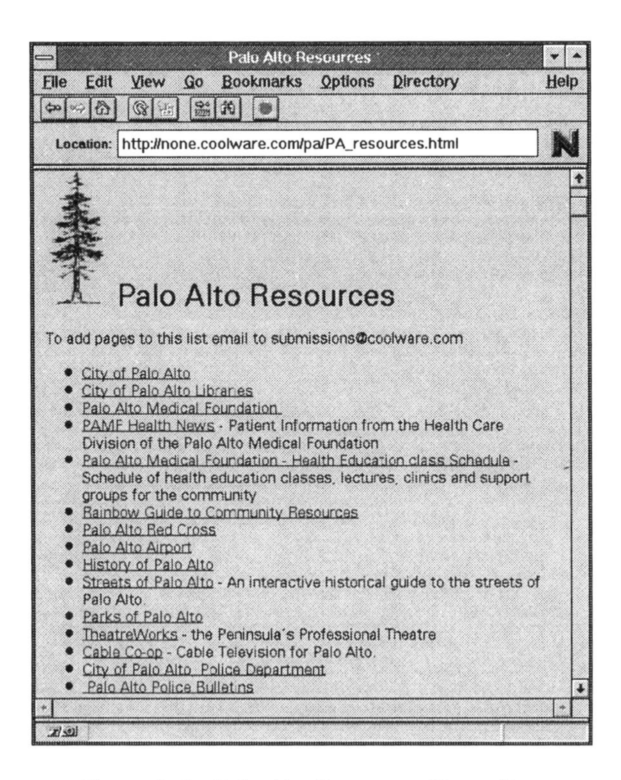

Figure 3-6. *Palo Alto Resources Home Page*

The city of Palo Alto probably has more Internet users per household than any other city in the world. It was natural for Palo Alto to go on-line. The example set by this city is sure to be followed by many cities throughout the world.

Chapter 4

INTERNET TOOLS AND THE ENTERPRISE LEGACY

By "enterprise culture," we mean the values and attitudes reflected in the enterprise's organizational structure, policies and procedures. In many older, more mature organizations, these cultural features have evolved over many years, and they are institutionalized. They are also reflected in the enterprise's legacy of information technology—in the platforms, applications software, networks, and data resources dispersed throughout the enterprise. Because this information legacy is so intertwined with the enterprise's culture, it is difficult, when building a new information system, to separate the constraints that are purely technological from those that are purely cultural. Hence, in this chapter, we have chosen to address the constraints imposed by the information legacy, the ponderous "installed base," in the larger context of those constraints imposed by the enterprise culture.

When you proceed to implement your Internet clone, your enterprise's culture will probably influence the degree of support or resistance you will receive. If your culture is dominated by a certain conservative mindset (stereo)typically associated with homogeneous, mainframe computing, you may encounter considerable inertia. If it effectively discourages the sharing of information, your plans may be greeted with skepticism. Such skepticism may be due to attitudes, habits, and work processes formed over many years by relying on legacy information systems—systems based on an older, perhaps archaic, computing and organizational paradigm. On the other hand, these legacy systems may represent nothing more than an extra challenge to your technical skills as an implementor of Internet tools and methods. Regardless, the enterprise legacy, whether cultural or technological, is a real constraint; you must be prepared to interface your new, Internet-based system with older systems—and you must be ready to deal with cultural resistance to change.

In this chapter, we discuss the various constraints arising from the enterprise legacy and offer advice on how to accommodate them. We consider the following three categories of legacy-related constraints:

- The Information Legacy
- Financial Constraints
- Technology Obsolescence

These three categories are loosely associated with the past, present, and future of the enterprise. While your information legacy derives from your enterprise's history, your financial constraints are realities that reflect your enterprise's current economic situation. Finally, the problem of potential technology obsolescence reflects the fact that today's hot technologies will be tomorrow's cold legacies.

4.1 The Information Legacy

Your enterprise's information legacy has both technological and cultural aspects. The former include your installed base of hardware, software, and data, while the latter are formed by the attitudes, habits, processes, and organizational structures acquired by your enterprise over decades of operation. These legacies may be founded on antiquated information technology.

We begin our exploration of these two aspects of the information legacy by examining some of the issues of technological legacy. These break down into the areas of hardware and software legacies. First we consider the problem of hardware legacies. Two kinds of hardware are pertinent here: platform and network hardware. Next, we look at the legacy of applications software and then proceed to discuss data legacies. Accordingly, the next three sections are the following:

- Platform and Network Legacies
- Application Software Legacies
- Data Legacies

Afterward we will return to the subject of cultural legacies and deal with the attitudes, habits, and processes embedded in your organization.

4.1.1 Platform and Network Legacies

In most large enterprises, the installed base of hardware represents a significant investment in information technology. Many Fortune 500 companies have spent hundreds of millions of dollars on computers, disk drives, terminals, printers, and tape drives. In the last 15 years many have also invested heavily in hardware needed for both local and wide area networks—bridges, routers, terminal servers, network interface units, modems, and cabling. A fact of life in many companies, this sprawling installed base of hardware presents a mammoth challenge to the designer of Internet clones. It is a challenge not only because of its sheer size, but also because it is largely heterogeneous: Within most large enterprises there are often several different mutually incompatible networks and computer systems. This heterogeneity is probably the biggest technical challenge facing the builder of Internet clones.

Fortunately, the Internet itself is a gigantic installed base of heterogeneous hardware. Virtually every kind of platform—from the supercomputing number cruncher to the lowly desktop PC—is connected to a network that is connected to the Internet. The local networks joined via the Internet are by no means homogeneous. There are Novell IPX, IBM SNA, and DEC DECNET networks all connected in some way—usually through multiprotocol routers or trusted, multi-homed hosts—to the Internet. The common denominator enabling these diverse networks to work together is the TCP/IP family of protocols and the application services built on top of TCP/IP. TCP/IP is the glue that makes the worldwide Internet work. For the problem of network incompatibility, TCP/IP is the solution par excellence.

In the following paragraphs, we provide a brief historical background sketch of the two areas of platform and network heterogeneity.

4.1.1.1 Incompatible Platforms

Many enterprises today own and use practically every kind of computer platform. In a single large corporation, for example, you can find nearly every imaginable configuration of IBM mainframes, DEC minicomputers, UNIX workstations, PCs, and Macintoshes. In the resulting islands of information, valuable enterprise data are segregated and locked away in incompatible file formats, unique operating systems, and incongruous applications software. Sharing information among users of incompatible platforms is difficult at best and often considered to be not worth the effort.

How did this chaotic situation come about?

In the early to mid-1970s, the computing environments in most large organizations were fairly homogeneous. The few desks that needed access to computing resources were generally equipped with what we now call "dumb" terminals. Most business computing was accomplished using centralized IBM mainframes, and scientific computing relied on more specialized high performance computers like those supplied by the Control Data Corporation. These two incompatible computing environments interacted hardly at all, and most companies saw little reason for these environments to interact. Communication between different workgroups was accomplished primarily by a steady flow of paper memos, reports, and charts prepared by secretaries using typewriters. This situation is depicted in Figure 4-1.

In the late 70s and early 80s, however, the situation changed dramatically. Minicomputers, like those in the PDP and VAX families produced by Digital Equipment Corporation, made their debut, and their relatively low cost when compared with monolithic mainframes made it possible for major divisions and projects to acquire their own systems. Administrative workgroups that previously lacked computers could now reap the benefits of computer access. Secretaries and human resource personnel, for instance, could now make use of word processing and database software to facilitate their work. The VAX/VMS (Virtual Memory System) operating system offered an interactive, multitasking environment, and the computing paradigm evolved from a batch-dominated model to one supporting extensive interactive use. In addition to traditional, number-crunching computational aids, this operating system supported a wide variety of office automation tools.

Scientific and engineering workgroups gravitated to this environment. Soon

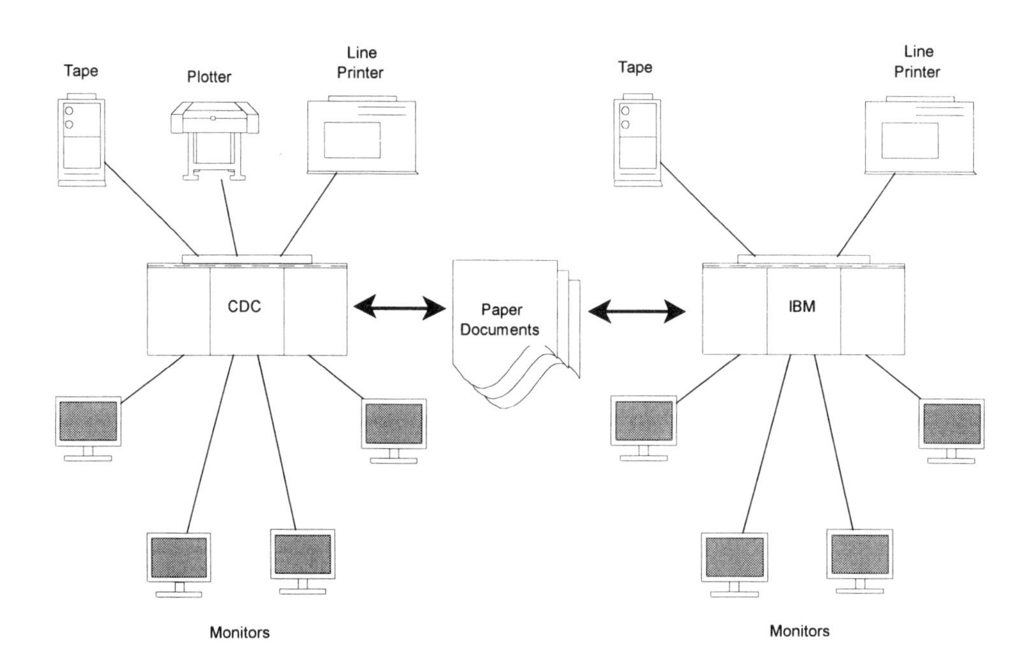

Figure 4-1. *Mainframe Computing Islands in the 1970s*

secretaries and engineers alike were using word processing software like Digital Standard Runoff to produce memos and documents. Electronic file sharing among users of a single VAX system—and across DECNET links between VAX computer systems—became quite common.

The UNIX operating system also made its corporate debut during the 70s and early 80s, and it was primarily popular with the younger generation of computer scientists and software engineers. The first hardware platform to support UNIX was the DEC PDP-7. In those days, few suspected that UNIX would ever have the far-reaching impact on business and general scientific computing it has in fact achieved.

Meanwhile, similar trends were evident in the MIS world. Interactive computing and office productivity tools became more popular. Although workgroup computing became more common across many different functions in the enterprise, MIS-oriented computing in many enterprises evolved separately from scientific and engineering computing. In simplistic terms, the MIS world tended to orient itself toward IBM-style mainframe computing, while scientific and engineering computing gravitated toward DEC and UNIX-based computing.

The second major shift in computing in the early eighties was occasioned by the introduction into the workplace of the desktop personal computer. As a standalone machine, the PC offered user-friendly word processing, spreadsheet, and database productivity tools. Integration and file sharing were achieved via application and hardware homogeneity. Files could be transferred among standalone desktop machines using the "sneaker-net" method in which files were copied onto floppies and literally carried from one machine to the next. Between standalone PCs and the larger mini and mainframe computers, however, very little information was transferred electronically.

The next stage of evolution was marked by the integration of standalone PCs to form local area networks (LANs). LANs allowed common local resources like printers and file servers to be shared. Until the late 1980s, however, connectivity between PC-based LANs, on the one hand, and minis and mainframes, on the other, was still uncommon in many enterprises.

The result of this evolution was the familiar heterogeneous enterprise computing environment of the early 1990s. Roughly speaking, each vendor prior to this era strove to dominate a specific market segment: IBM, the MIS segment; DEC, the engineering; Apple, Intel, Microsoft and Novell, the standalone desktop or PC LAN.

Although the foregoing description simplifies somewhat the actual evolutionary path leading to the current heterogeneous computing situation, it nevertheless provides a basic sketch of the hardware-oriented legacy inherited from the 1980s. It is probably not too different from the legacy situation within your own enterprise.

One approach to solving this incompatibility problem is to mandate standard hardware, i.e., to force homogeneity by purchasing hardware from only a few compatible vendors. Although many MIS organizations seem to prefer this approach, they often find that internal customers and users are dissatisfied with the limited choice of vendors. This is especially true of enterprises that standardize on a single-vendor. Lacking competition, these sole-source vendors can be slow to respond to user needs. A company that invests large sums in a single vendor solution is understandably reluctant to discard that investment and start over with another vendor. As a result, vendors are tempted to become complacent and exercise what is sometimes referred to as "account control."[1] Forced homogenization through overly restrictive hardware standards can be costly in the long run.

Although a heterogeneous environment is a fundamental constraint facing many system architects today, it is also the perfect opportunity for introducing Internet tools and methods. Developed independently of any one vendor (although often with the cooperation of many vendors), these tools and methods can bridge the communication gaps between proprietary machines. Many public domain Internet software tools are available today for a variety of widely-used hardware platforms, and third-party vendors are beginning to offer fully supported commercial versions of these public domain tools, often with significant improvements over the public domain versions.

To better appreciate the potential benefit of Internet tools and methods, we need to discuss the problems of networking in a heterogeneous environment and see how the TCP/IP protocol suite overcomes these problems.

4.1.1.2 Incompatible Networks

During the 1980s, many MIS professionals began to realize that islands of information placed limitations on workgroup computing. Each vendor responded by developing data communications protocols to interlink its various families of proprietary computers. At first these network protocols were limited to their own computers; later they tried to integrate equipment and protocols from other vendors. DEC, for example, first used its DECNET communications protocol to interconnect islands of DEC equipment. In the late 1980s and early 1990s, however, DEC extended DECNET-based networking to include both PCs and Macintoshes in their Pathworks LAN concept. In its day, Pathworks was considered a bold step forward; DEC, a major vendor of information technologies, set an admirable example by recognizing and respecting its customers' previous investments in non-DEC information technologies. Unfortunately, DEC's original strategy was limited to using the proprietary DECNET protocol to achieve this integration. The explosive growth of the Internet following the admission of commercial domains had yet to raise TCP/IP to its present position of prominence.

Similarly, IBM developed a network architecture called SNA (Systems Network Architecture), which was oriented towards its System 370 family of computers. Third-party vendors like Irma and Attachmate provided terminal emulation using the SNA protocol to link PCs and Macintoshes to IBM mainframes. Unfortunately, this approach rendered the desktop computer little more than a dumb terminal, effectively lobotomizing the desktop PC. In all fairness, however, we must mention that such terminal emulation at least eliminated the

---

[1] See Tapscott and Carston (1993).

need for having both a dumb terminal and a PC on a single desktop. Moreover, file transfer between PC and mainframe, though still somewhat cumbersome, was at least now possible.

Meanwhile, the UNIX world, already known for its relative vendor independence, was quietly adopting the TCP/IP family of protocols as its own basis for internetworking. The 1983 release of the Berkeley Standard Distribution (4.2BSD) added some layers of the TCP/IP protocol suite on top of the Ethernet datalink layer already implemented in previous versions. This fueled the rapid growth of Ethernet-based LANs and wide-area internetworks, including the famous ARPANET, forerunner of the Internet. Berkeley sockets, a convenient application programming interface (API) provided initially by the 4.2BSD version of UNIX, made it easy for UNIX programmers to develop client/server applications for file sharing, electronic mail, and remote login. This combination of UNIX and TCP/IP—both relatively vendor-independent technologies—was the enabling technological seed from which grew today's worldwide Internet.

Strictly speaking, UNIX is not fully vendor-independent, since there are several slightly incompatible vendor implementations of UNIX. Many vendors are still trying to unify on a common, standardized version of UNIX. However, precisely because there are so many different vendor implementations of UNIX, it is fair to say that UNIX is to some extent a vendor-independent, i.e., open, operating system.

4.1.2 Application Software Legacies

Perhaps the most important piece in the legacy puzzle is the application software legacy. Of prime concern to your enterprise are mission-critical applications. These programs—and the data they rely on—are what give your enterprise its unique competitive edge and support for day-to-day operations.

4.1.2.1 Mission-Critical Applications

The network strategist considering the long-term benefit of an Internet clone must consider the role to be played in this new environment by mission-critical applications. Most traditional applications of this sort run in environments foreign to or incompatible with the client/server, TCP/IP world of the Internet. Many legacy databases, e-mail systems, decision support software, and executive information systems have grown up in a mainframe environment without any hooks to the client/server world.

A number of strategies exist for integrating mainframe applications with the TCP/IP-based tools. One is to migrate the functionality provided by these applications to the new environment by purchasing or developing new applications. Although simple in concept, this approach can be expensive. It essentially amounts to a major software modification effort. Another approach is to port the legacy software to new platforms with the aid of software renovation or re-engineering tools. Still another approach is to upgrade to a newer version of the operating system, to one with interface functionality compatible with TCP/IP. New versions of MVS and VM for IBM mainframes, for instance, are appearing with the Open Software Foundation's Distributed Computing Environment (DCE) system of Remote Procedure Calls (RPCs). DCE functionality can make use of TCP/IP to provide application interaction between mainframe applications and DCE-compatible clients and servers in the networked world.

Regardless of strategy, application software legacies can be a major constraint affecting the seamless integration of mission-critical software with the Internet clone. There is no easy answer here. Considerable resources can be consumed in trying to accomplish this integration. We recommend that before trying to tackle this major problem you should first build a more modest internetwork in order to demonstrate the potential of Internet technologies. In this way, you can garner more support for a large scale integration of your Internet clone with mission-critical software. We also recommend that you first only implement read-only, browsable access to the output of mission-critical software. Later in this chapter we discuss some ways to do this.

Reliability is an important consideration in connection with mission-critical software. Because your company's financial health depends on it, financial software, in particular, must be extremely reliable. The same is true of databases containing marketing, customer, supplier, and competitive information. Many companies have invested huge sums in developing reliable, custom software and databases that provide mission-critical value to the business yet are tied to legacy mainframe systems. Given the mission-critical nature of such assets and the need for a high degree of reliability, many companies are understandably reluctant to embrace completely new architectures such as client/server without carefully considering all aspects of the migration problem.

One approach to dealing with the reliability constraints imposed by mission-critical applications and databases is to incrementally migrate portions of the application functionality to the new client/server domain. This is accomplished by leaving the original legacy application system intact and rehosting copies of the software and data sources to the new environment for integration with the newer TCP/IP-based tools. This can be done on a trial basis as part of the Internet clone pilot project. Extensive formal testing is, of course, always a good idea; the rule of thumb in such cases is that the more stringent the reliability requirement, the more extensive the testing.

4.1.2.2 Software Renovation

Unfortunately, many companies have lost sight of the internal workings of their legacy applications software. The original programmers have retired or otherwise left the company, and the documentation is no longer up to date. Bug fixes and enhancements incorporated into the software are perhaps undocumented. Even when the configuration trail has been kept in order, it is now probably so long and contorted that considerable effort is required to regain the insight that once resided in the programmer's head and was taken for granted. Even if the documentation was kept up to date, all familiarity with it may now be lost.

Looking for a way out of this jungle of legacy code, many companies are turning to software re-engineering or renovation tools and services to effect the transformation of their legacy applications into new software architectures better suited to the client/server paradigm. Not only do such tools and services offer a way to map legacy systems into more open architectures, they also offer the possibility of regaining the lost visibility into the logic and structure of the code. One such service is Lockheed's InVision® software renovation service, which we consider next.

One example of a software renovation service Lockheed Martin's InVision. It combines software tools, process methodologies, and professional expertise to help owners of legacy software understand their code. The InVision service relies on artificial intelligence, symbolic computing, software engineering, and compiler technologies to recover the design of an entire software architecture, not just provide a line-by-line analysis. After recovering the design structure, the InVision tools can be used to generate new code in a language better suited for a new platform environment, or to generate new documentation of the legacy software.[2]

4.1.2.3 Interoperability Standards

Another approach to integrating legacy applications with newer client/server, network-based applications is to impose interoperability standards on the applications and to augment these applications with middleware to enable compliance with these standards. The Open Software Foundation (OSF) has espoused this philosophy for years and has fostered the development of some key enabling tools and frameworks like the Distributed Computing Environment (DCE).

DCE relies on a remote procedure calling (RPC) approach. This allows monolithic applications software to be partitioned into various functional groups, which can then be distributed across a network and called remotely. An obvious application of this methodology is to separate legacy user interfaces from the computationally intensive data-serving portions of the code and allow access to the data server portions via DCE remote procedure calls.

Several companies are beginning to offer tools for encapsulating legacy applications in DCE. One of them, Kapsch AG, an Austrian company, offers a product called Kapsch-DCE/VM for the IBM VM operating system environment on IBM 370 and 390 hosts. This product offers the standard DCE components like the threads and remote procedure call

---

[2] For more information on InVision, send an e-mail message to Dr. Joe Sullivan at Lockheed's Palo Alto Research Center: *sullivan@aic.lockheed.com.*

runtime libraries, and the DCE time, directory and security services. Other platforms implementations of DCE include Transarc's version of DCE for the SunOS operating system, Hewlett-Packard's for the HP 700, and Gradient's PC-DCE for the MS-Windows environment. These implementations are all compatible with Kapsch's version of DCE for VM.[3]

4.1.3 Data Legacies

While hardware and software may be necessary to deliver information to your users, without data there would be no information to deliver. Because they contain information of proven value to your users, data legacies are important to you as a builder of an Internet clone. You already know that your users are interested in having access to these data, because they already have some form of access to it now. Therefore, you should be keenly interested in making sure that your new Internet-based system provides access—preferably enhanced access—to legacy data.

Another reason you should be interested in legacy data sources is that considerable investment has already been made in generating them. They have accumulated over the years. From a financial standpoint, it would be unthinkable to recreate these legacies from scratch in a new form. Ideally, you will devise some way to gain electronic access to these data legacies without "fat-fingering" the data all over again into new data stores compatible with your new client/server system.

Data legacies come in either structured or unstructured form. We consider now the constraints imposed by either sort of data.

4.1.3.1 Structured Data

Structured data sources organize their internal data components in a very formal, schematic way. A relational database, for example, contains data tables which consist of repeated records of information. These records, in turn, are composed of data fields. In raw form, relational databases are usually stored in a binary format accessible only by the database programs used to create them. Sometimes these formats are standardized and accessible by a number of different database programs. Even some flat files not created by a relational database program show repeatable patterns of data organization making them amenable to automated processing. In this section we consider these two types of data sources and discuss their implied constraints for an Internet-based information system.

---

[3] You can obtain more information on Kapsch's DCE product for VM from Karl Deininger, whose e-mail address is *Karl.Deininger@kapsch.co.at*.

4.1.3.1.1 Relational Databases

As mentioned above, relational databases are highly structured into tables, records, and fields. Each field contains data of a specified type such as numeric or ASCII string data. Because of their rigid and repeating structure, relational databases are particularly straightforward to integrate with an Internet clone.

Nevertheless, integration is not free. One method of access, for example, involves the export of database records into delimited ASCII records. This amounts to creating a text file consisting of separate lines of text in which the individual data fields are separated by special characters like asterisks or line feeds. The exported records can then be indexed by client/server tools like *waisindex* and thus fill a WAIS data source which is then accessible across your TCP/IP network. Most commercial database management programs have such export capabilities.

Some relational database systems have HTML publishing capabilities which allow direct queries against their databases to be returned to the HTTP server in HTML format. Both ORACLE and IBM's DB2 database have support for these features. There are also script gateways available that convert *NCSA Mosaic* or *Netscape Navigator* queries into ORACLE SQL SELECT commands.

Regardless of what approach you wish to take to gain access to relational databases, you must realize that some programming or periodic manual exporting of original database records will be necessary. More than anything, this translates into a cost requirement. We recommend that you survey your existing databases and prioritize them according to their relative value from the user perspective. You should also take into account how much programming will be required for each database.

4.1.3.1.2 Structured Flat Files

Structured flat files are documents or data sets not necessarily associated with a database engine but which have regular repetitive and hence predictable structure. If there are certain fields or lines that you can easily extract and treat as meaningful headlines for the whole document, then we would advise you to consider indexing this kind of document in a WAIS database. Again, there will most likely be a certain amount of script file programming required, but probably not as much as in a relational database.

Another example of a structured flat file is a standard SMTP mail message file. This kind of file has a standard header format that is well-understood by the *waisindex* program. This program will extract text from either the SUBJECT: or TO: fields in the mail header and make the extracted text the headline for the associated WAIS document. The body of the mail message then becomes the full-text document retrieved by WAIS after you select its associated headline. Since *waisindex* already knows how to parse SMTP mail messages, there is very little custom script programming associated with this kind of WAIS source building. You might wish, however, to create a script that will periodically retrieve mail messages from the mail folders of interest and feed them to *waisindex*.

The same remarks made about SMTP mail files hold also for USENET newsgroup postings. They have a standard header and body format (as well as some associated keywords—though not everyone is in the habit of supplying them) which can be parsed by the *waisindex* program.

4.1.3.2 Unstructured Data

There is only a fine line between semi-structured flat files and unstructured documents. Generally, the latter are less predictable in their internal data organization than the former. Here, too, WAIS indexing may be the best way to transform these documents into a searchable database. The only trick is to find a suitable item of information to serve as the headline. In the case of interoffice memos, for example, you might try writing a script file to extract the text phrases following the SUBJECT: header, if there is one. In odd cases, however, your script file may fail to extract the proper information, in which case you will have to massage the anomalies by hand. If you are lucky enough to belong to an organization that invariably produces interoffice memos in a standardized format, your job will be that much easier.

4.1.4 Cultural Legacy

Your cultural legacy is comprised of the attitudes, habits, processes, and organizational structures formed over many years of business practice. Your organizations are probably built upon basic premises regarding your business processes—processes that were perhaps developed long ago in a different information technological era. These items—attitudes, habits, processes, and organizational structure—mutually influence and reinforce one another and can be a formidable barrier to the introduction of new information technologies, especially Internet technologies.

Internet technologies were developed independently of the information technologies now dominating many enterprises, especially long-established business enterprises. Internet technologies grew out of the academic and government-sponsored research domains. These areas have significantly different attitudes, habits, processes, and even organizational structures than those found in many private businesses.

As a builder of an Internet clone, you may encounter considerable cultural resistance. This is a fact of life, a constraint you need to be aware of and deal with. Below we discuss some of these cultural constraints and provide some tips on how to accommodate them.

4.1.4.1 Attitudes

One attitude, unfortunately common in many enterprises, is to regard information technology as an expense rather than a strategic investment. Because past investments in information technology have been so costly, an attitude has evolved that is primarily and understandably focused on the issue of cost and cost savings. Yet over-preoccupation with cost-related issues can prevent you from considering the potential productivity and competitive advantages to be gained from effectively harnessing new information technology. In developing your internal clone of the Internet, you must realize that the attitude just described may be firmly entrenched within your organization and you may encounter it in abundance.

The cyberstrategy we recommend for dealing with this situation is for you to emphasize both the cost-effectiveness of Internet technologies and the value of enhanced communications and rapid access to high-value information. That Internet technologies, especially public domain freeware, are generally inexpensive to acquire and own,[4] is sufficiently clear and we have dealt with this topic in other chapters. It is also clear that these technologies provide a methodology for rapid access to information. Timely information is easily made available through the use of scripts and indexing tools, and user-friendly browsers make this information rapidly accessible from desktops across the enterprise. The key strategy, however, is to make sure that the information is of high value, and this means making sure that it has content related to the mission of your enterprise and that it is well-organized. This is a theme to which we have already alluded, and we will continually return to it. It cannot be emphasized enough: Your information resources must have content of high value and be well-organized. In later chapters we will provide more specific advice on how to structure your web of internal information in order to enhance its value.

4.1.4.2 Habits

Work habits can also present cultural barriers and constrain your alternatives when building an Internet clone. These habits are informal work processes developed by individuals and workgroups. For example, one individual in your workgroup may be uncomfortable with a computer keyboard and prefer to generate all memos by hand, passing them to the workgroup secretary for typing and distribution. And the secretary may be in the habit of typing memos and saving them on his or her own local disk drive, even though a shared file server is available on the LAN. In the former case, the individual uncomfortable with the keyboard may be indifferent to making use of a computer to access shared information, and may feel threatened when you wax eloquent about your vision of a paperless office. The secretary, too, may be disinclined to change his or her ways and start saving files on a common server, using standardized file-naming conventions and directory structures.

---

[4] The actual cost of ownership varies with each tool, of course. Some, being less robust than others, may in fact cost more to own than their commercial counterparts.

To deal with the habits of individuals and workgroups simply requires time, patience, understanding, and good communication skills. You have to listen to their concerns, understand the value they see in the old ways, and effectively communicate to them the value they and their workgroup will gain by developing new habits. The new technologies must be explained in ways that do not intimidate those whose habits must change. And you must be prepared to spend a little extra time going the extra mile and holding their hands while they take their first few steps with the new tools and methods. A little kindness goes a long way. Nobody likes the techno-geek who rushes in, plunks down some new techno-toy, and says he has no time to help anyone. Information technology can be impersonal enough all by itself. What people need and want is the personal touch. One of our cyberstrategies is to always maintain the personal touch. In the end, you are trying to help human persons achieve satisfaction in the work they do. You are trying to help them be more effective. Taking time to listen to their needs and to help them get adjusted will pay significant dividends in terms of making your new system a success. Internet clones are collaborative systems—if people aren't happy using them, they won't use them, and there will consequently be no system.

4.1.4.3 Processes

Processes are usually more formal than habits, and involve many individuals and often many different workgroups. Like habits, they are ingrained in the social and operational fabric of your enterprise and are difficult to change. Yet change they must, if they rely too heavily on archaic information technologies. As a cyberstrategist, you must survey the processes that are likely to be affected by your Internet clone, and select those that stand to gain the most from the insertion of Internet technology.

Determining exactly how the new technologies will affect processes for the better is one of the greatest challenges facing the cyberstrategist. In most cases, you must be prepared to visualize completely new processes enabled by the technologies. You must be able to recognize problems you never knew you had. This is very difficult and forms a large subject area outside the scope of this book; instead, we refer the reader to two important books dealing with process re-engineering. The first is *Re-engineering the Corporation: A Manifesto for Business Revolution*, by Michael Hammer and James Champy.[5] It devotes an entire chapter to "The Enabling Role of Information Technology." In this chapter, Hammer and Champy present the distinction between deductive and inductive approaches to the use of information technology. The deductive approach starts with a known problem and looks for a solution. By contrast, the inductive approach starts with information technology—i.e., a potential solution—and looks for unknown—i.e., unperceived—problems to solve. We are

[5] See Hammer and Champy (1994) in the reference list after Chapter 10.

indebted to Hammer and Champy for many inspiring thoughts that are quite relevant to the use of Internet technologies in the business environment.

The second book we highly recommend is *Process Innovation: Reengineering Work through Information Technology*, by Thomas H. Davenport.[6] This book points out the importance of examining the processes that information technology will be called upon to support. If it is not coupled to process innovation, information technology alone will fail to yield payoff in terms of significant productivity gains.

Against this conceptual framework describing the main components of enterprise culture, let us now explore some specific cultural features you are likely to encounter as a builder of an Internet clone.

4.1.4.4 Information Culture

The constraints imposed by the enterprise culture are elusive, because they are often embedded only implicitly in the behavior and attitudes of the enterprise stakeholders. They are seldom explicit. They manifest themselves in subtle ways such as unwritten and unspoken policies regarding the sharing of information. The cultural attitudes toward the sharing of information, for example, are particularly pertinent to the construction of an Internet clone, since the Internet itself is a paragon of information sharing and its implicit openness may clash with enterprise cultures that implicitly discourage such sharing.

Business enterprises are surrounded by many competing, and not always friendly, forces. They have to contend with a ruthless, unforgiving marketplace, wily competitors, suppliers with their own agendas, government regulators, and public opinion. To deal with these forces, a business needs to acquire considerable expertise in the form of knowledge. Stored up within the enterprise as information, knowledge is perhaps the greatest asset of a business enterprise. Knowledge enables a manufacturing enterprise, for example, to transform external raw goods into finished products for sale, and it provides a service organization with the unique know-how required to deliver valuable services to customers. It is no wonder, then, that talk of open information sharing may tend to raise eyebrows and occasion resistance.

As you introduce Internet technologies into your workplace, you need to be cognizant of various attitudes toward information sharing. The following paragraphs consider some of these attitudes.

4.1.4.4.1 Information Sharing

The attitudes of individuals within your enterprise toward information sharing may be significant in determining how well your Internet project is received. Since information is

---

[6] See Davenport (1994) in the reference list after Chapter 10.

power, those in power may be reluctant to endorse your enthusiasm for sharing information. Corporate management may well pay lip service to the idea of sharing and collaborating, but if the operative values—i.e., values-in-action—actually discourage such sharing, the implementation of Internet tools like USENET news may be met with indifference.

On the other hand, such indifference may only be a reflection of a lack of certain required work habits. For example, it takes persistent periodic effort to reap the benefits of a communications system like USENET. Newsgroups relevant to groups of people with whom you need to communicate should be checked routinely, perhaps daily. This is merely a habit that needs to be acquired.

Changing a corporate culture overnight is impossible. We have no illusions about Internet tools providing magical panaceas or silver bullets with which to slay the werewolf of a closed culture. It may be beyond the capacity of the system developer to influence the corporate culture in any significant way. Nevertheless, as a set of constraints, the culture is real, and the system developer needs to be aware of it as such. There are also ways of dealing with the constraints of culture to minimize their negative impact on the success of the project.

4.1.4.4.2 Not-Invented-Here Syndrome

Individuals who suffer from the so-called Not-Invented-Here syndrome, often referred to as NIH, are loathe to acknowledge originality and vision on the part of others. This sort of intellectual snobbery can also affect whole organizations. For example, an MIS organization clinging tenaciously to the mainframe paradigm, may react coolly to an upstart group of engineers who try to introduce Internet technologies into the workplace. They may simply ignore the efforts or "go limp" when the time comes to deploy the system in a full-scale manner. They simply don't want to acknowledge forward thinking on the subject of information technology, especially when it did not originate in their own shop.

Some managers, especially middle managers, show a strong NIH tendency. Some are unwilling to acknowledge the accomplishments of their subordinates for fear that their subordinates may appear to outshine them.

We have little advice to offer you if you find yourself facing NIH. NIH is a real malaise that can seriously affect the organization. Our only advice is that you need to find ways to get those suffering from NIH to become involved in your project so that they will begin to feel to some extent that it is their own project and their own idea. Keep them informed at every step, especially if they have the power to lay roadblocks in your way. Be patient. Keep smiling. And, if you have to, simply avoid them and spend your time and energy on those who will be more receptive and more generously recognize your efforts.

4.1.4.4.3 Incentivizing the Sharing of Information

In companies where information sharing is regarded as a strength, one common feature stands out: Individuals and workgroups are rewarded for producing infobases and documents that add value or provide utility to the whole organization. One measure of utility is the rate of access to the information (accesses per day, week, or month), the assumption being that people will refer to something often if they perceive it to be of value.

One note of caution, however, is in order here. In the case of multimedia electronic infobases, users may be attracted by the novelty and entertainment value of the presentation, rather than the actual usefulness of the content. In the case of the World Wide Web, this is always a danger. Slick graphics and snappy videos may attract the curious, but that is no guarantee they will derive any clear work-related value from their visit. USENET newsgroups are another example. High traffic newsgroups may attract a disproportionate share of lurkers who enjoy reading the threads of flame wars.

4.1.4.4.4 Information Ownership

A prerequisite to incentivizing the production of useful infobases is the clear assignment of ownership and accountability to the infobase. If employees who create infobases to be shared in an Internet-like environment are told that they must be accountable for the full life cycle of their infobases, they will think twice before simply dumping information of questionable value into the distributed enterprise repository. If their pay raises are tied directly to the quality of the content and presentation of the information, they will invest more time in structuring their infobase toward maximum utility. They will also see to it that their infobases are kept up to date. Our experience with Internet clones has been that many have created databases in order to show off the information delivery vehicles like WAIS and WWW, only to show no interest later when the data becomes stale.

It should be noted, however, that it is not always easy to judge the true utility of an infobase. If the cost to produce and maintain an infobase is almost negligible, then there seems to be no harm done in hosting it. However, one should avoid the temptation to dump information into the collective repository simply because it is easy to do so. The infoglut is already overwhelming as it is.

4.1.4.4.5 The Need for Cybrarians

We apply the term "cybrarian"[7] to someone who is adept at surfing the net (including your internal internetwork) and who keeps abreast of the rapid development of networked information resources. They are part librarian and part cybersurfer.

Because of the fast growth of both the Internet and corporate Internet clones, we can easily imagine larger corporations establishing full-time cybrarian positions. The traditional corporate librarian is typically already saturated with paper-based information and dial-up on-line sources (Dialog, Lexis-Nexis, etc.) and is probably already suffering from extreme

---

[7] Credit goes to Ken Wood of the Lockheed Martin Aeronautical Systems Company for coining the term "cybrarian."

information overload. They don't need the extra burden of having to surf the net and keep up with its developments.

Average knowledge workers will also soon be overwhelmed by the explosion of information on both the internal and external internetworks. Although they will need direct access to information, some will require the services of the cybrarian who is an expert searcher of electronic information.

Cybrarians, drawing on their library science skills, should also prove helpful in organizing the internal web of information. With independent departments and even individuals creating their own internal web pages, the potential for chaos is considerable. Cybrarians can offer guidance in organizing the internal web according to subject matter, organization, and importance for the corporation as a whole.

4.1.5 Overcoming and Working with Legacies

Besides the approaches we have already suggested for dealing with legacies, two others are worth considering. The first has to do with internal promotion of your Internet clone. The second deals with training and user support.

4.1.5.1 Internal Marketing

One approach to working with legacies, especially cultural ones, is to actively promote or market the use of the new tools within the enterprise. We have found that newsletters, magazine articles, briefings, and demos can spark interest in the new tools. This can help establish a critical mass of users. At one large aerospace firm, this technique was successfully used to arouse broad interest in a system that had been in existence for two years but was in danger of stagnating. Articles were written in corporate and company newsletters and in the corporate quarterly magazine to draw attention to the existence and potential use of the system. Points of contact were established at each of the major operating companies in order respond to requests for access.

In the example of this company, it also helped to have high-level corporate sponsorship of the program. Indeed, the original motivation for the system was a desire on the part of the chief technology officer to implement a system that would allow technologists at the different operating companies to share information and thus avoid duplication of effort in research and development. Research reports from each of the companies were indexed into WAIS and made available across the WAN, and special purpose company-internal newsgroups were set up on an NNTP news server.

Although this led to the establishment of some valuable R&D information repositories that were now widely available, few technologists at the operating companies actually knew about them. Many also lacked the appropriate computer equipment and client software with which to access the repositories. Thus the promotional campaign helped to publicize the availability of the information resources and to point potential users toward their own local company-level MIS support personnel who could then help install the right equipment and software.

4.1.5.2 Training and Support

One of the most effective ways to overcome cultural legacies is to provide training and support for users. Many users are intimidated or simply burned out by the tremendous onslaught of new information technology. Some hope their retirement date will arrive before they have to put their hands on a keyboard! The only way to reach and proselytize such reluctant recruits is to provide personal hands-on training and painstaking support.

A key element in developing a training and support program is to identify key in-house gurus and experts who already know about Internet technology and have used it extensively. These folks are natural proponents of the technology.

4.2 Financial Constraints

The financial resources at your disposal will be a major factor in determining the size and scope of your Internet clone project. A pilot project using only a few computers, existing infrastructure, freeware, and easily imported data sources will naturally require much less expenditure than a full-blown, enterprise-wide implementation bringing Internet technologies and access to every desktop in your enterprise and integrating the Internet clone with all your current existing information systems.

But what will determine the amount of financial resources available to you?

Although this is, of course, a difficult question to answer in general, it is a safe bet that those in your organization with their hands on the purse strings will want to know what the project will cost and what will be the likely return on their investment. They will want to know what substantial payoffs will result from implementing such a clone.

Thus, before you can even ascertain the fiscal realities constraining your project, you will need to do some homework to determine the probable costs of your project and the potential financial benefits that will result from system implementation. Therefore, in this section we shall consider the following topics:

- Non-Recurring Costs
- Recurring Costs
- Hidden Costs
- Conducting a Cost/Benefit Analysis

4.2.1 Non-Recurring Costs

Non-recurring costs are the initial, one-time developmental costs of engineering and building your Internet clone. They exclude all the operating costs you will incur later once the system

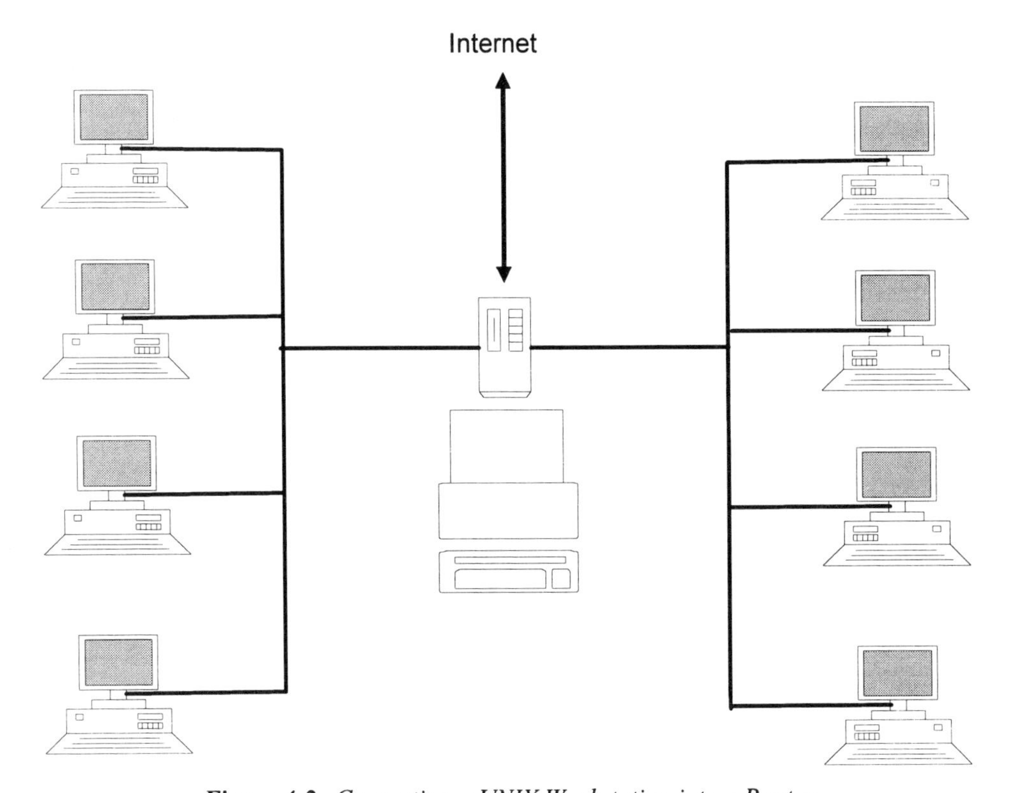

Figure 4-2. *Converting a UNIX Workstation into a Router*

is up and running. These latter costs are recurring and will be dealt with in the next section.

Many of the non-recurring costs of building an Internet clone are similar in nature to those of other information systems. One exception, however, is that an Internet clone can often be built with only minor investments in fixed capital assets. Assuming that you have legacy platforms that can be used as hosts for clients and servers, you can probably avoid

			Plan A	Plan B	Plan C	Plan D
Hardware						
	Computer					
		Servers				
		Clients				
	Network					
		Routers				
		Bridges				
		CSU/DSUs				
		NIUs				
		Modems				
		Cables				
		Connectors				
		Transceivers				

Table 4-1 *Worksheet for Figuring Non-Recurring Hardware Costs*

major purchases of new computing equipment.

Network hardware, however, may be a different story. If you do not already have some kind of TCP/IP network in place, you may have to buy a router to interconnect two or more of your enterprise LANs and connect your resulting internetwork to the Internet. In a pilot project aimed at demonstrating feasibility and assessing returned value, you can inexpensively convert an existing UNIX workstation into a router. To do this, you need to add an appropriate number of Ethernet cards. For example, in Figure 4-2, a UNIX workstation is endowed with three Ethernet cards and configured to route traffic between the two internal LANs and the Internet. Of course, this also entails some investment in cabling and purchasing a CSU/DSU to attach your internetwork to a dedicated line connected to the Internet.

Table 4-2 and Table 4-2 list items contributing to non-recurring cost. This worksheet can be used to total up these costs for various candidate solutions, but in the context of this chapter, we are primarily concerned with its use to work up ball park figures

Software						
	Computer					
		Server				
		Client				
	Network					
		Router				
Labor						
		Management				
		Engineering				
		Contract				
		Total Costs:				

Table 4-2. *Worksheet for Figuring Non-Recurring Software and Labor Costs*

with which to approach management. You and your management will no doubt want to know what the cost drivers are. Giving your financial managers a ball park figure of what you think the system will cost will (hopefully) result in a declaration from them of what your budget constraints will be.

4.2.2 Recurring Costs

Recurring costs are those you will incur periodically once your system is up and running. These costs should be no less important to you and your management than the initial, non-recurring, development costs. A system that is expensive to operate and maintain (because it is, say, labor-intensive) may in fact be easy to slap together; but it may end up draining your resources. There is a trade off between recurring and non-recurring costs, and you should take care not to be penny-wise and pound-foolish. One strategy that seems to work well is to avoid some of the up-front development costs by consciously allowing a few labor-intensive manual processes during the initial operation, while planning to automate these later when new development funds become available. These new funds may be easier to obtain once the sticker shock of financing the initial development is forgotten and the system's day-to-day operation generates enthusiastic support from the user community.

4.2.3 Hidden Costs

Some of the hidden costs often unanticipated by builders of Internet clones are associated with the following areas:

- User training
- Support
- Network management and trouble-shooting
- Application installation and upgrading

It pays at this stage in your project planning to reflect on how these factors will drive the recurring cost of your system. The last item above, application installation and upgrading, can be very labor-intensive and time-consuming if you do not properly plan for automating these processes.

4.2.4 Comparing Benefits and Costs

While costs are relatively easy to identify, benefits are not. Moreover, cost savings are easier to quantify than productivity gains. The major benefit we see from implementing Internet clones is the impetus they give to building new business relationships both inside and outside the organization. Most of the Internet tools foster communication in one form or another and enable knowledge workers to discover not only new information resources but also, more importantly, new sources of expertise. The human expertise distributed across a large corporation remains largely untapped because it is not widely known. The Internet technologies, when used correctly, can help publicize pockets of expertise and centers of excellence across the enterprise. This gives rise to new—both intra- and inter-enterprise—teaming arrangements among knowledge workers.

The benefit of such synergy, although obvious, is difficult to quantify. It is analogous to the benefit of the telephone. Telephone costs are certainly easy to determine and few question that business is unthinkable without the telephone; yet estimating the benefit of the telephone quantitatively can be very difficult, if not impossible. Similarly, it is very difficult to estimate quantitatively the benefit of Internet technologies and the communications they engender. But strong qualitative arguments can be put forth. The telephone analogy is a case in point.

In Chapter 1 we mentioned briefly some of the potential benefits to businesses of using the Internet and internal Internet clones. We now take a closer look at those potential benefits in the following areas:

- Synergy/Collaboration
- Time and Cost Savings
- Access to Resources

This detailed discussion will help you determine the potentially high payoff areas for your particular implementation of an Internet clone.

4.2.4.1 Synergy/Collaboration

The opportunities for collaboration over the Internet are endless and well documented (Cronin 1993). For large, highly decentralized and geographically distributed corporations, opportunities exist to enable internal synergy and collaboration between major operating units using Internet tools as part of an internal, corporate information system.

In the era of rightsizing, corporations cannot afford to have duplicate centers of excellence. Yet to stay competitive, they need rapid access to these centers. The logical solution to this problem is to give the whole corporation electronic access to these centers. Internet technologies can help provide that access.

Collaboration necessarily involves the sharing of information. This is certainly not a new discovery. People have been collaborating since the beginning of time and everyone understands that collaboration is built on communication. But with the advent of electronic networks, information can be shared in new ways, more rapidly, and on a larger scale. Previously, a large paper document had to be copied and distributed at considerable expense. It would take days for the document to arrive on the desk of the intended recipients. The reader would then have to visually scan the document carefully from beginning to end, hoping to catch sight of relevant passages. To extract these passages and incorporate them into a new document, the reader would often have to manually re-enter the text passages. Later, with the advent of personal computers, floppy disks with text file versions of the document could be distributed. This distribution method was often referred to as "sneaker-net."

Homogeneous local area networks (LANs) have made it possible for workers to share files electronically without leaving their desks. The Internet technologies now make this possible in heterogeneous, wide area networks (WANs).

While the TCP/IP protocol suite can help you create an underlying internetworking infrastructure that facilitates the sharing of information, it is more important to discuss the Internet applications that enable sharing and to consider ways in which these applications can be used to share information. More specifically, it is important to consider the kinds of information that can be shared using Internet applications.

We have already mentioned the Internet applications associated with e-mail, USENET news, and the World Wide Web. Although we will discuss these and several other Internet technologies in later chapters, it is appropriate here to indicate the kinds of uses to which these tools can be put within an Internet clone.

Most Internet tools fall into one of two categories:

- Communications
- Information Search and Retrieval

E-mail and USENET news are examples of communications tools. They facilitate communications between individuals or among groups of individuals. The World Wide Web—consisting of information repositories, servers, and browsers—is a collection of information search and retrieval tools.[8] Among the tools integrated into the Web are HTTP, gopher, WAIS, and FTP servers.

In considering the benefit of these communications technologies, you should bear in mind the telephone analogy presented above. Although difficult to quantify, this benefit is undeniable. However, to realize the potential, the users must actually use the Internet-based system. Even the telephone is useless unless people use it.

Search and retrieval tools are best suited for making information repositories available throughout the enterprise. For example, a file containing common MS Excel spreadsheet macros developed by the accounting department can be shared throughout the department—or across the corporation—using FTP. This would consist of a directory on a

---

[8] For the moment, we will ignore the fact that Web-related tools can also be used for communications.

server containing all macro files to be shared. Unfortunately, unless some clever file-naming convention is imposed, simply listing the files in a directory will not reveal to the interested user much information about the contents of the files, in this case the macros that were made available via FTP. This situation can be improved, however, by adding creating a few HTML pages describing each file and containing links to the FTP archive. Provided the accountants have browsers like *lynx* or *Netscape Navigator* on their desktops, they can now browse through the descriptive information and download only those files that appear to be useful.

A more interesting example is the following. Suppose your CEO is a particularly forward-thinking woman who is an avid Internet user and who has discovered the virtues of Mosaic and the World Wide Web. She decides she wants to make use of this Web technology to improve the reporting of company status. She thus mandates that all of her division vice presidents will henceforth create their weekly status reports using HTML. A single top-level home page will contain hyperlinks pointing to each of these individual HTML files. The vice presidents create their HTML files by summarizing the status reports they receive from their department managers. The CEO has mandated that the reports of each manager should also be composed using HTML, and that the vice presidents' reports will contain links to the original reports of their subordinate managers. The managers do the same with their first line supervisors, who in turn do the same with their project personnel. In this way, everyone in the company "submits" a weekly status report in HTML. These reports are completely interlinked.

Using her Web browser, your CEO can now call now call up her top-level home page with pointers to each of the vice presidents' status reports, and, at the click of the mouse, immediately retrieve, say, the report from the vice president of manufacturing and read from his report a summary of the past week's accomplishments and activities in manufacturing. Although she reads at this level the summaries prepared by the vice president, she can easily delve more deeply into any of the news items presented there by simply following the mandated hyperlinks to the status report of the responsible managers. If she has the time and inclination, she can even follow these hyperlinks all the way down to the lowest level worker and acquaint herself firsthand with the efforts of the troops in the trenches.

Naturally, our CEO has little time to read every single report. By reading the summaries of her vice presidents, however, she can quickly home in on the hot topics or key issues, and drill ever more deeply into the organization in her quest for more detailed information on those hot topics. One value to this is that she can gain from the variety of perspectives that are represented. She does not have to rely only on the "sanitized" or "filtered" version provided by her vice presidents.

Imagine trying to accomplish the same thing with paper reports. The mountain of paper that would find its way up the chain would take days to accumulate, and searching through this mountain for the equivalent of hyperlinks would be extremely inefficient.

But your brilliant CEO does not stop there. She now decides that it is important to have rapid access to historical archives. She asks her CIO to implement a distributed virtual archive of all status reports and to make it searchable by keywords. The CIO has one of his staff programmers write some scripts that use WAIS to index each of the weekly HTML status report files. Moreover, she asks everybody in the organization to be conscientious about inserting appropriate hyperlinks in their reports to refer back to reports from previous weeks. In fact, she finds this very worthwhile, because she can directly verify if milestones promised in previous reports are eventually achieved as promised.

This example shows the power of simple Internet technologies like the World Wide Web for integrating enterprise communications and information repositories.

4.2.4.2 *Rapid Development of Tactical Alliances*

It is widely recognized that the ability to make rapid alliances with tactical partners will be important in the virtual corporation of the future.[9] Internet technologies can help establish the electronic links between tactical partners. While it might be possible to standardize computing platforms and software applications within a single corporation, it is hopeless to expect other corporations to choose the same "standards" for their work environment. The most one can hope for is some degree of interoperability, and this is what open systems—and the Internet—are all about. Thus the Internet technologies, or their robust, commercial descendants, might become the standard tools that businesses in the future use to communicate.

4.2.4.3 *Time and Cost Savings*

Businesses are always looking for ways to reduce costs. There are two kinds of cost savings: direct and indirect. Direct cost savings are easy to measure. In the case of computer hardware, for example, the cost of two machines can be compared side-by-side, and—if all else is equal—the less expensive one would yield a cost saving. But life is seldom that simple, because all else is not equal and complex assets like computers are multidimensional. They have many parameters that characterize their performance. More important, however, are the associated indirect costs. A UNIX workstation, for example, may run circles around a mainframe in terms of MIPs, but what about disk access times, and the labor costs to convert legacy code from the mainframe to the workstation? Companies thus run the risk of being "penny-wise and pound-foolish." It does no good to buy the cheapest software in town, if you end up paying for it in lost time trying to work with it. As this is already true of commercial software, is it not even more true of public domain freeware? Surely, software

---

[9] See, for example, Davidow and Malone (1992) and Hammer and Champy (1993) in the reference list after Chapter 10.

developed by gurus for gurus ends up being intelligible only to gurus (although "gurus" is a relative term).

These are serious concerns that must be squarely faced by the business user of Internet tools. Although ruggedized commercial versions of these tools are showing up every day, many of the baseline Internet tools are freeware developed often by gurus for gurus. Why should a company endorse FTP, for example, with its arcane command-driven user interface that few business users outside of scientists and engineers are eager to learn?

4.2.4.4 On-Line Support

The traditional model of support for software within a business usually involves documentation, a company-internal help desk, and, ultimately, vendor support. Software documentation is usually within reach of the end user, perhaps on his or her desk, but certainly within reach of the local workgroup. The help desk may be within the same building or physical plant. Problems not solved by consulting the documentation are referred to the help desk first via telephone or e-mail. If after a telephone call to the help desk the problem is still unresolved, the support personnel at the help desk might come to the user's workstation to debug the problem on-site. Finally, if all these measures fail, the support personnel may call the vendor for assistance.

The Internet offers a new model for support. First, via USENET newsgroups a problem can be discussed among peers. If the problem has to do with commercial tools, the vendor will usually assign someone to monitor the newsgroup and answer questions that come up. The feedback is also useful to the vendor, since sometimes innovative workarounds, previously unknown to the vendor, are discovered by interested user group. Many vendors also offer direct on-line support through archives of patches and compilations of bug reports.

This model also applies to public domain freeware. The associated newsgroup serves as a meeting place not only for users but also for those computer scientists who have helped developed the software. Although this last set of software experts may be in a certain state of flux—people move on to other interest and greener pastures—the collective historical experiences of both users and maintainers make the newsgroup repository a valuable source of support.

This model, when imported into the corporate Internet clone, adds a new dimension to the traditional model of support. In the case of freeware, where documentation may be lacking, this forum for comparing experiences and sharing insights fills a real need. The challenge is to add value and structure by assigning someone to monitor and moderate the newsgroup. Help desk personnel are logical candidates for this.

4.2.4.5 Access to Resources

The information resources on the Internet are huge and growing exponentially. For smaller businesses or those wishing to right-size and reduce costs for information search and retrieval, the Internet represents a golden opportunity.

Another opportunity afforded by the Internet is access to remote devices and services too expensive to maintain in-house. Supercomputers are an obvious example. One of the main purposes of the high speed NSF backbones is to interconnect the U.S. supercomputing facilities. Many of these facilities are actively looking to collaborate with industry in a variety of ways. Businesses too small to purchase their own supercomputers can gain access to these supercomputing centers through the Internet.

HPC Select News, an on-line journal dedicated to high performance computing and delivered over the Internet, maintains a weekly column devoted to accumulating information regarding supercomputing facilities having Web sites. Called "Mo' Web Watch," this cumulative listing serves as a directory pointing to nearly all the high performance computing centers connected to the Internet and publishing information about their machines, their capabilities, and their services. For more information on this service contact HPC Select News at *info@hpcwire.ans.net*.

Similarly, corporations with supercomputing assets can make them available for hire over the Internet.

4.2.4.6 Calculating the Benefit-to-Cost Ratio

If you can see your way clear to quantify the benefits of your specific Internet clone implementation, then the next step is to compute the ratio of benefits to costs. This involves not only benefits and costs, but also disbenefits. Disbenefits are the disadvantages that accrue to your company as a result of using your new system. For example, a benefit might be expressed as time (in terms of dollars) saved in finding information that would otherwise be laborious and time-consuming, while a disbenefit might be the time that will be wasted by people surfing the Internet for frivolous items of no use to your company. The classical benefit-to-cost ratio, then would be expressed as follows:

$$\text{BC Ratio} = (B - D)/(NRC + RC)$$

where B = benefit, D = disbenefit, NRC = non-recurring cost, and RC = recurring cost. Here the RC implicitly includes the recurring operations and maintenance (O&M) costs. Some analysts prefer to include the O&M costs in the numerator and treat it like a disbenefit. In this case, formula would be:

$$\text{BC Ratio} = (B - D - RC)/NRC$$

In either case, the ratio should be a number greater than 1 in order for the proposed project to be advantageous to your company.

4.3 Technology Obsolescence

Today's Internet technologies will become tomorrow's legacies. No matter how effective and robust your suite of Internet tools is today, they are bound to become obsolete in very short order. This is a fact of life with almost all kinds of information technology today. One of the unique features of the information revolution is that information technology actually fuels its own growth. Every advance in storage capacity and processor price/performance enables new applications which in turn speed the development of new chip designs with higher densities and more capable logic.

The collaborative nature of internetworking also speeds the development of internetworking technologies. As internetworks like the Internet enable high bandwidth communications and sharing of ideas across the global community, new concepts of information access, dissemination and utilization are rapidly incorporated into new software tools.

The Internet saw three stages of this rapid succession. The first stage was dominated by rather prosaic command line tools like *ftp* and *telnet*. When the Internet was the sole province of UNIX gurus and academic researchers, this was clearly adequate. Easy-to-use GUIs were still a long way off. The second stage of development was marked by the advent of protocols like Gopher and WAIS, which allowed non-technical researchers in the humanities and librarians to get into the act. Finally, the appearance of *NCSA Mosaic* and the World Wide Web spawned an explosion of Internet use by all walks of life, from academic users to business persons to elementary school kids.

Note that Gopher was popular for only a couple of years before *NCSA Mosaic* all but obsoleted it overnight. Although there is still a very large installed base of Gopher information resources across the Internet, today there is very little new development of Gopher archives.

Although the applications layer tools are sure to become obsolete almost overnight, the underlying network protocols are expected to show more stability. TCP/IP, for example, though it needs some drastic upgrades like expanded addressing capabilities, will undoubtedly remain the mainstay of network computing.

One of the reasons for this is that the TCP/IP suite and associated protocols have already become de facto standards. We think this fact is important enough to warrant further discussion, as it points to a strategy you should consider when making bets in the technology horse race.

Standards: De Facto and De Jure. Someone once said, "The nice thing about standards is that there are so many to choose from!" This anecdote highlights the fact that there are sometimes several competing standards in any one technical area. One conflict is between de facto standards and de jure ones. De facto standards are those that have emerged for one reason or another from the competitive marketplace. They may have inherit technical merit or they may merely reflect the technical approach of the dominant player in a given market area. In PC operating systems, for example, Microsoft is the clear victor; both MS-DOS and MS-Windows are clearly de facto standards. The large installed base of applications programs that run in these environments virtually eliminates any other competing operating system standard for PCs for the foreseeable future (not that there aren't contenders out there).

De jure standards, on the other hand, are produced by vendor-independent standards generating bodies like IEEE and ISO. Examples are the IEEE 802.3 Ethernet standard and the ISO X.11 X-Windows standard. The Internet Society and its technical subgroups, the Internet Engineering Task Forces (IETF), strictly speaking, do not produce any standards. However, they produce documents called RFCs (requests for comments) that are respected by the Internet community and independent software (and hardware) providers as standards. In a sense, they are a compromise between de facto and de jure. (Perhaps this middle ground approach is one of the many reasons for the overwhelming success of the Internet.)

One major difference between de facto and de jure standards is that the former are here today—by definition—whereas the latter require vendors to take a chance on them. Thus de jure standards are frequently impeded in their adoption by a wait-and-see policy, in which few vendors want to risk implementing the standard until there is sufficiently broad market support. It may then take a long time to develop a critical mass of vendors to support the standard. For example, while SMTP was already becoming the de facto standard for e-mail, the ISO X.400 e-mail standard was only slowly being adopted by industry.

Similarly, some companies are slow to evolve their internal information systems, adopting instead a wait-and-see attitude. Rather than cast their vote with an existing de facto standard like SMTP, they choose to wait for full industry acceptance of X.400. Unfortunately, at one aerospace firm this policy of inaction led to a proliferation of incompatible e-mail systems. To solve this, this company chose to purchase a comprehensive e-mail switch to bridge existing applications and pick particular vendor's proprietary system as the standard for the future. The latter choice, however, will end once again in vendor dependence. The better choice, in our opinion, would have been to mandate a de facto yet non-proprietary standard like SMTP. In this way the desired interoperability would be achieved yet vendor dependence would be minimized. On the other hand, provided that minimal interoperability requirements are met, a single vendor solution can indeed yield considerable cost savings based on economies of scale.

Today's popular technologies will inevitably become tomorrow's installed base. Potential obsolescence is always a constraint, albeit a rather soft one. One option is to wait and see which standard prevails. However, since de jure standards are generally uncertain and at best are slow to materialize, it seems prudent to opt for de facto standards, especially those that are relatively vendor-independent. In this regard, the "standards" specified in Internet RFCs are hard to beat. In fact, many vendors have already realized this and are becoming more directly involved in IETF activities aimed at generating application and protocol standards. Rather than wait and see what the IETF comes up with, they are proactively helping to steer the result.

Chapter 5

SECURITY REQUIREMENTS

Security is an essential aspect of many business processes. In the daily course of business we process and convey confidential correspondence, financial information, and intellectual property. The information contained in these transactions, if not properly protected, may cause severe damage to a company's competitive and financial position.

When you combine the benefits of internetworking with the ongoing requirement for security, you are in many ways exploring new territory. Besides establishing a framework of relative risk, you may still need to tailor your strategy to meet individual corporate needs. For example, higher levels of security translate into higher costs. Are these costs appropriate for the data that is being protected? Each and every security strategy will have its own unique profile both in terms of cost and configuration.

Those who connect their private networks to the Internet will have concerns beyond the risks of building a system for internal use. The Internet, with a multitude of opportunities for electronic commerce, is still a hostile new frontier. Edward J. Markey, chairman of the House Subcommittee on Telecommunications and Finance, reminds us to remain cognizant of the "sinister side of cyberspace." With this warning in mind, we must adopt proven methods of locking out intruders so that business efforts can proceed unhindered.

In this chapter, we will introduce the reader to the potential threats associated with an Internet-based information system. We will explore the weaknesses of open internetworks and explain the issues associated with developing a network security strategy. An overview of some essential tools and technologies for securing an Internet clone will provide the network and system administrator with starting points for managing this environment. Finally, we will look at methods for maintaining system security and provide resources for independent study.

5.1 Understanding the Fundamental Security Problem

The fundamental security problem facing networks has two aspects, threats and vulnerabilities, which mutually condition each other. If there were no threats to your system, its vulnerabilities wouldn't matter. If your system were perfect and had no vulnerabilities, you wouldn't care about threats. Unfortunately, the world is neither that perfect nor that simple. You have to carefully consider both threats and vulnerabilities. And you have to be diligent in considering these two aspects of security, because your adversaries are diligent in considering them as well.

In this section, we discuss these two aspects of network security. We consider threats first.

5.1.1 Threats

Threats to your network's security stem from both external and internal sources. External threats originate outside your organization. They may come from adversaries or trusted associates. Some intruders are clearly intent on breaking into your system to steal or destroy your intellectual property. Others are merely careless with the information to which you have granted them access. Internal threats come from employees and other trusted users of your system who through malice or negligence steal or destroy some of your mission-critical information. In the following paragraphs, we treat external threats first and then proceed to discuss internal ones.

5.1.1.1 External Threats

External threats are either intentional or unintentional. Intentional threats come from various kinds of adversaries, including info-terrorists, competitors, and pranksters. Unintentional threats, however, usually result from the negligence of those who are in some way your trusted associates. They may be strategic allies, teaming partners, vendors, or customers.

5.1.1.1.1 Intentional

You can further classify intentional external threats according to the types of adversaries you face. They may be info-terrorists, competitors, or pranksters. Info-terrorists are persons who, perhaps for political, religious, or psychological reasons, are strongly opposed to your enterprise and its mission. They feel threatened by your organization and its work and want to destroy, disrupt, or disable your operations. Competitors, similarly, are intent on preventing you from succeeding in the marketplace. They may be less intent on your demise than on their own economic advantage to be gained from obtaining inside information. Pranksters, however, like overgrown adolescents, seem to be interested primarily in the challenge of breaking into your system and stealing system resources in order to continue their merry pranks.

Info-Terrorists. Info-terrorists want to destroy your organization's information because they perceive your organization as a threat to their value system. They may base their values on politics, religion, or simply the result of psychological disturbances. Political fanatics on both ends of the political spectrum may feel threatened by your enterprise and feel obligated to disrupt it in some way. The Oklahoma City bombing reminds us that political terrorism is not necessarily identical with foreign terrorism. Similarly, members of fanatic religious cults may feel it is their divinely appointed mission to prevent your enterprise from succeeding. The Jonestown mass suicides, the Branch Davidian disaster in Waco, Texas, and the nerve gas attack in a Tokyo subway are sad reminders that some religious extremists are prepared to take drastic measures in acting out their internalized system of beliefs. Finally, certain psychologically disturbed persons may see your enterprise as an opportunity to vent their frustration and anger. The so-called Unabomber, believed to be pathologically opposed to modern technology, is a case in point.

In his book *The Cuckoo's Egg*, Clifford Stoll describes how a hacker from a small West German apartment managed to steal information from the Lawrence Berkeley Labs in California. The chase began with a 75-cent bookkeeping discrepancy in the lab's accounting records and led to an international search involving the FBI, the CIA, and the German Bundespost.

This episode reminds us that the Internet community transcends national borders and that attacks can come from anywhere in the world. Because of the worldwide extent of the Internet, info-terrorists can operate from safe havens in countries where you are legally powerless. In other words, your laws against computer break-ins may fail to deter info-terrorists operating from other countries.

Competitors. Industrial espionage tempts businesses faced with decreasing profit margins and increasing competition. Access to your internal private information can easily tip the economic scales toward your competitors.

Your competitors are always on the lookout for information that will give them an advantage. They are particularly interested in information regarding your strategic plans, research and development projects, and cost of doing business. For example, suppose you host your internal research and development reports on an internal Web server. If you fail to use a firewall to protect your server from outsiders, you invite the whole world to browse through your strategic research program. Similarly, if you set up internal newsgroups to facilitate proprietary discussions and let those newsgroups propagate beyond the firewall, you invite the whole world to eavesdrop on your proprietary discussions.

Pranksters. Pranksters in the world of computer break-ins are crackers and hackers—often brilliant people who enjoy the technical challenge of breaking into a computer system. They often do not have any particular motive beyond the thrill of succeeding. Once inside they leave signs of their visit, perhaps deleting a few files or leaving a spooky message to haunt the system administrator. Often, they are less interested in stealing your property than your passwords. A password file will give them the opportunity to use your system as a base of operations for further exploits and forays into other machines. Pranksters tend to invade computers either directly by hacking or through the transmission of viruses, Trojan horses, and similar backdoor programs.

Pranksters commonly replace your system monitoring programs with their own. This helps them continue to operate and yet remain undetected. UNIX system administrators, for example, routinely use the *ps* command to display a list of processes executing on their computer. Whenever a user logs in, the operating system creates a process. The *ps* command displays information about all such created processes. It displays the name of the user and the names of programs the user is executing. However, pranksters can install their own version of *ps*—one which does not display any information about the pranksters' processes. Thus, if you logon to your system and attempt to list all the processes running on it, you will actually execute the prankster version of *ps*. Of course, this phony version of *ps* will not report processes belonging to the prankster. Thus, you will not detect that the prankster is executing programs on your computer. The prankster has installed what is often called a ***backdoor***.

Hackers. Hackers seek to exploit the vulnerabilities in systems and networks in order to gain unauthorized access to information and resources. Whether for fun or profit, these cyberpunks represent a real threat to corporate security.

Many people blame Kevin Mitnick, a supposed career hacker, for break-ins at Bell Labs, Digital Equipment Corporation, and most recently Netcom, an Internet service provider.[1] Although they failed to apprehend him for years, authorities finally caught him in 1995 thanks to the collaborative efforts of many Internet citizens.

Viruses. A favorite creation of computer pranksters, computer viruses primarily affect the PC and Macintosh world of computing. Once inside your computer they replicate themselves and attack your system's resources. The bad guys may have programmed them to erase your hard drive. Viruses have the potential to destroy data, consume or crash system resources, and play tricks on unsuspecting users.

Some people lump viruses together with other forms of malicious programs like Trojan horses and worms, but they are actually different. A Trojan horse entices someone to use a malicious program. It is a program that promises one thing and does quite another. One such program promised to turn your CD ROM into a writeable device, which is physically impossible. Yet many people downloaded and ran this program and discovered that all data disappeared from their hard drives. If it seems too good to be true, it probably is.

A worm is a program that tries repeatedly to gain access to your network from a network connection. It tries to worm its way into your system by repeatedly trying to find vulnerable ports of entry. The most famous worm to ever plague the Internet was the so-called Morris worm, named after its alleged inventor Robert Morris.

---

[1] See Quittner (1994).

5.1.1.1.2 Unintentional

Although some of the most serious external threats are intentional, many are unintentional. In this age of telecommuting, some employees and strategic allies may have legitimate access to your computer networks from outside your walls. Thus, the opportunity for negligence has grown, and the distinction between external and internal has become somewhat blurred.

Allies. Even in the best of business relationships, accidents may happen. We usually expect our friends and allies to safeguard our private data. Yet they may be working outside your Internet clone and need access using TELNET or FTP. Such programs usually transmit passwords in the clear, and other not-so-friendly programs may intercept them. Or they may retrieve proprietary information from your system and carelessly transmit it to unauthorized persons. Thus, your sensitive information may wind up in the wrong hands.

Vendors, Customers. Vendors, too, may have legitimate access to some of your information systems. They may need to track the inventory of products they supply you with. In order to track inventory, however, your vendor needs to have access to your information systems. Yet the vendor may provide the same service to one of your competitors. In this case, you must ensure that your vendor understands the sensitive nature of your information, is accountable for the right to access it, and safeguards against unintentionally disclosing it to unauthorized persons.

You must be especially careful that your vendor does not receive more access than is necessary. For example, suppose your vendor needs TELNET access to your UNIX machine in order to support an inventory database program. You probably would not want your vendor to run a Web browser to connect to your private internal Web servers.

The same holds true of customers. To place orders and give feedback to your personnel, customers may need access to product support information and communications channels. But you need to carefully review and appropriately restrict their access privileges.

5.1.1.2 Internal Threats

You can manage your internal networks and systems according to various standards. One network may serve an engineering department consisting of fairly sophisticated users needing very little hand-holding. In such cases, the system and network administrator may empower the individual users to make back-ups of their data and roam external information sources at will. On the other hand, a human resources department may have less sophisticated users handling very sensitive information like employee records. The system and network administrators in this case may need to implement more stringent system and data management procedures. These diverse environments, when thrown together, face a host of security issues. Finding a common denominator on which to build a security strategy may range from trusting no one to trusting everyone. The need to protect information and resources varies from system to system, network to network, and department to department.

Like external threats, internal threats are either intentional or unintentional. Since most internal users of your system are trusted associates with a vested interest in the success of your enterprise, the danger of an intentional attack from inside your system seems less likely than one from outside. On the other hand, your system is probably most vulnerable to attack from the inside. Regardless, unintentional threats appear to loom larger than intentional ones on the inside than they do on the outside.

5.1.1.2.1 Intentional

You should focus your internal security efforts on the movement and protection of data within your private network or Internet clone. Information exchanges among employees and other legitimate insiders may be at risk from several threats. Disgruntled employees, subcontractors, teaming partners, and pranksters can compromise your internal information resources. Your goal here is to prevent the transfer of technology, proprietary information, and other sensitive data beyond the corporate perimeter.

Can nonemployee contractors, for example, casually view or browse through your private or sensitive information? If so, then you may need different levels of security to match the different kinds of workers within your organization. Levels of security must be consistent with the information being provided and may have a direct bearing on cost. If you have many nonemployee contractors, we advise you not to put private or confidential information on an internal Web server unless you also add some additional layers of authentication. Of course, this will add the cost of auditing access logs and maintaining password files. When the cost of maintaining information is negligible, then it is fairly easy to justify the dumping of information into Web archives. However, if adding layers of data security and maintenance increases your recurring costs, you need to carefully consider the proverbial bang for the buck.

It is risky to let unintended eyes simply view sensitive information. It is even riskier to allow them to quickly download such information via FTP, store it on a local floppy disk, and carry it out the door.

You may have subcontractors who need access to your information systems. Although they probably have clauses in their contracts prohibiting misuse of company information and restricting disclosure to third parties, subcontractors certainly do not have the same sense of loyalty to your company that employees are expected to have. Often, your subcontractors have relationships with your competitors. You may wish to consider adding a few layers of authentication and modification to the software your subcontractors use to gain access to your network of information.

Today's business relationships call for teamwork. Teaming arrangements allow companies to share the risks and benefits of jointly negotiated opportunities and acquired technologies. Teammates on one project may, in fact, be competitors on another. Since these partnerships usually restrict their scope to a particular deal or joint development effort, companies are wise to segregate these project-dedicated information systems from their other proprietary systems.

Still another threat is the possibility that employees may be surfing the external networks frivolously, eating up bandwidth and disk storage—not to mention labor hours. This may not be a malicious destruction of property, but it is certainly a very costly consumption of resources your enterprise pays for.

Despite new opportunities for the network distribution of sensitive information, the human factor in the security equation remains static. The old adage "locks were meant to keep honest people honest" is still true today. Employees intent on stealing information may have little or no problem doing so.

Employees may steal information over a phone, through a fax machine, or via a public computer network. They can also physically remove or copy documents. Electronic theft, however, differs from physical theft by being less conspicuous.

To keep internal information private and reduce the risk of compromise, you should tailor your security policies and procedures to fit the circumstances of an electronic environment. Your policies and procedures should address new risks by providing information to employees about their responsibilities for handling sensitive electronic information. Additionally, you should expand the scope of ethics training, if necessary, to address risks and responsibilities in a computer-based environment.

Enemies. Internal enemies are a major risk. Regardless of medium, misplaced trust can result in information compromise. You must be able to trust employees who have daily access to important information. Disgruntled employees can exploit the networked resources for their own gain or plant time bombs that will execute when they leave. However, even with many layers of security applied to your network, you still have no effective mechanism for ensuring the trustworthiness of the people using it. We see this primarily as a management problem, not a technical one.

The prevalence of theft and sabotage within a corporation probably has significant implications for corporate cultural health. Low morale resulting from downsizing and large-scale layoffs can undermine an employee's sense of loyalty. In this situation, no amount of technology can rebuild the broken trust between employees and their employer.

Pranksters seem less of a problem inside the corporation than they are outside. Probing into unauthorized areas may cost internal pranksters their livelihoods. Although it is prudent to periodically monitor the computer-related activities of all your personnel, it is generally sufficient to make would-be pranksters aware of the consequences of perpetrating pranks. Examples of pranks are internal "game playing." Such amusements as displaying cartoon characters on other people's screens and shrinking displays can cause productivity losses, and they can snowball as others try to outdo and emulate the prankster. Pranksters may also cause severe damage to systems that cost many hours to repair.

5.1.1.2.2 Unintentional

One of the greatest internal threats comes from accidents and negligence. There is no malice or pranksterism here, just plain carelessness. Users leave terminals unattended. They employ passwords that are easy to crack. They leave sensitive information on unsecured disk drives.

Your financial obligations to your stakeholders require that you not compromise or jeopardize your sensitive information and crucial system resources. Moreover, legal consequences may be in store for your enterprise if you neglect to properly educate, monitor, and control your network users. The legality of interstate commerce and export rules governing the transfer of technology represent legitimate concerns. In addition, employees directly delivering inappropriate information to customers—without going through the normal formal channels—can seriously damage business dealings and credibility.

Easily guessed passwords are still one of the major causes of system compromise. You should implement appropriate guidelines for password selection. For example, it is a good idea to have users generate passwords with six characters, at least two of which are special or numeric characters. If you suspect that user passwords are not secure, you can retrieve a program called *crack* from CERT that tries to hack the system password file. *crack* will systematically attempt to break password files by applying an encrypted dictionary with various rule sets. When we have run this program, we have achieved a crack rate as high as 30 percent. You should also encourage users to change their passwords regularly.

5.1.2 Vulnerabilities

The variety and complexity of today's security problems have made the Internet more dangerous than ever. Unfamiliarity with internetworking concepts, terms, and configurations only serves to obscure the underlying reasons for examining security issues in the first place. In this section, we describe some of the weaknesses in the networking protocols themselves and discuss the need to apply security throughout the network infrastructure.

5.1.2.1 Datalink and Network Layers

At the lower layers of the OSI reference model (see Figure 5-1), TCP/IP networks are inherently insecure. They often rely on underlying datalink protocols that use broadcast methods to transfer data. All nodes—whether on an initiating network, a receiving network, or any network in-between—have the potential to capture and interpret information being passed across a shared communications channel.

Every device on an Ethernet network, for example, examines the data traffic to determine if the local system is the intended recipient. Similarly, on a token ring network, a system not holding the token operates in copy mode, passing frames from the incoming wire

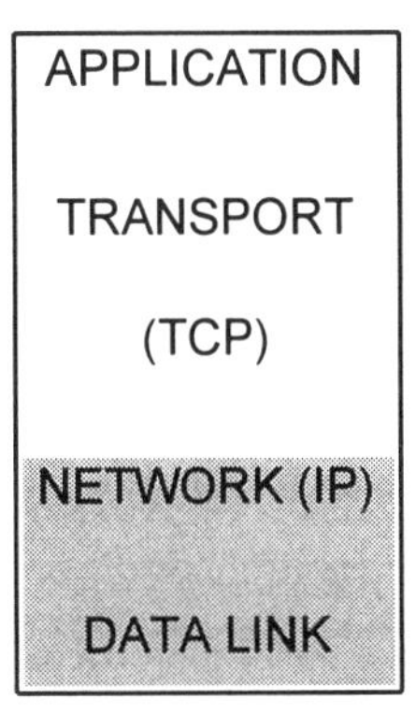

Figure 5-1. *Datalink and Network Layers*

to the outgoing wire. In principle, you can reconfigure these interfaces to ignore the recipient address altogether and process or store the network frames locally.

Network interfaces that collect all frames regardless of their intended destination are said to be in ***promiscuous mode***. Applications called ***sniffers*** or ***snoopers*** take advantage of this capability on TCP/IP networks to read and translate data from a network interface. Sniffers are useful in diagnosing network problems. Some system vendors include packet sniffers in releases of their operating system software. The *snoop* utility in Sun Microsystem's Solaris 2.X is one example.

The widespread availability of sniffers opens the door to network and system compromise. On a corporate network, for example, a user with a network connected PC and a sniffer application can read information like logon IDs, passwords, and other data commonly passed over the net.

This activity is virtually impossible to detect. Aside from a physical inspection of all network interfaces and connections, there may be no other way to detect a snooper. Even if you have a physically secure environment and can account for every device, you cannot rule out the possibility that a trusted employee is using a packet sniffer.

Spoofing is a method of programming a transmission so that it looks like it came from somewhere else. Servers masquerading like this can gain the trust of unsuspecting clients in order to get users to reveal sensitive information. Since you can easily reprogram network addresses, your host can masquerade as another and thereby gain user trust.

Spoofing attempts are attacks from highly skilled individuals who seek to manipulate system and network resources into accepting phony connections. They involve highly technical methods for reprogramming packets to spoof both a source address and predict TCP sequence numbers to gain access to workstations. Intruders use the results of such attacks to seize control of remote sessions and plant bogus configuration files and backdoors for the purpose of gaining unauthorized entry.

Tsutomu Shimomura, at a presentation in Sonoma, California in January 1995, described a scenario in which an aggressor could use a spoofing technique to gain system privileges on a remote node. The technique uses the UNIX utilities *finger*, *showmount*, and *rpcinfo* to discover possible relationships between computers. Intruders then manipulate the network interfaces to block traffic on one end and impersonate it on the other. Upon gaining access to the remote system, the compromised computer passes a *.rhost* file (a configuration file that identifies allowable remote hosts) to the impersonator. The attacker then uses a program to take control of terminal devices on the remote system.

5.1.2.2 Transport and Application Layers

TCP (Transmission Control Protocol) is part of the third layer of the OSI model. This protocol layer resides just above the Internet Protocol, the second layer. An explanation of TCP's relationship to applications and higher level protocols is necessary to illustrate two key security points. First is the concept of port numbers, their restrictions, privileges, and other characteristics. You need to understand how to use this information to filter packets. Second is TCP's relationship with the application layer on individual systems and how they address one another over a network. (The higher layers of the simplified OSI model are shown in Figure 5-2.)

5.1.2.2.1 Ports

TCP establishes connections to a remote system by specifying two pairs of numbers: the source host IP address and its port number, and the destination host IP address and its port number. For example, you determine a connection from host 204.30.247.10 to host

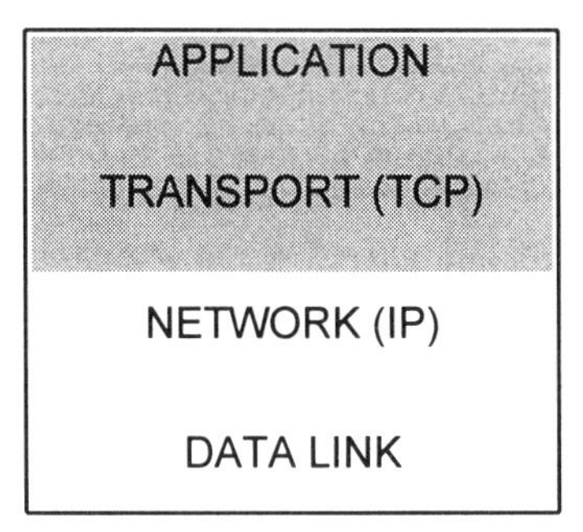

Figure 5-2. *Application and Transport Layers*

134.5.35.65 on TCP port 25 by the source pair (204.30.247.10, X), and the destination pair (134.5.35.65,25). Note that the source pair need not have a unique port number.

Ports with numbers less than 1024 are commonly referred to as *well-known* or *privileged* ports. Each of these port numbers belongs to a standard application found on many machines. The concept of a privileged port comes from UNIX, in which the superuser (usually the root account) is the only user who may bind applications and communications to one of these ports. Although this is the case among UNIX systems, it is not enforceable on systems like PCs that do not make any distinction between the superuser and other users.

Port number assignments are the result of consensus. No one enforces them. You can assign any port number you want to any application you want.

5.1.2.2.2 Processes

Most applications using TCP/IP communicate using a client/server model of interprocess communication. Many server processes wait for inbound connections and do not require any authentication before accepting a connection request from a remote client process. Although applications like TELNET and FTP pass user authentication information from the client to the server, snoopers can grab this information. Since the connection resides outside the system's internal control, the server application must perform any necessary authentication before permitting an inbound connection. This contrasts with the normal interactive session in which a preliminary application like *login* on UNIX machines controls all access of interactive users to the system.

SMTP e-mail, for example, uses the well known service port 25. The e-mail server process uses system resources (CPU cycles and disk space) just like any other application. Clients transmit e-mail messages to the mail server. The mail server processes these messages and stores them in the appropriate mail file. There is no provision in the SMTP standard for authenticating each and every system that may attempt to relay mail to the server over port 25.

The situation just described establishes the basis for a mail bomb. Attackers repeatedly send mail to a valid user account and overwhelm system resources trying to process the incoming mail. Such an attack can render a system useless by eating up CPU cycles and disk space.

Many applications that support the flow of information over a network lie outside direct operating system control for authentication. Network-based applications are not required to pass through the same authentication mechanisms as other system users. That is why applications without secure user interfaces may pose a risk to system security.

Here we have identified two concerns with network-based applications. First, many applications do not authenticate remote users (this may or may not be a concern depending on the accessibility of your network as a whole and the environment in which your systems reside). Second, the possibility of snooping negates the effectiveness of application-based authentication.

Applications with internal authentication mechanisms may employ a proprietary scheme or work within the larger framework of a protocol like the Open Software Foundation's Distributed Computing Environment. Either way, there is a fundamental shift in the way that we must handle network-based applications in an open environment—applications, not the operating system itself, must be accountable for all transactions.

5.1.2.3 Other Layered Security Concerns

Security concerns can affect many aspects of designing and building an Internet-based information system. System administrators, networking specialists, application programmers, data administrators, and end users must all be cognizant of the role they play in maintaining a safe and secure work environment.

This interdependence is what we mean when we talk about *security layering*. Protection mechanisms are layered on top of one another to achieve a complete security solution. Changing the way one layer works requires that you revisit the other layers to evaluate the impact of the change.

At the datalink layer and at each layer above, security policies must address the fundamental openness designed into the network. The future will provide better, more standard, and easier security systems.

Providing optimal system security does not mean that you can neglect physical security. Physical system security must remain an integral part of your overall defense strategy.

The need for physical security results from the risks of unsupervised access to computer system consoles. On most computer systems physical access to the system console or the system itself means that a privileged user is just a reboot away.

What is the point of securing a system from internal threats if anyone can walk up to your system and take the disk drive out? In most cases, physical access to a computer system console is the equivalent of being granted system manager authority. The vulnerability of PCs is already familiar. We use power-on passwords, floppy boot disable, and a variety of other methods for increasing the difficulty of system compromise. Yet, a knowledgeable hacker can quickly overcome these barriers.

Physical barriers go a long way toward protecting a computing environment, but they are not enough. Someone in Australia, for example, who's intended destination was New York would have to cross thousands of miles and pay for the transportation. On the Internet, time, space, and, to some extent, cost are no longer major barriers.

If you know that a neighborhood has a high crime rate, you can always stay away from it. On the Internet you cannot choose your neighbors. Companies that connect their private networks to world-wide networks like the Internet have millions of computer users as their virtual electronic neighbors. In order to protect information you must depend on electronic mechanisms that extend the familiar security of physical locks and keys. Businesses must construct networking barriers that discourage criminals, adventurous hackers, and those who stray from their intended destinations.

5.2 Developing a Network Security Strategy

Businesses, in order to minimize any negative impacts that electronic commerce may have on internal processes, should carefully map out a security strategy that achieves a balanced and cost-effective approach to enterprise-wide information management. By examining the threats, trade-offs, and limitations of an internetwork security plan, companies can select a cost-effective approach and plan for contingencies.

As distributed information technologies become more common, data protection concerns are escalating. In the world of client/server applications, operating system security alone provides little security for data. You should employ network and application-based protection methods to secure the expanded perimeter these technologies create.

Previously we mentioned the phrase "the network is the system." Just as a computer transfers and processes bits and bytes within its own enclosure, the network provides the connections between users and systems that make information distribution and dissemination possible within a business infrastructure. When a corporate network is down you will often find that in many areas work stops.

Physical security is the cornerstone of an information protection strategy. Safeguarding a physical office structure and its premises is the first step in establishing a secure environment. Placing locks on entry points like windows and doors and installing alarms help to deter theft and vandalism. In some cases, depending on the environment and what we have at stake, we may even hire guards or construct security fences.

We illustrate the need for physical security in order to establish its relationship with computer systems and network security. In much the same way as physical security, we structure our networking and computing security methods to reduce the risks of compromise. Instead of locks and security fences, however, we depend on a web of authentication schemes and networking components.

Thinking of this virtual environment in terms of the physical environment helps to clarify security issues and provides key insights into security methods and mechanisms. To protect our business information internally, we lock our office doors, desks, and filing cabinets. To some degree, this prevents accidents. Yet, in other cases, we are actively engaging in deterrents to theft and the misuse of information resources. Even the casual disclosure of an important piece of information may adversely affect a company's competitive position. This is why security policies define ethical behavior—in order to establish clear expectations from employees.

We often trust employees with critical information. They are usually free to move in and out of an office without constraint. We provide them with keys, alarm codes, and a company ID that permits them access to information and resources of all types. Within the internal structure we assign authority to individuals that permits them to access certain information. Even casual observers may be suspect.

Confidence in a security implementation develops over time as a result of continued testing and as a result of troubleshooting. As we become more familiar with our surroundings, we understand the risks, and we know how to prevent and respond to the everyday threats that we might encounter. When we leave important documents on our desks or in our computer accounts we feel secure because we trust those we work with and we have a reasonable sense of protection from external threats.

Just as with physical security, concerns about the protection of information from external threats involves securing a network's perimeter. This strategy focuses on reducing the risk of fielding undesirable requests for inbound connections. Any inbound connection, whether through a modem or from a public network, presents an equally great risk. Establishing a firewall provides a granularity of control between these two entities.

5.2.1 Assessing Your Risk

The process of risk assessment begins with the analysis of your threats to determine the severity of the impact of penetration. The next step is to determine the probability of occurrence of security breaches by examining your vulnerabilities. The threats have to pass the "so what" test, and vulnerabilities indicate your level of exposure and hence the likelihood of an undesirable event.

Networked computer systems and the information they contain face these threats on two fronts—physical and electronic. Now that many systems are located in public and often well-known sites on the Internet, steps must be taken to protect them from electronic threats above and beyond the physical threats that have always been a part of the business environment.

How well do you implement your information protection strategy? What are the risks? How do your policies address each specific risk?

Barbara Fraser outlines the following growing trends in system abuse:[2]

- Increased networking provides greater access to many systems;
- Computers are such an integral part of American businesses that computer-related risks cannot be separated from general business risks;
- The widespread use of databases leaves the privacy of individuals at risk;
- Increased use of computers in safety-critical applications increases the likelihood that accidents or attacks on computer systems may cost human lives;
- The ability to use and abuse computers is becoming increasingly widespread; and
- The international political environment is unstable while international corporate, research, and other computer networks are growing.

So what are the real risks of doing business on the Internet? Companies and individuals stand to lose the most from exposed intellectual property, private or official correspondence, and the destruction or compromise of systems and other computing/telecommunications resources. Unlike credit cards which provide liability limits (like an insurance policy), intellectual property may have cost millions of dollars to develop or acquire. Correspondence that contains strategic marketing information, for example, may open the door to competitive theft.

Assessing risks at the system level must take into account the operating environment (public or private), protection mechanisms already built into the operating system, and the availability of commercial security mechanisms. You must adequately address these risks both in terms of the physical and logical systems environment. Securing individual systems also requires the implementation of guidelines designed to ensure a safe and secure

---

[2] From a presentation entitled "Security Incident Planning: Resources and Responses," given at the Open Systems Summit in March 1994.

environment. Whether you are selecting passwords, performing backups, or installing new software, you need to apply common sense.

Assessing risk is a collaborative task. It involves data owners and computing specialists. Data owners should establish the value of the information requiring protection. Computer specialists should provide technical means to secure information assets without making them difficult to use.

Risk assessment is a good alternative to "cookie cutter" security implementations. Risk assessment accepts the premise that all computers are not created equal. In addition to varying degrees of information content, differences in computing platforms often make it

Risk Assessment Case Study—Credit Cards and the Internet

Are credit card transactions on the Internet really all that risky? Perhaps not. Below, we have provided a comparison of the risks associated with credit card transactions both in normal use and over an electronic network like the Internet.

At dinner, a waiter or waitress brings you a check. After glancing over the bill to make sure it doesn't contain the next table's drinks, you cheerfully put your credit card on a little plastic tray—signifying that you are ready to pay. When your server comes back, he or she picks up your card and takes it away, sometimes for as long as five minutes. What happens to your card during this time? Are you certain that no one in the meantime has copied down your number and expiration date? After you sign the charge slip, do you destroy the carbon copies?

The use of credit cards greatly simplifies financial exchanges. People normally use their credit cards at hundreds of merchants every year—locally, on travel, and over the telephone. For the most part, we conduct business with strangers. So what's the big deal about passing a credit card number over the Internet? A credit card transaction on the Internet might take few hundred milliseconds to complete. In order to steal a credit card number a thief would require the right hardware and software positioned at just the right location at just the right time. Even if someone steals your credit card number, in most cases you are only liable for up to $50.00. (For merchants, however, the liability is greater.)

On the other hand, packet sniffers arc very easy to obtain and install. Moreover, with a little programming to analyze the content of sniffed packets, someone can install a computer program to sift through thousands of packets looking for specific patterns matching the submission of credit card information. Thus, there may be some vulnerability, but as just mentioned, the severity of impact to consumers appears fairly small.

difficult to consistently implement protection policies.

The next step in developing an overall security plan is to evaluate and understand the environment that will be supporting the flow of business information. Many factors should influence your security plan. Attitudes, business goals, corporate culture, and the layers of physical security already in place should drive the content of your security plan. This information taken as a whole offers a balanced approach to individual Internet security requirements.

It is sometimes helpful to categorize the computing environment in terms of the physical environment and virtual (or logical) environment. The physical environment involves computer platforms, office accessibility, and network topology. The virtual environment involves operating systems, client and server software, and specific information resources.

Lacking adequate knowledge of the environment they need to secure, developers of security solutions will almost always miss their mark. It is important to understand all aspects of a particular computing environment in order to avoid the development of inappropriate policies and procedures. Developing policies and procedures in a vacuum can lead to unnecessary expenses and unrealized security risks. Attitudes, cultural constraints, customer-driven security requirements, infrastructure, and the physical limitations of systems will all play a role in providing a secure Internet based information system.

Opportunities for exchanging information include telephones, FAX machines, dial-up communication channels, sneakernet disks and paperwork. You should assess the risks associated with Internet clones in the context of this larger framework of information and communication technologies.

You should determine how the typical threats described earlier in this chapter are relevant to your enterprise information systems. You should identify which threats are most likely to occur. You should study several factors, including your work environment (public or private), the types of external connections you maintain, and the people having access to your network and systems.

To assess your vulnerabilities, you must first determine what you are trying to protect. Attacks can come against resources and information. For example, attackers may destroy data, consume system resources, bring systems down, and consume valuable labor resources in troubleshooting and reinstalling applications.

Resources to be protected include computers, storage devices, telecommunications channels, and software applications. Today, hackers seem to be less interested in stealing CPU cycles than bandwidth. In fact, CPU cycles have become so plentiful and inexpensive, we hardly pay any attention to whether and by whom they are being consumed. Bandwidth and telecommunications channels, however, are still at a premium. Many hackers simply want to gain access to your telecommunications links. For example, suppose your company has a dedicated T-1 connection to the Internet and a hacker in your town can break into one of your computers with a local telephone call. He or she thereby gains high-speed access to the Internet, limited only by the speed of the modem link. They may also gain an anonymous staging area from which to launch further attacks on other machines across the world.

For most companies, however, the primary concern is the potential loss of sensitive data: "It's the data, stupid!"

In the past, companies secured their information physically by guarding against unauthorized resource utilization. Now that more information resides in digital format and more computers interconnect via open networking protocols, emphasis has shifted from resource protection to information protection.

Ultimately, we are concerned with the information that is transmitted between systems. Since there is very little we can do to enforce authentication at the datalink layer, we must enforce it at the application layer. The primary method of achieving this is encryption.

To assess your vulnerabilities, then, you must examine your whole array of information. You must consider how you currently protect that information. Assuming you have prioritized your various classes of information, you must determine, based on your current protection scheme, what the likelihood is of someone accessing and misusing your information. Then you can decide what extra mechanisms you need to implement.

Security policies and practices are often designed around avoidance—taking concrete steps to protect an environment and avoid the loss of data or other valuable resources. As a contingency, however, you can also employ mitigation and containment to stop a security problem from spreading once it has occurred. Avoidance is a proactive posture, as compared with mitigation and containment which are, for the most part, reactive. Nonetheless, mitigation and containment take on a proactive flavor and are highly effective if considered well ahead of the event.

5.2.2 Formulating Your Security Goals

Once you have analyzed your risks both in terms of severity of potential breaches and their likelihood, you should prioritize the risks to be mitigated and then formulate clear goals regarding the level of mitigation to be achieved in carrying out your plan. For example, you might decide that the *crack* program should not be able to guess user passwords correctly more than 5 percent of the time. You might then formulate this as an explicit goal to be achieved in, say, three months from when you set the goal.

Using a rough assessment of information protection needs, you should articulate a clear vision in your security plan. Clarity is important because others will have to interpret these goals during the development of specific policies and practices. Misinterpretation at this level could propagate through to the specific practices designed to secure a network or system.

Security goals should also be realistic and attainable. You cannot ensure complete security. You should counter relative risk with an appropriate security response. You can determine acceptable levels of risk by comparing the value of information and specific resources with the cost necessary to protect them. This approach is not unlike that found in an insurance policy—the greater the risk, the higher the cost.

Next, we take a closer look at security tradeoffs and the idea of acceptable risk and how you can manage risk to achieve the optimal security solution for your environment.

5.2.2.1 Basic Security Policy

The primary stance you take toward security will affect the entire process of developing an internal strategy for information protection. There are two ways in which you may approach a security strategy. Corporate culture, the sensitivity of information within the business, and the level of experience and education of end users will influence your stance.

There are two extreme approaches to formulating a basic security policy. One extreme denies all access to information except that which it explicitly permits. It grants access only on a case-by-case basis. The other extreme grants blanket permission but denies access in specific cases. We call the first approach closed and the second open.

The closed approach, although more conservative, consumes more administrative resources than the open approach. Administrative overhead is required to explicitly grant individual users access to individual information items. Although this provides a detailed audit trail of who has access to what, it can be very labor-intensive. The open approach, on the other hand, usually indicates a highly trained staff empowered to be accountable for their actions. However, it may be more costly to establish, since it usually involves considerable investment in technical training to minimize the threat of inadvertent compromise of sensitive information. Open systems may be easy to use, but they also make it easy to give away sensitive information.

We favor the open approach because it is more in synch with the overall open systems approach of which the Internet itself is a prime example and because it is more cost-effective than the closed approach. Further, we feel the investment to train people on how to use information technology can pay big dividends in productivity.

5.2.2.2 Implementing the Open Approach

The open approach to security involves three basic models of information distribution: the library, the trusted system, and the trusted user.

The library concept involves the distribution of bookshelf information to everyone on an Internet clone. It provides an "open stack."[3] For businesses, this information may be newsletters, insurance forms, or reference materials. The World Wide Web and other Internet tools like NNTP, Gopher, and Anonymous FTP are well suited to this type of information distribution.

The concept of trusted systems—distribution only to specific groups—is the next level of information protection. In an Internet clone, you can implement this kind of security with IP address filtering and application-specific authentication. IP address filtering, however, is weak, owing to the possibility of spoofing. In traditional systems, group authentication is built on individual user authentication. Each user belongs to a group of users. Group access is then restricted on a file-by-file basis.

Information provided to trusted users is usually sensitive or private and requires limited distribution. Often, only those with a "need to know" have access to this type of information.

Using encryption or other application-specific user authentication mechanisms is the best way to keep private data private within a TCP/IP network. Often, however, this involves access control lists maintained by the data owner or the system administrator.

When formulating your security goals, you should consider these three models of information access and determine which one is the most appropriate for each given situation.

5.2.3 Considering Alternative Strategies

As the benefits of distributed open systems and client/server applications generate a demand for more secure interactions between applications, improved security solutions increase the demand for and accelerate the migration to client/server technologies. Thus, the increased reliance on client/server technologies fuels the demand for security, while increased security makes client/server technologies more attractive to businesses.

Which of the many possible information protection strategies best fits your needs? It is important to consider alternative strategies in order to achieve the best overall plan.

One approach, suggests Dr. Sanford Sherizen, is to integrate security into company-wide quality efforts. "If a company is to function as a secure quality organization, information protection activities must be an integral part of the quality effort. This can be

---

[3] A "closed stack" model is also possible. In this approach, only catalogues and directories are available. In order to actually access source materials, user authentication and tracking are required. This approach is sometimes a reasonable compromise between the open stack and the trusted system.

achieved by positioning information protection as a way of ensuring the confidentiality, availability, and integrity of information."[4] In addition to sharing similar goals, a combined security awareness and quality assurance effort is more cost-effective than separately initiated programs.

Too much security wastes money; too little security puts information and resources at risk.

5.2.3.1 Host-by-Host

In an environment where a comprehensive security solution is only as strong as its weakest link, individual systems must provide the first line of defense against the accidental or malicious loss of data. For this reason, we must analyze security beginning at the host system level. Evaluating security on a host-by-host basis provides a foundation for progressing to network-based security solutions. Hosts are links in the network chain.

Hosts can be single or multiple user systems. Most Macintoshes and PCs are single-user systems. Most also run client rather than server software.[5] On the other hand, UNIX, VAX/VMS, and IBM mainframe machines are generally multi-user systems. These systems run both client and server software, though traditional mainframes mostly run standalone applications in which the client and server are identical. Most corporate environments today involve both these elements, and we are tacitly assuming in this book that your environment fits this description.

To ensure network information protection even in this desktop-rich environment, you can install login software on each desktop machine. Such software should be capable of notifying a centralized security server of the user name, IP address, and time of each login session. Since most Internet information distribution systems like the World Wide Web and gopher can log the IP addresses and times of client connections and downloads of information, you now have all the data you need to associate individual users with specific kinds of information access. This can help track down unauthorized use of passwords and frivolous net surfing. For example, you can determine from the logs of Web proxy servers which IP addresses within your corporate clone are accessing external Web sites unrelated to your organizations work charter and ethic.

Traditional PC operating systems like MS-DOS have no built-in authentication mechanisms. All you need to do to access the computer is flip the power switch. Since the boot sequence is easily interrupted, it is nearly impossible for login software to be fully

---

[4] See Sherizen (1995).

[5] With the advent of Microsoft's Windows 95 Operating System, ordinary desktop PCs can support multi-user and multi-tasking software, including server software.

effective. You can nearly always interrupt the *autoexec.bat* batch file with a few control keys. Once inside a system like this, an unauthorized user can gain access to network resources, since most TCP/IP packet drivers do not distinguish between sessions that are initiated through login software and those that are not. However, if central systems periodically collect login records from each computer and compare these records with the access records of all available information repositories, it is possible to correlate repository accesses with missing login records. Naturally, it is most cost-effective to automate these logging and correlation tasks.

Each entry point added to your network enlarges its perimeter, making it increasingly difficult to judge which elements are inside and which are outside the system. In the days of mainframe computing, it was easy to point to the exact location of your data, define exactly how it was protected, and limit access to it both physically and through the operating system. With a network-based system composed of widely heterogeneous computers, it is difficult to achieve such consistency.

If your network is like a house, your end user desktop machines are the windows and doors. They are the access points through which intruders will come and the primary points at which you should apply security measures. However, it is a good idea to have some centralized command and control for security. In your house, an intrusion at a window may well trigger a single, central alarm loud enough to be heard from any room in the house. This is an effectively centralized security alarm system. Similarly, a secure network should be able to signal the command and control center.

5.2.3.2 Tradeoffs

The primary tradeoffs associated with security are effectiveness, convenience, and cost. In this subsection, we discuss how these three items are related and how they affect each other.

Effectiveness is often inversely proportional to convenience (see Figure 5-3). For example, most highly effective security measures involve user authentication mechanisms. These are generally login procedures employing user names and passwords, or encryption mechanisms requiring dissemination and management of public and private encryption keys. If a single-user login procedure is used to gain access to the whole network, the inconvenience to the end user is minimized. The cost of corporate-wide management, however, goes up. Network administrators must still maintain the centralized user name and password files. Data owners still have the burden of determining and specifying which end users are to be granted or not granted access to their data stores, which usually means maintaining access control lists. Many data owners would rather not share their data than be bothered with that administrative burden. It is not hard to see that security effectiveness drives cost.

Figure 5-3. *The Security Tradeoff*

The cost for security is primarily one of development, implementation, operation, and maintenance. To develop an effective corporate-wide security scheme requires many hours of planning and analysis, discussion and consensus building, documentation, and promulgation. To implement effective security often requires the purchase of equipment and software, personnel training, extensive testing, and continual monitoring of security-related events.

An Internet-based information system should also strive to establish a balance between ease-of-use (primarily a user concern) and adequate security for the protection of sensitive information (a business concern). In general, these are opposite concerns. When higher levels of security are applied, the system generally becomes more inconvenient—if not more difficult—to use. This may be due to an increase in the number of steps required to authenticate the user. For example, access software with built-in security methods may have to pass tokens to a security server, resulting in network delays or the inability to access information when the remote security server is unreachable.

Firewalls, proxies, and additional logins may further complicate the process of retrieving information. Besides presenting difficult user interfaces, these security measures can also result in performance bottlenecks.

These opposing concerns must be balanced by a single common objective that provides the highest levels of security without impacting an end user's ability to perform productive work.

Security management comes with a price tag. Increased file system capacity for log files, additional processor overhead to record transactions, and extra staff hours to develop and implement procedures all amount to higher costs in a security-conscious environment. If you develop software internally, you will need to explicitly allocate budget to adding security functions to applications.

Security personnel are necessary to review logs and make judgments on risk assessment and information control. The greater the requirement for security, the more qualified and higher paid the staff must be.

Although you can automate some of the security auditing process with properly designed applications, you still need humans to interpret and follow-up on the alarms triggered by these auditing processes. You still need staff to perform audits, review their results, and enforce policies.

The amount of information you log or monitor directly impacts system and network performance. Attempts to perform detailed security monitoring may result in substantially degraded system performance, leaving less capacity for productive efforts. Security-enhanced software and systems may be slower and require remote authentication, which, as mentioned previously, is a potential bottleneck.

Whether purchased or home-grown, additional software and hardware in a networked environment means more pieces to configure and integrate. Complexity always increases as the number of interfaces increases, and in a system of networked computers, this translates into higher personnel training and system management overhead. For example, enhanced security options on bridges and routers means that you have to train personnel how to effectively configure the filters and logging mechanisms. Since these interconnection devices bring together sometimes heterogeneous environments, you'll need extensive testing to verify that you can pass or filter all combinations of user data packets.

5.2.4 Communicating Your Security Policies and Procedures

Many experts agree that one of the best ways to foster good security practices is to provide training aimed at promoting increased security awareness. An organization's best defense against security threats is a cadre of knowledgeable and concerned users and systems support personnel. The ability to quickly identify resources that address specific security concerns will help to prevent accidents and insure that data integrity is maintained.

Before you communicate policies through command media, however, you should first supplement them with operational procedures. Policies, response procedures, and network management methodologies must all work together to provide a comprehensive security solution for systems and data. Security management operating procedures depend on policies to define the limits of the operating environment. Operating procedures are, in turn, conditioned by challenges inherent in a distributed application environment. Only through the careful coordination of operational procedures, computer security concerns, and established corporate policies, can a balanced approach to overall security management be achieved in such a complex environment.

From network-based license pools to authentication schemes, distributed computing imposes an inherently complex set of security technologies. As these technologies evolve, so must the policies that govern their implementation. It may be necessary to revisit policy decisions more often during periods of rapid growth. This type of ongoing revision calls for flexible security policies; you should be able to rapidly modify your security policies in response to an ever-changing technological landscape. Policies must also be robust enough to adapt to the changing organizational environment.

Finally, to achieve a heightened awareness of security issues, the security command media must be effectively communicated to all stakeholders. This usually entails a comprehensive promulgation and training program.

5.3 Tools for Carrying Out Your Strategy

5.3.1 Encryption

The Internet value chain discussed in Mary Cronin's *Doing Business on the Internet* defines a methodology whereby internetworked companies become extensions of both their customers' and suppliers' value chains. A key element in making this scenario work is the ability to maintain data integrity and security. Many encryption products have emerged to fill this security gap in internetworking products. RSA's public/private key cryptography method, in particular, seems to have attained the necessary momentum to become the standard underlying encryption for the World Wide Web and Privacy Enhanced Mail.

In the RSA encryption scheme, an individual generates both a "public key" and a "private key." These keys are used to scramble and unscramble the data to be protected. Only a user's private key can decrypt messages that were encrypted with the corresponding public key. Additionally, items encrypted with a private key provide a digital signature to those who have verified the validity of a public key. This solves two problems—authentication of the sender with a digital signature and security of data transfers to the recipient. Encryption alone, however, does not guarantee that a message will remain private. One must still depend on both the message recipient and the remote system security to keep the information from becoming public.

5.3.2 User Authentication

Providing secure connections for the transmission of data is a critical concern for many businesses today. Without widespread and consistent security techniques at the application level, the development of multi-platform information architectures would be of little value.

The Open Systems Foundation's Distributed Computing Environment (DCE) and Distributed Management Environment (DME) comprise a framework for developing, implementing, and managing applications and systems in a heterogeneous environment. The thrust of this effort is to provide secure solutions to problems industry has identified as critical to the further expansion of open systems.

DCE's platform-independent architecture offers single sign-on, network-wide user authentication, and security services for systems and applications. Based on MIT's Kerberos, information can be centrally registered and securely passed across a network to validate transactions of different types. This approach reduces the costs of security management by eliminating the need for redundant administrative chores. In addition, end users no longer have to remember a multitude of logon IDs and passwords.

5.3.3 Firewalls

Conceptually, a "firewall" is a network device positioned between a public and a private network in order to prevent unauthorized public access to private information resources. Firewalls often consist of a router—sometimes other systems—programmed to accommodate only approved connections. A single server host can also act as a router, provided it has two network interface cards, one for each network connection.

Firewalls filter incoming and outgoing data traffic. Routers, the primary control point for a firewall, can filter packets based on IP address and port number. Proxies provide further control at the application level by utilizing filters based on user, system, or application function. You can configure a firewall to permit connections initiated from within your private network but to deny access from external systems. Many firewalls, for example, allow SMTP e-mail to permeate in both directions. You can also program them to allow public USENET newsgroups to permeate in both directions, yet prevent private newsgroups from leaving your private network.

In interfacing your private Internet clone with the public Internet, you should place public information on hosts residing outside the firewall. For example, a Web server hosting publicly available press releases or marketing materials, should reside outside the firewall and be readily accessible to all users of the Internet. From within the firewall, you can maintain this Web server by allowing outbound TELNET and FTP traffic to reach the server host. However, you only need to open up the firewall to outbound traffic of this sort. Allowing inbound TELNET and FTP is asking for trouble.

One of the things you may be wondering is how a router can permit interactive outbound access and still deny inbound traffic. A router can distinguish between packets originating from within your clone and those coming from external sources, because they use different physical ports. Further, you can program routers to permit only certain kinds of outbound packets. Therefore, users on one side of the firewall can enjoy interactive access over permitted application ports while users on the other side are denied service. Users on the inside can thus interact with Internet hosts on the outside as if there were no firewall at all.

The basic premise behind a firewall is that you can selectively filter incoming and outgoing connections based on IP address and port number. Protocol filters may be applied to network routers permitting only "specified" port numbers to pass. This provides a certain layer of application-level security, since certain application services like TELNET and FTP, for example, are associated with well-known port numbers.

5.3.4 Proxy Servers

Proxy servers allow users behind a firewall to access the external World Wide Web. They run Web server software specially designed to execute on multi-homed hosts functioning as firewall machines. The proxy receives connection requests from inside the firewall and forwards these to remote servers outside the firewall. It then reads responses from the remote servers, and forwards these back to the original requesting client. Thus, a proxy server can make your firewall permeable for internal users, without opening a potential security hole through which intruders could possibly penetrate your defenses.

Most commercial Web browsers can handle proxy servers. You merely need to tell them the host name of your proxy server. Moreover, most of these browsers can also travel through the proxy server with other protocols such as FTP, Gopher, and WAIS.

Internal clients using a proxy server do not need to have DNS nameserver support. They only need to know the IP address of the proxy server. With a multi-homed proxy, your internal users can access the Internet even if your internal network addresses are private as in the case of a class A network.

More pertinent for our security discussion, proxies can log client transactions, including the client IP address, the date and time, the URL of the resource accessed, and the byte count of data passed to the client. You can also log the information in the meta-information tags of accessed HTML files. Note that this goes beyond logging at the IP and TCP levels.

Proxy servers can also filter client transactions at the application protocol level. They can control access to services for individual methods, hosts, and/or domains.

Proxy servers can also cache, i.e., temporarily save, a recently requested HTML file. This file is then available for other clients inside the firewall to access. This ability to cache reduces the traffic load on the external network. It also saves disk space, since only one copy of the file needs to cached at the proxy server rather than at each of several clients. With caching you can also access files even when the original source platform for those files is otherwise inaccessible due to outages or congestion.[6]

The TIS Firewall Toolkit from Trusted Information Systems provides the ability to proxy FTP and TELNET transactions (without special client applications) beyond a firewall. The drawback, however, is that users must learn a special syntax in order to make the existing software work with the proxy server.

	HTTP	FTP	TELNET	Gopher	Network News
TIS Firewall Toolkit [1]	N	Y	Y	N	N
CERN Proxy Server [2]	Y	Y	N	Y	Y
SOCKS [3]	Y	Y	Y	Y	Y

[1] The TIS Firewall Toolkit requires no special client software, but end users must receive special instruction on how to interact with and use the proxy.

[2] The CERN proxy does not have facilities for user level authentication (FTP transactions are only permitted to anonymous FTP servers—a limitation of most W3 browsers).

[3] SOCKS proxy services are essentially transparent to the end user, but require special versions of client applications that have built-in socks facilities (FTP and TELNET applications are included with the SOCKS package. Gopher, HTTP, and Network News may be proxied through one of several W3 browsers supporting SOCKS).

Table 5-1. *Proxy Comparision Table*

To provide granularity not achievable with a router alone, you can use inbound proxies. Proxies like the TIS Firewall Toolkit have the ability to limit functionality within supported applications. For example, if you wish to allow FTP file transfers to, but not from, a private network, you can use a router and bastion host running the TIS Firewall Toolkit. Table 5-1 compares the TIS Firewall Toolkit with other proxy mechanisms.

---

[6] For more information on proxy servers, see the information maintained by the W3 Organization at *http://www.w3.org/hypertext/WWW/Daemon/User/Proxies/Proxies.html.*

You can obtain the TIS Firewall Toolkit from *ftp.tis.com/pub/firewalls/toolkit*. TIS also makes a firewall system called Gauntlet, packaged for Pentium-class machines running the BSD/OS version of UNIX. Based on the TIS Internet Firewall Toolkit, the Gauntlet firewall adds commercial quality documentation, management tools, reporting tools, "smoke alarms," transparent proxies, encryption, protection against IP spoofing attacks, and commercial support. Information on Gauntlet can be obtained from the TIS Web site at *http://www.tis.com/Home/NetworkSecurity.html*.

5.3.5 TCP Wrapper

On UNIX servers, the TCP Wrapper provides additional capabilities for monitoring and filtering incoming requests to processes spawned by the *inetd* daemon. *Inetd* listens for incoming service requests and spawns server processes as needed to handle inbound connections. This conserves system resources by alleviating the need for numerous server processes to wait for inbound connections. On the other hand, you pay a performance penalty by having to launch the server daemon at the request of *inetd*. Examples of application servers launched by *inetd* are *telnetd*, *ftpd*, and *fingerd*. Once the TCP Wrapper accepts a connection, the resulting communication between the client and server is not impaired in any way.

The TCP Wrapper can log and filter incoming requests based on the remote host name (or IP address) and the service requested. It can provide additional security against host name spoofing by verifying DNS name resolutions against more than one server—essentially asking for a second opinion about the authenticity of the remote host. The wrapper may optionally provide remote user name lookups with the addition of an RFC 931-compliant daemon (refer to the README file that accompanies the TCP Wrapper toolkit for more information).

Use of the TCP Wrapper is common and provides a good way of building an audit trail. In most cases, an experienced system administrator can build and install the TCP Wrapper in less than a half hour. So, if you need a way to track remote accesses to common system services, the TCP Wrapper is a good choice. The TCP Wrapper is available at *ftp.win.tue.nl/pub/security/*.

5.3.6 WWW Security Features

Web providers acknowledge the importance of security and the need to validate certain types of transactions. The inclusion of security features like authentication (username/password facilities or IP address filtering) and encryption provide convenient methods of achieving user accountability and privacy over insecure networks.

The use of encryption with WWW browsers is not new. NCSA's Mosaic has supported PGP-style encryption, for example, since its early implementations. The hooks for both of these encryption mechanisms are for their client and server products.

Several security enhancements to WWW are underway. These include the following two protocols:

- S-HTTP (Secure HyperText Transfer Protocol)—S-HTTP, proposed by Enterprise Integration Technologies, provides secure communications between HTTP clients and servers. It relies on message-based security similar to that of Privacy Enhanced Mail; and
- HTTP-S (HTTP over SSL—The Secure Sockets Layer)—HTTP-S attempts to establish a security layer beneath the HTTP application protocol. SSL can provide security for other protocols like NNTP and TELNET as well.

The need for such security features added to HTTP is apparent. In February 1995, the Computer Emergency Response Team at Carnegie Mellon University reported a vulnerability in the NCSA HTTP daemon (*httpd*) version 1.3 for UNIX. This version of *httpd* can be tricked by client software into executing shell commands. Such shell commands could be used to destroy the integrity of data used by the server and also to alter access control files. Exploiting this vulnerability, remote users could gain unauthorized access to the account under which the *httpd* process is running. Patches to plug this hole are available from NCSA. Subsequent versions of *httpd* have fixed this problem.

5.3.7 Privacy Enhanced Mail (PEM)

Privacy Enhanced Mail (PEM), as described in RFC 1421, defines a standard for message encryption and authentication procedures for Internet mail transfers. It is designed to be compatible with both private and public key encryption methods and provides services like confidentiality, authentication, and integrity assurance without imposing additional requirements on your system's mail transfer agent (MTA).

With PEM, you can use a preferred encryption mechanism that depends on your environment. Until an inexpensive and widely-available encryption package is developed, however, PEM may not be widely implemented because of the differences in encryption technology. PEM also does not necessarily guarantee security. The recipient must decrypt and store the e-mail message. There is nothing to prevent the recipient from forwarding the decrypted version of the message to unauthorized persons.

5.3.8 Other Protocols

CERT (Computer Emergency Response Team) maintains a set of anonymous FTP guidelines at *http://ftp.cert.org/pub/tech_tips/packet_filtering.*

Because of flaws in the respective protocol or chronic system administration problems, the CERT Coordination Center recommends that the following services be filtered:

- DNS zone transfers—socket 53 (TCP)
- *tftpd*—socket 69 (UDP)
- *link*—socket 87 (TCP) (commonly used by intruders)
- SunRPC and NFS—socket 111 and 2049 (UDP and TCP)
- BSD UNIX "r" cmds—sockets 512, 513, and 514 (TCP)
- *lpd*—socket 515 (TCP)
- *uucpd*—socket 540 (TCP)
- *openwindows*—socket 2000 (UDP and TCP)
- *X windows*—socket 6000+ (UDP and TCP)

To obtain information on how to configure an anonymous FTP server in a secure manner, consult CERT's FTP archive at *ftp.cert.org/pub/tech_tips/anonymous_ftp*.

Securing a multi-homed USENET environment containing both private and public newsgroups can present several problems. First, without clear naming conventions, sensitive information may be posted inadvertently to public groups. We suggest that you ensure a division between these two areas by establishing guidelines for group creation and by educating your user population. Second, NNTP administrators, in order to limit the propagation of internal information beyond the corporate perimeter, must take precautions when configuring and maintaining their servers.

USENET content may be at risk from other threats as well. You should seriously consider the potential for contractors and teaming partners working in-house to eavesdrop on your internal newsgroups. You can use the INN news server, for example, to restrict newsgroup access based on specific domains or IP addresses. We know of no news servers that offer individual user authentication. However, restricting IP addresses may help reduce the likelihood of information leaks.

5.4 Maintaining Network Security

In order to maintain adequate security, you should monitor the day-to-day usage of your networks, systems, applications, and data. You should also be proactive in anticipating new kinds of security threats that may confront you in the future. To do this, you should keep abreast of security related warnings issued by CERT, the Computer Emergency Response Team at Carnegie Mellon University. You should also monitor the postings in various security-oriented USENET newsgroups and exercise good netizenship by sharing your own experiences and discoveries with the USENET security community. Subsequent paragraphs deal with both aspects of maintaining security on your Internet clone: monitoring system use and staying informed.

5.4.1 Monitoring System Use

Servers within your Internet clone are generally multiuser systems already endowed with monitoring applications capabilities. They are crossroads of data traffic and fewer in number than client hosts. It makes sense, therefore, to focus your system monitoring efforts on server platforms. Servers usually provide two kinds of monitoring facilities: operating system logging capabilities and applications program proxy services. The discussion below draws primarily on our personal experiences with the UNIX operating system. Many of the monitoring features of UNIX have counterparts on other multitasking, multiuser operating systems such as VAX/VMS and MS Windows NT.

The log files of multiuser operating systems are primarily concerned with tracking user logins and activities. They are not necessarily intended to log processes created in support of client/server interactions across the network. Nevertheless, it is primarily through illicit user logins that security breaches are first made. Intruders often try to modify the configuration files of server applications in order to open up access to otherwise unauthorized users. Thus, it is important to understand the various types of user logging facilities provided by the operating systems on your server platforms.

The main information provided by log files for each user process is the time of user login, the commands run by the user, and the time of user logout. On the UNIX operating system, for example, there are several files to capture this kind of data. One such file is the */etc/utmp* file, which logs a record for each user login. Another is */usr/adm/acct*, which logs the commands executed by each user.

Enabling the logging that goes into */usr/adm/acct* puts extra overhead on your CPU and can gobble up disk space in a hurry. Depending on how many users you have on any given platform, this log file can grow by several megabytes per day. It is a good idea, therefore, to enable this kind of logging only on machines requiring this extra level of security and having the required performance and storage capacity. Certain kinds of gateway machines are good candidates for this kind of logging.

Another useful log file on Berkeley UNIX systems is *syslog*. This file logs messages such as alerts, warnings, and errors generated by kernel routines and various applications programs. The program that monitors the system for generated messages and which records these message events in the *syslog* is called *syslogd*. It runs in the background as a daemon process and is configured based on specifications in the */etc/syslog.conf* configuration file.

Besides interactive user sessions, *syslog* can also monitor messages generated from other machines on your internetwork. It is an important defensive weapon in the security arsenal of any Internet clone administrator.

5.4.2 Staying Informed

As Internet technology continues its relentless drive toward the future, security issues change rapidly. Chances are that your adversaries will discover new security holes long before you do. It is imperative, therefore, that your organization stay informed of new developments on the security front. One of the best sources of new Internet security information is CERT, the Computer Emergency Response Team at Carnegie Mellon University in Pittsburgh, PA.

5.4.2.1 The Computer Emergency Response Team—CERT

The Computer Emergency Response Team (CERT) was formed by the Defense Advanced Research Projects Agency (DARPA) in November 1988 in response to the needs exhibited during the Morris Internet Worm incident. This incident was the result of a self propagating program, called a worm, that took advantage of a hole in the finger server (*fingerd*) and the debug mode of the UNIX sendmail application. The spread of this worm clogged the net and affected public and private institutions across the country. This incident demonstrated the need for a central clearing house to facilitate better security-related communications.

CERT's charter is to facilitate the Internet community's response to security events involving Internet hosts, to raise the community's awareness of computer issues, and through research to help improve the security of existing systems. CERT communicates with the Internet community through its FTP server maintained at *cert.org* (see Figure 5-4). This site contains both CERT advisories and bulletins regarding vulnerabilities in various applications as reported by Internet citizens.

It is CERT's policy to neither confirm nor deny Internet related security incidents. This makes it possible for reporting companies and organizations to maintain anonymity. Anonymity achieves two goals. First, it constrains what might otherwise be a publicly embarrassing situation for an individual business. Public knowledge of a security breach could have prolonged effects, for example, among corporate stockholders and customers who may question the basic underlying mechanisms for protecting information. Second, it prevents the misuse of information for malicious purposes.

Security bulletins, known as CERT advisories (see Figure 5-4), provide the global Internet population with up to date information on known security problems, incidents, related cures, and patches. Advisories provide general information on problems or incidents, a description of the problem, its impact, and known solutions. CERT circulates information about a vulnerability only after a workaround or patch becomes available. Working with a variety of software and system vendors, CERT is able to quickly contain the spread of security problems.

CERT Coordination Center

Carnegie Mellon University

Pittsburgh, PA 15213-3890

U.S.A.

24 hour hotline: 412-268-7090

The anonymous ftp server at CERT offers a variety of security tools and advisories—the URL for this server is: ftp://cert.org/

To join the CERT advisory mailing list, send e-mail to:

cert-advisory-request@cert.org

Figure 5-4. *The CERT Announcement*

CA-94:12 Cert Advisory

July 14, 1994

Sendmail Vulnerabilities

This advisory supersedes all previous CERT advisories about sendmail(8) for the vendors listed below.

There are two vulnerabilities in some vendors' versions of sendmail(8). One, in the debug option, enables local users to gain root access. The other, in the error message header option, enables local users to read any file on the system. Both vulnerabilities are known in the intruder community.

I. Description

There is a problem with the debug option (-d) and/or the error message header option (-oE) in some vendors' versions of sendmail(8). An exploitation script has been circulated for sendmail -d, and intruders are actively exploiting this vulnerability. As of the date of this advisory, we have not received reports of the sendmail -oE vulnerability being exploited.

II. Impact

The sendmail -d vulnerability allows local users to gain root access. The sendmail -oE vulnerability allows local users to ready any file on the system.

III. Solution

Obtain and install the appropriate patch according to the instructions included with the patch.

Figure 5-5. An Example CERT Advisory

5.4.2.2 USENET newsgroups

USENET newsgroups provide another forum for Internet users to discuss security issues. Several USENET newsgroups host discussions on security topics. The information in these newsgroups is often broader in scope than that found in CERT advisories and bulletins. It is CERT's policy to withhold the specific details of a security incident until patch fixes are available. USENET newsgroup participants, however, will often provide in-depth technical descriptions of bugs with examples of how they work. The rationale here is that, in order to verify problems and develop protection mechanisms, the good guys should have access to the same information as the bad guys. With up-to-the-minute information, many system managers can develop interim problem fixes or simply disable an offending program or network facility. Some of the newsgroups providing information on security-related topics are:

- *alt.security*—an unmoderated discussion group for general security issues, including computer security;
- *comp.risks*—a moderated discussion group for risks to public computers;
- *comp.security.announce*—a moderated newsgroup dedicated to the distribution of CERT advisories;
- *comp.security.misc*—an unmoderated forum for the discussion of computer security ; and
- *comp.virus*—a moderated newsgroup focusing on issues pertaining to computer viruses.

Gathering security-related information from CERT and the various USENET news sources provides a starting point for ongoing security analysis and troubleshooting. By regularly reviewing these resources for security information and recommendations, system and network administrators have a better chance of preventing serious problems.

You should review and test system and application patches or workarounds prior to implementing them. This will help minimize incompatibilities and other side-effects that can result from hastily performed upgrades. Further, you should only acquire patches through known, reliable channels, either directly from your system or application provider or from a trusted Internet resource like CERT.

5.4.2.3 Other Internet Resources

There are a number of security-related resources on the Internet. Organizations that have a financial stake in Internet security often use their own sites to market security-related products and services. These sites often contain useful information, guidelines, and in some cases free software. An excellent place to begin looking for security-related sources on the

Web is Yahoo's security and encryption page.[7] You will find there pointers to information on cryptography, computer security books, commercial products and services, conferences, digital cash, firewalls, hacking, viruses, and, in particular, WWW security.

5.4.2.4 Security Patches and Vendor-Specific Information

Security patches can be retrieved alongside other trouble fixes from first-party vendor sites across the net. Companies like DEC, IBM, HP, and Sun provide customer service information and archive sites containing the latest information on their products, and services.

Patches and trouble fixes are as varied as the vendors that develop applications and the hardware platforms they run on. The details of retrieving and installing a system patch will vary from application to application and system to system.

The most reliable way to secure system patches (sometimes referred to as PTF's—Problem Trouble Fixes) is to contact the vendor directly either by phone or the Internet. Hewlett-Packard, for example, offers a number of Internet-based services for their customers. In addition to product catalogs and service information, they utilize the Internet to deliver updated drivers, system software revisions, and patches for their products.

5.4.2.5 Keeping Your Users Informed

In addition to keeping yourself informed of security matters, you must make the effort to keep your internal user community informed. You can do this by establishing prominently displayed hyperlinks on your internal home page to places like the CERT FTP archive. You can also mandate by policy that all home pages belonging to operating units within your enterprise have the same set of prominently displayed hyperlinks. In addition, you can put yourself on the CERT advisory electronic mailing list and forward any pertinent advisories to cognizant parties within your organization. You should also employ more traditional methods of sharing information such as face-to-face meetings, and audio and video teleconferences.

You should also consider establishing internal USENET newsgroups dedicated to discussing computer security as it pertains to your own internal organization. You can replicate postings from related external newsgroups to facilitate further internal discussion. You should be careful not to discuss too openly the vulnerabilities of your own internal systems. Even within the corporate walls, you can never be sure exactly who is reading the postings. In order to prevent sensitive information from being posted on this very sensitive topic, it is prudent to have a knowledgeable person moderate these newsgroups. If you desire even more security, you can implement IP address filtering to permit only authorized personnel to read and participate in these private newsgroups.

---

[7] Located at *http://www.yahoo.com/Science/Mathematics/Security_and_Encryption/*.

Chapter 6

SYNTHESIZING AND EVALUATING ALTERNATIVE SOLUTIONS

After you thoroughly understand your stakeholders' basic requirements, i.e., their primary goals and constraints, you should carefully articulate your understanding to the stakeholders and receive from them explicit buy-in in order to proceed with the project. Once they give you this go-ahead, you should proceed to *synthesize* and *evaluate* various candidate solutions. During system synthesis, the system architect considers each individual requirement and surveys candidate technologies and components that promise to fulfill the requirement. By selecting combinations of compatible components and considering the details of their mutual interfaces, the architect synthesizes the system. In this way, the components of the candidate system are mentally integrated into a cohesive whole.

Although the process of synthesis is sometimes referred to as *system design*, we prefer to use the phrase *system synthesis*, in order not to confuse this activity with that of detailed system design. Some prefer the terminology *system architecting*[1] rather than *system synthesis*, because at this stage the top-level physical architecture is laid out for various alternative systems, and trade offs are made based on evaluations of the system. This process, which is iterative and presupposes that a functional architecture has already been established, is intended to converge to a near-optimal system architecture.

In this chapter, we explore some alternative architectures and indicate in broad brush strokes how those alternatives might be evaluated using criteria based on previously established goals and constraints. Since the number of architectural variations for any given set of requirements is practically limitless, we will keep matters simple here by focusing on a

---

[1] Rechtin (1991).

small but illustrative set of nominal requirements. To do this, we presuppose a scenario based on the following set of hypothetical requirements:

1. The system shall be a prototype, spanning a wide geographical area for a moderate size corporation comprised of three operating companies or divisions.
2. The users shall be limited to less than 100, with 50 drawn from engineering, 25 from the MIS organization, and 25 from the marketing or business development organization. (Although our hypothetical corporation may be much larger than indicated here, we restrict the experimental pilot project to 100 users of the types mentioned.)
3. The project leader shall be dedicated near full-time to the project, but shall not have a significant budget for any major purchases of new equipment or software. Any major purchases have to come out of the operating companies. The labor resources shall be drawn from the three operating companies and provided on an almost "volunteer" basis. The project support community will be drawn from the MIS organization with some support from the engineering ranks. The project leader shall also function as the chief system architect for the project.
4. Each of the three operating companies already have an Ethernet infrastructure. Companies A and B are already interconnected via a dedicated 56-Kbps line; however, Company C is not connected to the other two. Company A, the R&D arm of the corporation, is dominated by Macintosh and UNIX workstation users who are already interconnected and using TCP/IP. Company B is primarily a PC-oriented company with a Novell Netware LAN, while Company C has an IBM 3090 mainframe, a VAX minicomputer, and a few PCs also interconnected via a Novell Netware LAN.
5. The initial network configurations of the three companies are shown in Figure 6-1.
6. Company A has a dial-up connection to the Internet used only by the company librarian. At the request of the engineers and marketing personnel, the librarian uses the Internet to perform literature searches, download documents, and gather demographic and market analysis data. At the start of the project, the librarian is the only person at Company A who uses the Internet. He uses it to send SMTP e-mail, to post inquiries and answers to USENET newsgroups, and to gather information using gopher, WAIS, and Jughead. He has browsed the World Wide Web using the text-based browser lynx. His serial line connection to the Internet gives him access only to a UNIX shell account, and he cannot currently make use of a GUI browser like Mosaic.
7. The only electronic means currently used within the companies to share information is e-mail. Company A and B use SMTP, while Company C uses OfficeVision/VM and the VAX Mail utility. Company C e-mail users cannot exchange e-mail messages with employees at Companies A and B.

8. The goal of the proposed pilot system is to

- enable information sharing by means of e-mail, file transfer, and shared databases;
- foster collaboration among the companies; and
- provide more rapid and direct access to Internet resources.

If the project participants perceive the prototype system to be useful and can convince upper management of its usefulness, the system shall be implemented on a broader scale and made available to the whole corporation.

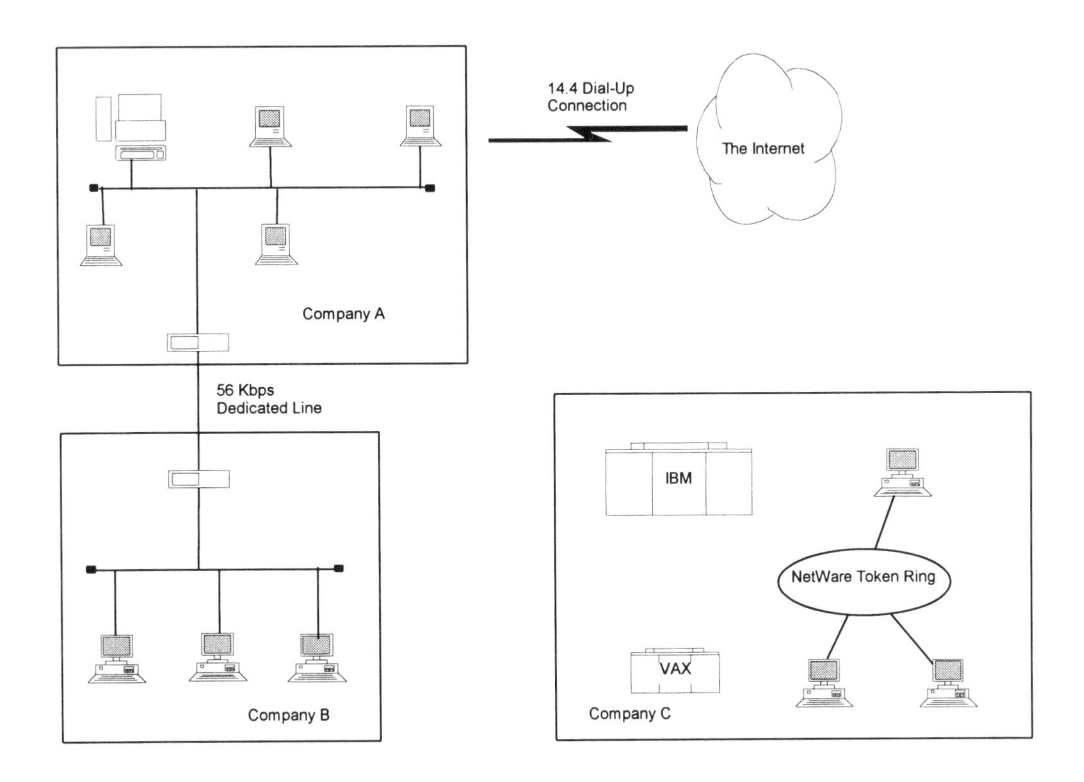

Figure 6-1. *Company Internetworks Prior to Upgrade*

6.1 Synthesizing Alternative Solutions

6.1.1 The Network Architecture

The first order of business for the system architect is to survey and document the existing network infrastructure. The architect should consider the computers the intended users are currently using and how these computers are connected (if at all) to the underlying network infrastructure. One of the main technical products of this phase of the project is a set of schematic network drawings showing both the existing and the proposed network architectures. The difference between these architectures will give the architect insight into the size and scope of the proposed upgrade.

An equally important product of this survey should be a user-centered inventory of system components. This can be a database consisting of information about the users, their current computer resources, and their requirements as perceived by themselves. We call this the *User Requirements Database*, or URDB. As a minimum, this database should contain the following information items:

- User Name
- User Location
- User Functional Organization or Specialty
- User Job Description
- Usage Requirements (as perceived by the user)
- User Level of Computer Sophistication (as perceived by the user)
- Computer Hardware (type and capacity)
- Relevant Application Software
- Operating System Software (including version numbers)
- Network Interface Software (packet drivers) and telecommunications software
- Modems
- Network Interface Units (or cards)
- Current LAN Access
- Associated Routers

The order in this list is not arbitrary. It represents a layered approach to organizing the information needed to assess the current status of the network. As users are the driving force behind the project, their profile is listed first. The purpose of the project is to empower them with tools and resources that will help them be more effective in their work.

Using a database management tool, you can sort and summarize these data in several useful ways. For example, a tally of the existing network interface cards will give the project sponsors an accurate measure of the budget required to procure cards for those users who don't have them. It is not necessary, however, to go out and purchase an expensive database management tool. Many spreadsheet programs like MS Excel contain database features adequate for our purposes.

Note the two fields "usage requirements (as perceived by the user)" and "user level of computer sophistication (as perceived by the user)." The first represents the user's perception of his or her need for system access. These requirements can be thought of as personalized goals. On the other hand, the second item represents a constraint. It tells the system architect and project sponsors how much assistance and individual attention the user will need in order to be productive in using the system. In other words, the architect (as project leader) can infer from this information how much labor will be required to satisfy each user's needs and constraints.

Next in the list is an inventory of the user's current computer and network resources. These are also constraints. This information helps the architect quantify the computer upgrades required for this particular user.

In our hypothetical scenario, one of the goals is to provide rapid and direct Internet access to all participants regardless of location. Here the terms "rapid" and "direct" are subject to interpretation. Here we assume the users and builders have agreed on the following interpretation: Rapid and direct access to the Internet shall mean access from each desktop without having to dial-up or emulate a terminal. For our hypothetical corporation, this is a radical departure from the current approach in which only the technical librarian at Company A has any access at all, and that is limited to dial-up. The first implication, therefore, of the requirement to have rapid and direct access is that the project will need a dedicated line connecting one of the companies to the Internet.

Alternative approaches for achieving the desired type of Internet access are numerous. There are several good books on the subject of implementing connections to the Internet.[2] There is no need to explore all the details here. It is sufficient to consider some of the key factors. One of these key factors is the capacity or *bandwidth* of the connection. The bandwidth requirement is driven by the number of users and the manner in which they will use the Internet connection. These user-driven requirements can be gleaned from the information in our user requirements database.

---

[2] Estrada (1993).

Determining the capacity of the "pipe" connecting our system to the Internet will require some detailed computations. In our example, there are 100 users. If the main focus of our experiment is merely to interconnect the companies by means of a private backbone of leased lines and support only occasional (but direct) access of the Internet, then several low-speed, shared SLIP or PPP lines would probably suffice. This approach, which requires only a bank of 14400 or 28800 modems and a few phone lines, can be relatively inexpensive.

What's a CSU/DSU?

The CSU/DSU is a digital device that converts V35 or RS-232 data from your router to 56 or 64 Kbps channels on a dedicated digital line. It translates data emanating from your router into the standard DS0 format used for multiplexing according to the international telecommunications standard for T-1 data communications.

The T-1 standard was developed by AT&T and is widely adopted. It consists of a 193-bit frame divided into 24 channels of 8 bits each. (Although $8 \times 24 = 192$, the T-1 standard adds an extra bit to each frame.) Since according to the AT&T standard, DS0 channels contain 7 bits of information (or data) and an additional bit for control, the *data* rate of these channels is only 56-Kbps. (The coder-decoder, or codec, samples signals at a rate of 8,000 samples per second; thus 7 bits × 8,000 samples/sec = 56,000 bits per second.)

The T-carrier system was invented by AT&T to enhance its plain old telephone service (POTS) by multiplexing many conversations together for transmission over twisted pairs of copper wires. The scheme uses two pairs of wire to multiplex 24 channels. One pair is used to transmit, the other to receive. This allows simultaneous transmission and reception of communications signals, commonly referred to as *full duplex mode*.

Because the T-1 standard uses two pairs of unshielded twisted pairs, it is important to determine if the wiring in your facilities satisfies the T-1 requirements specifications. The way in which the cables are spliced, the kinds of junction boxes you have, and the number of twists per foot are all important considerations when installing a T-1 system. It is best to have the T-1 provider inspect your facility.

If, on the other hand, our users plan to make more than occasional use of the Internet—exploring its resources daily—chances are that shared SLIP or PPP connections will soon become a bottleneck and a source of user frustration. The users will eventually contend for the limited number of modems and phone lines. For a pilot project of 100 users, a 56-Kbps dedicated line is probably a smarter choice than a single low-speed SLIP or PPP connection.

However, even a 56-Kbps line does not leave much room for growth. As the network system comes on-line and other potential users outside the original intended set discover its potential, they will find a way to get connected. It is very difficult to restrict the number of users, especially when the technologies enabling the connection are inexpensive and readily available. Moreover, when users—intended or not—begin to see the attractive, multimedia features of the World Wide Web, their appetite for bandwidth will grow. It is prudent, therefore, to make room for such growth.

One way to accommodate bandwidth growth is to implement a fractional T-1 connection to the Internet. A fractional T-1 connection can provide an initial 128-Kbps of bandwidth and all the equipment needed to upgrade the connection later to a full T-1. The change from a fractional T-1 connection to a full T-1 is painless. The access provider and the telecommunications company can easily grant access to more channels that are already physically connected via the channel service unit/data service unit (CSU/DSU).[3]

Even at this preliminary stage of system synthesis there are many considerations and many alternative solutions. For our hypothetical pilot project, we recommend a 128-Kbps fractional T-1 connection, because this can accommodate not only the expected 100 users, but also any additional users who might show up; it allows for a graceful upgrade to a higher speed connection using the same equipment.

Given that the connection will be a fractional T-1, we must now decide where to locate the Internet connection. In other words, which of the three companies shall host the dedicated leased line to the Internet access provider? The answer depends on several factors. Since cost is a major driver, we are inclined to choose a dedicated line minimizing the distance between our internal network and the access provider's point of presence (POP). Since we will have to add a dedicated leased private line anyway between Companies B and C (or between Companies A and C), any one of our three companies is a candidate to be the Internet connection site. We might consider choosing the company closest to the most desirable provider's POP as the site for the connection. On the other hand, if the pilot project is to proceed in incremental phases, it might be desirable to first demonstrate the utility of the connection by giving access to those who already have the most elaborate infrastructure in place. Presumably, these users will have the greatest initial appetite for Internet access and probably show the steepest utilization growth trend. It also makes sense to place the link where there is the greatest number of people already using TCP/IP, since these users will have less trouble in learning how to navigate the Internet. In our scenario, this would be Company A. It certainly does not make sense to establish the Internet link at Company C, since only its users would have access to it, the other companies having to wait for the link between B and C (or A and C). Thus, while users at Company A are already experimenting with the Internet

---

[3] Andrew S. Tannenbaum, *Computer Networks*, Prentice-Hall, 1981, pp 104-106.

connection, the project can then turn its attention to setting up the link between Companies B and C (or A and C, whichever makes the most sense).

We must also consider the compatibility of each company's existing routers with those of the Internet access provider. Router manufacturers, among them Cisco, Bay Networks, and Proteon, have preferences for particular routing protocols. In our hypothetical

Speed	Type	Protocol	Equipment	Growth	Uses
9.6	dial-up	SLIP/PPP	modem	up to 28.8	e-mail
14.4	dial-up	SLIP/PPP	modem	up to 28.8	e-mail, text files, minimal graphics
28.8	dial-up	SLIP/PPP	modem	none	e-mail, text files, graphics, minimal audio/video
14.4	dedicated	SLIP/PPP	modem	up to 28.8	e-mail, text files, minimal graphics; server applications
28.8	dedicated	SLIP/PPP	modem	none	e-mail, text files, graphics, minimal audio/video; server applications
56	dedicated	RS-232-DS0	CSU/DSU	up to T-1	e-mail, text files, graphics, full audio/video; server applications; moderately many users
128	dedicated	RS-232-DS0	CSU/DSU	up to T-1	e-mail, text files, graphics, full audio/video; server applications; twice as many users as 56-Kbps
1.544 Mbps	dedicated	RS-232-DS0	CSU/DSU	none	e-mail, text files, graphics, full audio/video; server applications; many users

Table 6-1. *Bandwidth Options for Initial Internet Experiment*

corporation, there may already be an investment in certain kinds of routers, and we should verify that the Internet access provider can accommodate that protocol.

Besides the access provider's installation and monthly charges there will also be a charge by the local telephone company for the local loop tail circuit, which is the dedicated line from the company site to local exchange carrier's central office. The monthly cost for the local loop can vary depending on location (e.g., local loop rates may be higher in Los Angeles than in Houston).

In Figure 6-2, we show the additional equipment installations at each of the three companies. In this figure, we show the additional routers and dedicated lines but not the CSU/DSUs. You should note, however, that all new routers with an external leased line connection do require a CSU/DSU. In this architecture, we have proposed replacing the 14.4 dial-up connection with a dedicated fractional T-1 line with an initial capacity of 128 Kbps. We have also proposed to upgrade the previous 56-Kbps line between Companies A and B to a 128-Kbps fractional T-1 line. This is to avoid a potential bottleneck between these two companies.

Given that this pilot system is to be low-cost, it might make sense to see if some cost savings can be reaped by multiplexing other kinds of telecommunications with your dedicated data connections. If dedicated voice and video connections already exist between Companies A, B, and C, piggy-backing on these systems by way of multiplexers might yield significant cost savings.

After deciding on the dedicated point-to-point WAN links—one between Companies B and C, and one between Company A and the Internet access provider—it is time to register your domain and reserve a block of Internet addresses for computers and routers on your own internetwork. This will probably involve replacing the IP addresses already in use prior to installing the Internet connection. Unfortunately, this is often a tedious and labor-intensive operation. It requires that you walk around and manually configure each computer on your network, and change the routing tables in any pre-existing router. In our sample project, we will assume that Company A, which already had an extensive TCP/IP LAN in place, requires this change. Indeed, since the only access before was a dial-up shell account used by the librarian, there was no need for Company A's network users to have IP addresses registered with the InterNIC. Changing the IP addresses will be a thankless task for the "volunteers" at Company A.

Finding the priority to accomplish this address change may require some extra pleading by the project leader with Company A's MIS management. This is one area where cultural clashes may become visible. Here it will be helpful to enlist the help of those intended users at Company A who can be counted on to share their enthusiasm.

If the political energy required to effect the change of network addresses is more than the project leader can muster, consideration might be given to a different kind of Internet access. A *trusted host* approach might be appropriate. In this case, only one computer (preferably a large, multi-user one) needs to be connected to the Internet. Users of the Internet would have to login to this computer and run client software on this machine. This approach also provides an added layer of security: Users within the organization would have to have authorized usernames and passwords to access the trusted host. This is a security paradigm whose risks are already well understood and minimized.

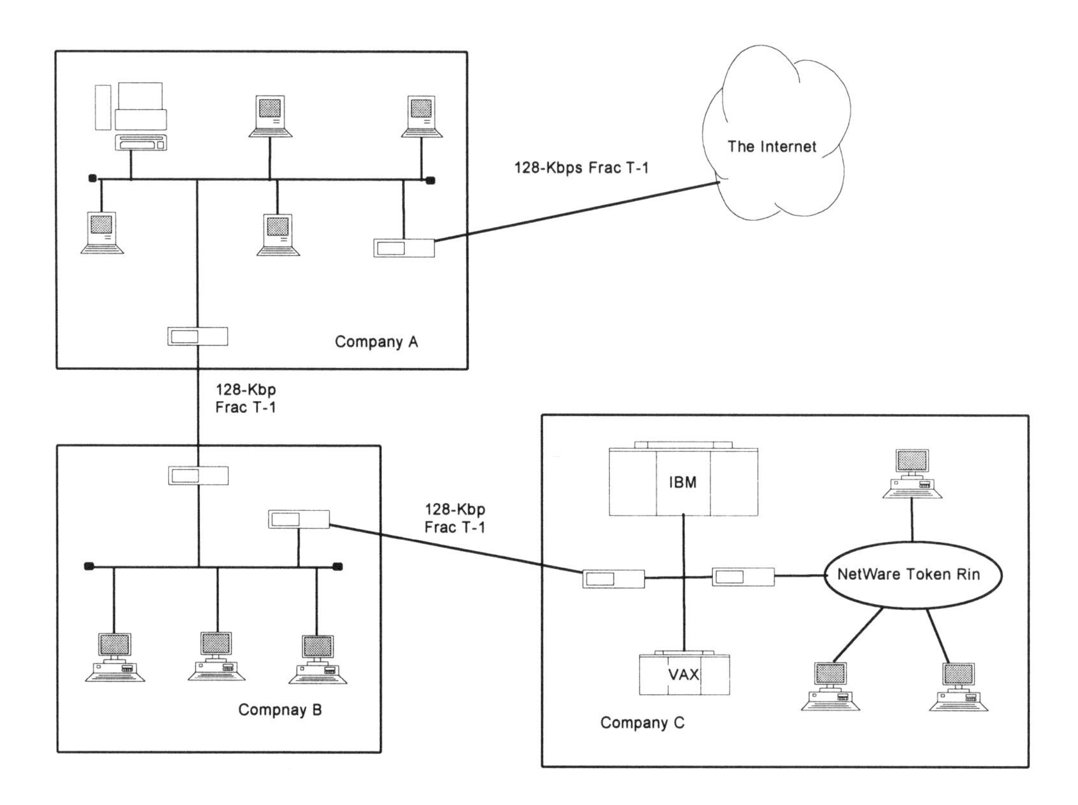

Figure 6-2. *Additional Company Interconnections*

There are disadvantages to the trusted host approach. First, it will not allow full multimedia access to the Internet. Users will have to emulate a "dumb terminal" on their workstations and use text-based browsers like lynx and gopher. Although there is a wealth of text-based information on the Internet, the trend is toward multimedia access, which takes full advantage of the visualization potential of the World Wide Web. It is safe to bet that before long your users will clamor for full multimedia access from their desktops to the Internet.

Nevertheless, even without full multimedia access to the Internet from the desktop, a full Internet clone can be built within the organization. Corporate-internal Web servers can be set up that give users full multimedia access within the corporation to enterprise-internal information. Our experience, however, is that this only whets the user's appetite for expanded multimedia access to Internet resources outside the enterprise.

The discussion thus far calls attention to some of the design decisions that have to be made at a fairly high level. These decisions focus primarily on the point-to-point dedicated

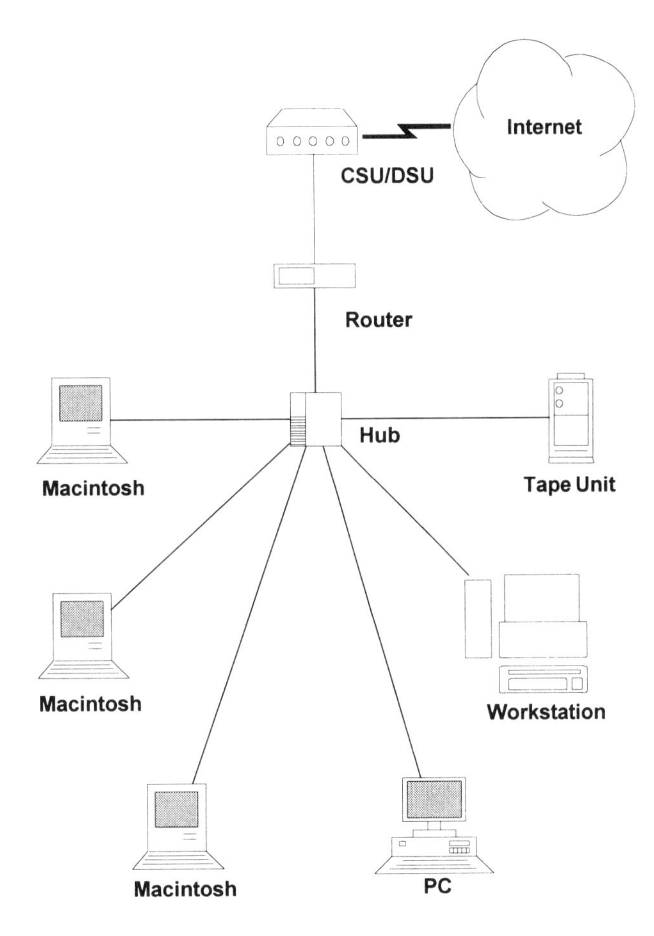

Figure 6-3. *Proposed Connection to the Internet at Company A (Connection to Company B not shown)*

lines between the companies and between one of the companies and the Internet access provider. The next step is to take the top-level context diagram and decompose it into smaller component pieces. It is time to look at the internal LAN architectures at each of the companies. For company A, the architecture might look like that depicted in Figure 6-3.

6.1.2 Application Software: Make, Buy or Barter?

For the pilot project with very little budget, neither alternative of the traditional make-or-buy decision is attractive. Making software is difficult if not impossible to accomplish with "volunteer" personnel. Buying can only be accomplished on a small scale. Fortunately, there is a third alternative for Internet clones: to "borrow" software by downloading it from the Internet. We call this borrowing, because we feel that organizations that take from the Internet ought to give something in return; they should either contribute expert advice in newsgroup discussions or establish archives of potentially useful information or software and make them freely accessible to the Internet community.

For a full-scale implementation, however, a make-or-buy decision may be in order. We consider in the next section some of the key factors affecting the outcome of that decision.

6.1.2.1 Factors in the Make-or-Buy Decision

The following three factors are most important in the make or buy decision:

- Cost
- Benefit
- Risk

We consider each of these factors in turn. While analysis of these factors is certainly imperative in a full-scale implementation, their consideration to some degree is also advisable even in a pilot project.

6.1.2.1.1 Cost

As previously indicated, software cost is a major consideration in building a network-based information system. Not only must software be installed at several different layers on desktop machines, but server software and network facilitating software must also be installed at strategic points within the network. Some software may be unobtainable for your particular configuration and may have to be custom-built.

The cost of software is usually directly proportional to the number of features (i.e., the functionality), the quality, the documentation, and the level of support available. At one extreme are primitive tools available at no cost via the Internet. Some of these have only limited features, at best a README file for documentation, and nobody to call when they break down. At the other extreme are fully supported, well-documented, full-featured, and robust tools costing several hundred dollars for client software and several thousand for server software.

For the low-cost or even no-cost software solution, you must be careful in case the software's lack of features and documentation ends up requiring the construction of custom-built "glueware" to achieve the desired level of interoperation between software components. For example, shell scripts are often designed to make software components interoperate with other hardware, software, and data components in the system. Although this is sometimes unavoidable and at other times even desirable in order to enhance the functionality of the whole system, it can represent a hidden cost unanticipated at the beginning of the project. It does not take many such hidden costs to break the meager budget of a pilot project. It is a good idea to prepare for such situations by allocating some budget in the beginning to cover unanticipated software development requirements.

Generally speaking, it is much more expensive to develop software from scratch than to buy it. The reason is simply that commercial developers strive to amortize their development costs over a large base of customers. Developing code yourself, you don't have that advantage. Nevertheless, some niche applications and glueware specific to your system will not be available commercially. Your only option in such cases is to develop that software.

The cost of custom software development can be minimized, however, by taking advantage of software components available via the Internet. In one spectacular example, Ken Wood of the Lockheed Aeronautical Systems Company compressed a one-person, six-month software development project into a three day integration project using software components found on the Internet.

6.1.2.1.2 Benefit

The benefit of the software usually refers to the utility or value the software offers to users of your system. Whether user interface, server, or glueware software, the architect must carefully examine the contributions the software makes to the cohesive operation of the whole system.

Sometimes users are unaware of the presence and hence the contribution of the software to the system as a whole. This is something that only the software architect can appreciate. In fact, the more the detailed workings of your system are hidden from or transparent to the users, the happier they will be. Users are generally uninterested in knowing, for example, that 132.12.7.45 is the address of the device that routed their e-mail message from host A to host B. They want the system to appear like one big seamless entity that simply works all the time.

As there are usually not enough resources and time to thoroughly investigate the functional features of all required and available software, it helps to prioritize the list of software components in terms of the contributions they make to the success of the system.

For example, user interface software, being obviously very visible to the users, should rank high on the priority list. If users are dissatisfied with the interface you give them to your system, they won't be inclined to rave about how much their system does for them. The user interface software is their window into the system and greatly determines their perception of system utility. In fact, good interface software can make the difference between a system the users love and one they hate.

NCSA Mosaic and its derivative browsers provide illuminating examples of the difference a friendly GUI can make. These browsers have a way of hiding system details like resource location and enable the user to locate information sources without ever touching the keyboard. For senior managers with minimal typing skills, this is a welcome tool; they can point-and-click their way through the web of information your system provides.

6.1.2.1.3 Risk

Risk consists primarily of two factors: likelihood of occurrence and severity of impact. To quantify risk it is helpful to assign a probability measure to the former and any linear numerical scale to the latter. Both these measures are generally subjective estimates and must be based on best engineering judgment. When multiplied together, these factors combine to generate a single measure of risk. Minimizing the risk, either by reducing the likelihood or the severity of the occurrence becomes the goal of risk management.

For software components, the technical risks involved are associated with the performance and reliability of the components in the system context. As a general rule of thumb, these risks, like the benefits, are dependent on their relation to the users. If bugs and system crashes become all too visible to the user, their severity ratings need to be high. By the same token, system glitches deep within the system are unnoticeable to the users and naturally less severe.

6.1.2.2 Publicly Available Software

Because of its prominent role on the Internet, and its low cost, public domain software deserves special consideration. Our experience has shown that both client and server software is robust enough to use in a pilot project situation. In this section we discuss some of the aspects of this publicly available software. We distinguish between freeware, shareware, and public domain software, and provide some pointers on how to locate, download and examine such software from the Internet.

6.1.2.2.1 Freeware vs. Shareware vs. Public Domain Software

There seems to be much confusion regarding the difference between freeware, shareware, and public domain software. The distinction is important, especially for the commercial user of Internet tools, since the legal implications are different for each type of software.

Freeware is the term given to software that is available to use free of charge, subject to certain restrictions on the software's use and redistribution. A typical example of freeware licensing is afforded by the GNU family of software products.

Shareware, on the other hand, usually requires payment in order to make full use of the software. Shareware is often distributed at no cost for evaluation purposes, but the author or owner demands payment after a trial period. Such software sometimes contains only partial functionality or expires—i.e., no longer functions—after the trial period. To receive full functionality, documentation, and user support, the user must be willing to pay.

Strictly speaking, ***public domain*** software is owned by no one. But you are advised to be careful. What may appear to be in the public domain may in fact have some restrictions attached.

In any case, you should always consult the relevant README files or other licensing documentation accompanying the software you download. You could be incurring significant liability on the part of your company if you fail to heed the proprietary markings associated with any file you download.

6.1.2.2.2 How to Locate Publicly Available Software

There are several methods for locating archives of software. One approach is to obtain one of the many books cataloging the vast resources of the Internet. Another is to use some of the Internet's search tools like FTP's Archie and Gopher's Jughead. Archie can give you a list of all the anonymous FTP servers on the Internet, which contain files matching your search criteria, much as does the MS-DOS DIR command on your own PC. There are also several Web-based sources of publicly available software. Check the University of North Carolina's Sunsite Web server for more details.[4]

Yet another approach is to procure one of many CD-ROMs which have been compiled from archives on the Internet. Such distribution media often contain not only the binaries of the tools you need, but also the associated FAQ, README files, and licensing data. Several vendors provide CD-ROM distributions of such archives.

6.1.2.2.3 Downloading and Scanning

The most common method for downloading files from the Internet is anonymous FTP. This technique, described in more detail later, uses a simple command-line syntax for transferring files from the remote host to yours. Care should be taken to download not only the binary executable files, but also any associated documentation like FAQs, README, and licensing files. It is advisable to invest in a copy of a user-friendly interface to assist in the download process. A tool like Chameleon from NetManage can make the transfer of files quite simple.

---

[4] *http://www.sunsite.unc.edu.*

The investment in a tool like Chameleon will pay for itself in time saved downloading files from the Internet. Many Web browsers like the *Netscape Navigator* now also have easy-to-use FTP interfaces.

6.1.2.3 Insourcing and Outsourcing

The subject of insourcing vs. outsourcing is a vast, complex, and current topic. For the Internet-based information system there are many options. Our advice is for managers and architects to keep an open mind. Offloading some of the details and headaches of day-to-day operations can certainly be well worth the cost, other things being equal. However, there is always the danger of losing control of and insight into the inner workings of your information system.

Although there are many companies that offer outsourcing services for traditional information systems, there are few that know about Internet-based technologies. Companies such as Andersen Consulting and EDS are exploring these areas, as they are generally becoming more familiar with client/server technology. Most of the consulting companies specializing in TCP/IP networking are small outfits with requisite technical expertise but not necessarily established track records in designing large-scale, business computing systems.

Nevertheless, the mainstream consulting companies will continue to gain expertise in TCP/IP networking and client/server computing and begin to offer consulting services that take advantage of Internet-based technologies.

6.1.2.4 Strategic Alliances

One possible strategy for staying ahead of the technology curve is to establish alliances with key developers and vendors of technology. The publicity value alone can be significant for all parties to such alliances. Many software vendors have partnership programs. Perhaps your organization can contribute in some way to the technical development of the software and thus steer them in a direction that serves your needs.

6.2 Evaluating the Alternatives

6.2.1 Requirements Analysis

Although requirements analysis should be mostly completed during the initial phases of the project, its methods and results are also useful when you are evaluating alternative system architectures. This is because the evaluation criteria should reflect your perception of the relative importance of the requirements. It is also a good idea to make sure at this point that the requirements are testable, so that the degree of satisfaction will have some basis in measurable, objective fact.

Accordingly, we discuss in the following subsections two aspects of requirements analysis that are relevant to the evaluation of alternative system architectures:

- Must-Haves and Nice-to-Haves
- Requirements Testability

6.2.1.1 Must-Haves and Nice-to-Haves

Hard requirements are goals and constraints that must be satisfied. Soft requirements are those you'd like to satisfy, but which are not critical to your system. Many a system development project has frittered away valuable time and resources for failure to clearly distinguish between these two kinds of requirements, the "must-haves" and the "nice-to-haves." Consequently, it is very important that your system architect spend adequate time analyzing the system requirements and carefully separating them into each of the two categories.

Hard, or must-have, requirements are "binary" requirements in the sense that the project will surely fail if they are not met. It is not a question of relative importance; each hard requirement is equally important and must be satisfied. Otherwise, there is no system at all. They are like logic gates determining the system success. The system architect must look long and hard at each supposedly hard requirement and eliminate from that category any such requirements that are in fact only soft requirements masquerading as hard ones.

Soft, or nice-to-have, requirements display relative importance—some are simply more important than others to the success of the system. Prioritizing these requirements is an important task for the system architect. The higher a requirement's priority, the greater is its relative hardness. Although it may be impossible to satisfy all the system's soft requirements, it is important to make sure that, if any are satisfied, the higher priority ones are satisfied first.

6.2.1.2 Requirements Testability

Requirements are considered to be testable if you can devise a step-by-step procedure to verify that they are indeed satisfied. Admittedly, not all requirements are directly testable. Some can only be verified by analysis and are thus susceptible to bias and superficial treatment. Nonetheless, by examining the degree of testability of requirements at this stage, you can flush out those that are ambiguous or unsatisfiable.

6.2.2 From Requirements to Weighted Evaluation Criteria

Having completed a thorough requirements analysis in which each soft requirement is prioritized, you are now ready to quantify the assigned priorities by giving each requirement a numerical weight. Strictly speaking, you should develop these weighted evaluation criteria before synthesizing various system alternatives, so that you will not be tempted to assign weights according to your subjectively favorite, or "pet," solution.

6.2.3 Gathering Data

Performing the evaluation requires that you collect data on the various components of your system. Two cost-effective methods we have used are the following:

- Product Demonstrations
- Bidder's Conferences

6.2.3.1 Product Demonstrations

With your checklist of criteria in hand, you should begin to gather data on various components needed for your system. In the case of commercial components, product demonstrations given by vendors are a good way to gather the required data. With previously developed evaluation criteria, you can call the shots at the demo session. Without preconceived evaluation criteria, however, you are no longer in the driver's seat—the vendor is. Vendors will show you primarily what *they* want you to see, not necessarily what *you* want or need to see. Having evaluation criteria thus saves time and focuses the demonstrations on your needs, not your vendor's.

A variation on vendor product demonstrations is an extended trial period during which you can evaluate the products in your environment. This gives you more time to concentrate on verifying that the product does indeed or does not satisfy your requirements. It also gives you time to discover other unanticipated features or bugs latent in the vendor's product. Moreover, subtle interactions between the product and the rest of your system are best observed over a long period of time.

In sum, product demonstrations can provide a cost-effective approach to gathering data on prospective pieces of your system. For a pilot project on a shoestring budget, this can be a real windfall.

6.2.3.2 Bidder's Conferences

To gather data on the more complicated components of your system, especially whole subsystems consisting of both hardware and possible customized software, a public bidder's conference can be effective in gathering data on potential solutions. By giving bidders advanced notice through a request for proposal (RFP) that contains your requirements and their relative importance to you, you may be able to extract from the vendor considerable interest in and commitment to helping you find a solution.

A vendor may view your pilot project as the beginning of a potentially lucrative business relationship, and may decide that expending extra effort initially to meet your requirements with a rapid prototype is a good strategy for establishing a beachhead not only within your company, but also in a specific market niche. Many forward-thinking vendors routinely look for ways to learn more about the problems of their potential customers.

With the RFP and bidder's conference approach, you may actually enlist the support of vendors to assist you in analyzing requirements and finding synergistic components that fit into your system. The value of this to both you and your vendors should not be underestimated.

6.2.4 Scoring

For each soft requirement, you can now assign to each candidate system or subsystem solution a relative numerical value indicating the degree to which the candidate satisfies the associated requirement.

Suppose, for example, that you have to evaluate routers from three different manufacturers, call them vendors A, B, and C. Suppose further that all three of these routers meet a certain minimum requirement for the mean-time between failures (MTBF), say, 2000 hours. If Router A has an MTBF of 3000 hours, Router B of 3500 hours, and Router C of 4000 hours, then clearly Router C should receive the highest score with respect to the MTBF requirement. On a scale of 1 to 10, you might assign Router C the score of 10, and B and A the score of 8 and 6, respectively, depending on how important extra MTBF hours are for your system.

Once scores for each individual candidate and criterion are assigned in this manner, they are multiplied times the relative weight for that requirement. This helps ensure that less important requirements will not contribute more to the final score than more important ones. Final scoring is practically a mechanical task; all that remains to be done for each system or subsystem solution is to total the weighted score to yield a composite score for that solution.

6.2.5 Analyzing Risks

While scoring based on weighted evaluation criteria often focuses on expected technical performance, risk analysis is more concerned with the possibility that system components fail to fully meet expectations. It also looks at non-technical factors affecting your system's ability to achieve your goals.

In this section we look at the following three risk-related topics:

- Acceptable Levels of Risk
- Vendor and Product Risk
- System Risk

6.2.5.1 *Acceptable Levels of Risk*

Realizing that we live in an imperfect world and that few components in the system will work exactly as expected, the system architect must seriously consider—for each component—what level of risk is tolerable. Since system success depends greatly on user perception, it makes sense for the architect to the focus on determining the probability that the failure of certain components will impede the users in accomplishing their work.

Some key questions to consider in this regard are:

- What kinds of user dissatisfaction are possible?
- What level of user dissatisfaction is acceptable?
- Which components contribute potentially to user dissatisfaction?

As you already learned in Chapter 5, knowing the acceptable level of risk is especially important with regard to system security. Some associated questions are:

- How do you value your internal information?
- Which information is critical to your competitiveness?
- What is the time sensitivity of that information?
- What kinds of intrusion, if any, are tolerable?
- How much do you trust "insiders," whether they be employees or not?
- How much monitoring and control information can you deal with?

6.2.5.2 *Vendor and Product Risks*

After determining for each component the level of risk you are willing to accept, you should examine next the risk contributions of each proposed, individual component. In particular, you should examine the risks of both vendor products and the vendors themselves. Only by thoroughly testing and wringing out a product can you determine how prone it is to malfunction or introduce harm into your system.

For a full-scale deployment with commercial software, it is also important to know how risky your vendor is. Is the vendor a fly-by-night garage shop likely to go out of business in a heartbeat? What is the vendor's track record? Will the support really be there when you need it? Many an MIS procurement has ended up being penny-wise and pound-foolish in this regard.

For the pilot project, this concern is mitigated by a number of factors. First, the size of your investment in hardware and software is considerably lower. Second, some of the Internet software may be available in source code form, and it may be possible to support the software internally.

6.2.5.3 System Risk

Up until now, we have considered risk from the point of view of each system component. This obviously has limitations. A perfectly good component can still introduce risk into a system. The way in which the system components interact can cause unexpected failures. A thorough analysis of the functional and physical interfaces within your system should help illuminate potential areas of hidden synergistic risk.

6.2.5.4 Contingency Planning

One reason for analyzing risk is to develop contingency plans to be executed in case something goes wrong. This is a way to soften the impact of certain undesirable events. For example, users tend to be less annoyed with bugs when they have been forewarned and informed that you are looking into the bugs. Known bugs are always more tolerable than unexpected ones.

Contingency plans should be developed for possible failures of all key components, i.e., for components that tend to be single points of failure like routers and servers. When a router is down, everybody knows it. Likewise, when a server is down everybody knows it. The prudent system architect will be prepared with the phone numbers of support personnel and perhaps vendor-supplied contingency plans.

6.2.6 Opportunity Awareness

While risk tends to focus on what can go wrong, opportunity awareness emphasizes what can go right. A good system designer will not only be prepared to avoid and/or mitigate the effects of negative events, but also to exploit unexpected successes. In our experience, the appearance of *NCSA Mosaic* offers a case in point. Prior to the appearance of this easy-to-use Web browser, one of our systems relied heavily on the use of USENET news and WAIS. Although the WAIS client software was not very difficult to use, many users disliked having to know the server address of information sources and having to configure their client software with such information. (We did not have a server of servers implemented in our system.)

When *NCSA Mosaic* came along, however, this became moot: Our frustrated managers could now point and click their way to valuable information resources without having to know or care about the location of these resources. Thus, *NCSA Mosaic* became a way for the system to promote itself. Instead of having to convince managers of the valuable resources provided by our system, we could now simply let them convince themselves. To exploit this opportunity, we put the NCSA browser in the hands of as many managers as we could. Suddenly, critical skeptics became enthusiastic advocates almost over night.

Another way in which we exploited the features of *NCSA Mosaic* was in the area of documentation. Previously, we relied on traditional paper documentation—user guides—to introduce users to the system as a whole and to show users how to use the various client tools—USENET clients, WAIS clients, etc. But with *NCSA Mosaic*, there was no longer a need for paper documentation. We could put the documentation on-line using a Webserver, and it found its ways instantly into the hands of nearly every user. The documentation also became much more timely. As new info sources came on-line, we could simply make an announcement via the Web. Just-in-time documentation of the system became a reality.

Chapter 7

SPECIFYING AND IMPLEMENTING THE SOLUTION

After completing evaluations and trade studies, the system architect must pick the final system configuration and communicate it to those who will sponsor and those who will actually build the system. The fully elaborated system design specifications form the basis for implementing. In this chapter, we consider both the specification and implementation of the system solution.

7.1 Specifying the Solution

The process of specifying the system solution has the following three aspects:

- Working Out the Details
- Documenting and Communicating the Solution
- Selling the Solution

In this section we consider each of these aspects and then proceed in the next section to the subject of implementing the system.

7.1.1 Working Out the Details

Although by this time you should have already selected the top-level architecture and made most of the major design decisions, numerous details still remain for your team to work out. You have to refine the top-level functional architecture. You have to cluster related lower-level functions into meaningful groups. You have to identify all the detailed functional and physical interfaces. You have to identify specific network components, both hardware and software, and you have to determine where you will locate key interfacing equipment like routers and telecommunications equipment. Finally, you have to specify the architecture, the source, and the format of key information repositories that will populate your framework.

The project manager also has to work out many details of the project plan. He or she will have to describe, schedule, and assign to personnel tasks like software installation, router table configuration, component and system testing, infobase creation, domain nameserver installation, and training. In short, you will have to ensure that your implementation team carefully transforms the high-level system concepts into concrete physical reality.

At this stage and depending on the size and complexity of the project, the system architect can play various roles. On a large project, the system architect should probably stand aside and let a team of systems engineers work out the details of the system to be built and let a separate project manager work out the details of the project plan. The system architect will then serve the team as a consultant to help resolve conflicts and arbitrate requirements changes. As your team works out the details of the system, you will need to maintain system integrity through configuration control; the system architect will have a major authoritative role to play in the configuration control process.

On a small pilot project, however, the system architect may be the system architect, the systems engineer, and the project manager all rolled into one. Regardless, even on a small project you should ensure that your team documents the most important architectural and engineering decisions, as well as all major milestones and task timelines. This will ensure that all participants are "singing from the same sheet of music." Your system architect has a key role to play in all of these activities. In the discussion that follows, we will use the terms "systems engineers" and "project manager" with the understanding that the system architect may be the only person playing each of these roles.

At this stage, the systems engineers need to specify the detailed functional and physical architectures and design the detailed interfaces. The next few paragraphs consider these topics.

7.1.1.1 Functional and Physical Specifications

In the previous phases of the project, your system architect may have modeled the high-level systems architecture using a variety of representation schemes, including data flow diagrams, control flow diagrams, state transition diagrams, and functional requirements specifications. Now, it is the job of your systems engineers to analyze, refine, and express these items in greater detail.

7.1.1.2 Interface Design

Of particular importance at this stage are the system interfaces, both internal and external. Information systems like Internet clones are both data- and software-intensive. This means that the data and control interfaces between software components are numerous and predominant. However, there are still numerous critical hardware interfaces, including environmental interfaces such as power and thermal, not to mention interfaces between hardware and software. Your system architect should make your team members aware of each of these types of interfaces and help them determine the relative criticality of each interface.

To illustrate the kind of interface analysis and specification that goes on at this stage, let us consider an example. Let's suppose that you have decided to create a server that automatically and periodically generates custom Web pages consisting of hyperlink

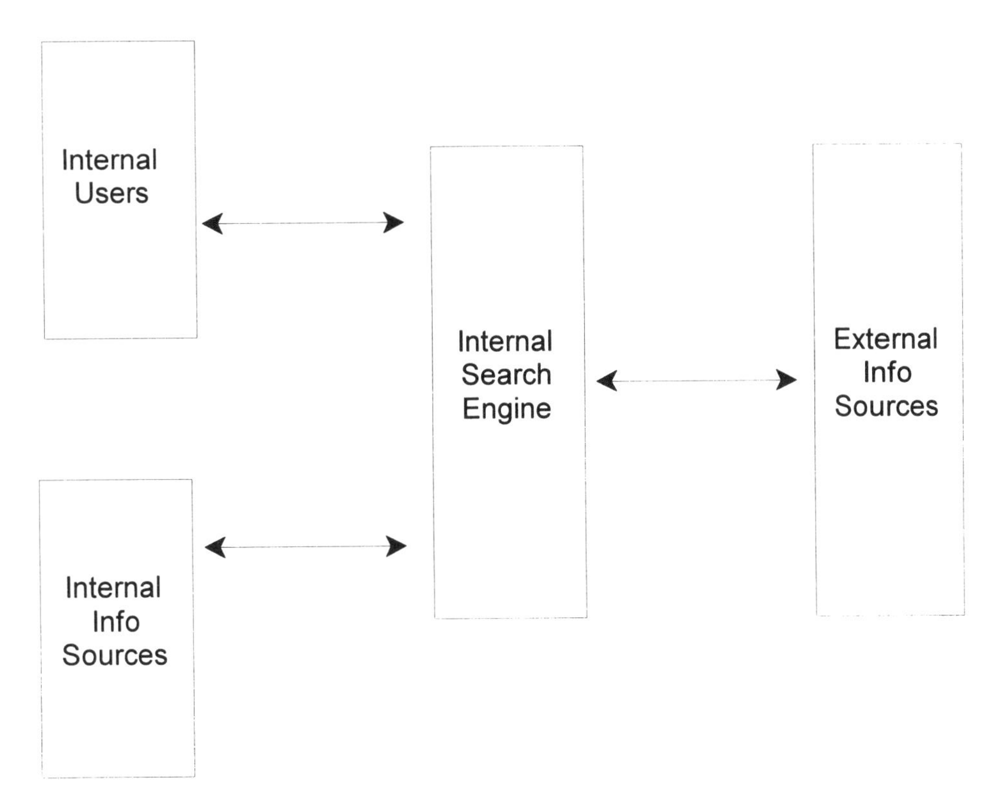

Figure 7-1. *Functional Interface Block Diagram*

references to internal and external Web sites and other types of information sources (gopher, WAIS databases). These custom Web pages are based on periodic searches of Web sites (and other sources) using search terms and keywords important to users.

From the standpoint of interfaces, it is advisable to specify as many information sources as possible. Unfortunately, the number of external sources on the Internet are growing very rapidly and you cannot accurately predict the emergence of new sources. Even your internal sources will be somewhat unpredictable. From a top-level perspective, therefore, the best you can do is depict the functional or logical interfaces in a diagram such as Figure 7-1. This is a good starting point for analyzing the detailed interfaces. In Figure 7-1, three types of functional interfaces are relevant to the example search engine we are considering. Two of these—between the search engine and the internal and external information sources—are functionally similar. The interface with the user, on the other hand, is quite different.

Refinement of our sample top-level interface diagram reveals some additional detailed interfaces. A data flow diagram at the next level illustrates the data flows and logical processes involved. Consider Figure 7-2. This figure shows a data flow diagram that refines the top level functional interface block diagram given in Figure 7-1. While Figure 7-1 shows that the search engine has three major functional interfaces, Figure 7-2 shows more of the search engine's internal functionality and internal data interfaces. This sheds more light on the original interfaces retained from Figure 7-1.

This type of analysis uncovers important design issues. For example, in Figure 7-2 we see that the interface between the search engine and the user involves not only the delivery of requested custom Web pages, but also the performing of searches on behalf of the user. This raises some interesting questions: Should this search be performed in real-time, i.e., in response to the user's input and while the user waits for the custom page to be built, or should it be performed off-line in a separate session, according to a general profile of topics of interest to the user? With the second method, the search engine—as an independent agent—would search periodically the external and internal info sources and accumulate off-line a custom Web page. Instead of requiring the user to wait for the custom page, the second method uses previously supplied search terms of interest to the user and has the pages ready to be consulted. Maybe your users would like your system to accommodate both approaches.

This example illustrates several important features of interface analysis. First, it reveals the ambiguity of the original requirements. It shows how an attempt to interpret the requirements gave rise to some new questions. At this point, your system architect should return to the users for clarification. The second feature this analysis illustrates is how important design trade-offs can surface in the course of detailed functional and functional interface analysis. Lastly, this analysis shows the danger of merely assuming a particular interpretation. If your systems engineers simply proceed without returning to the users for clarification, they may end up building an unsatisfactory system.

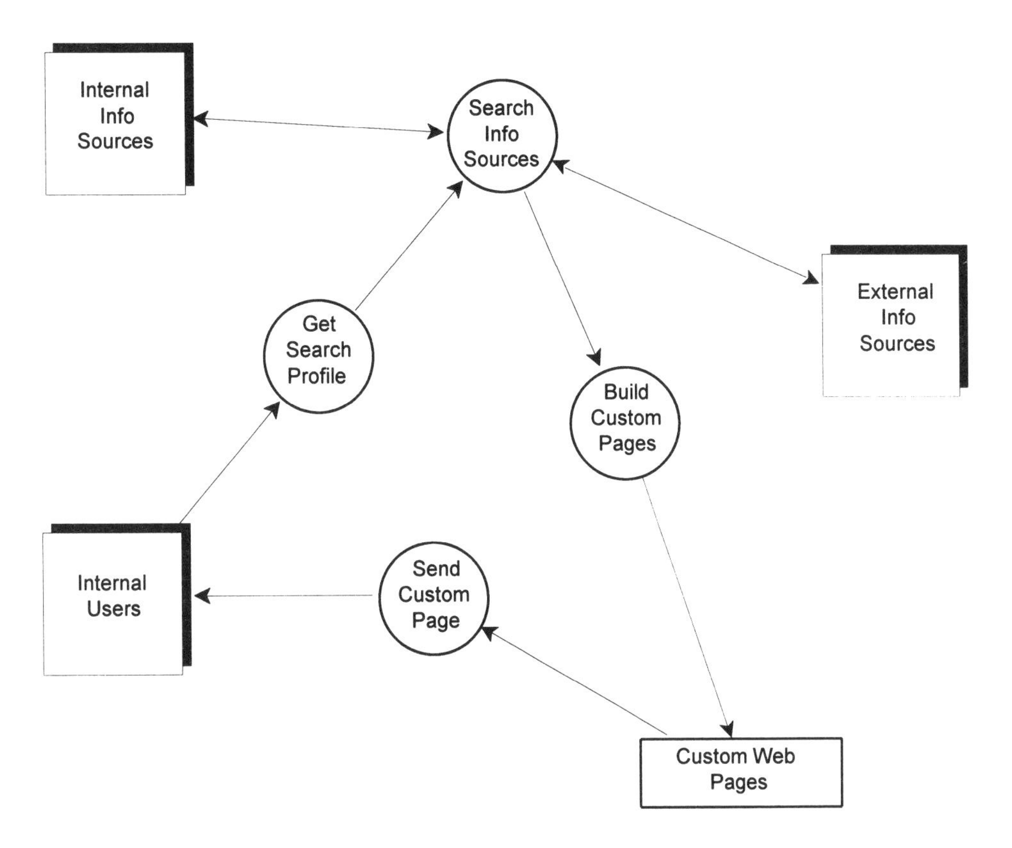

Figure 7-2. *Data Flow Diagram*

To resolve design issues like these, the systems engineer can resort to the methods presented in the previous chapter, those of proposing and evaluating alternative candidate solutions. Again, the benefit to the end user should be the guiding principle. Once a detailed design decision has been made, it should be carefully recorded in the appropriate detail design document. This facilitates revisiting the decision should you later run into unanticipated negative consequences.

7.1.2 Documenting and Communicating the Solution

In documenting the system, you will accomplish two things. First, you will be specifying the system so that those who are supposed to constuct it will know what to do. Second, you will be setting expectations of those in management who will sponsor the construction of the system. Both these aspects of documenting and communicating the system solution are crucial to the success of your program, and we discuss both aspects in the following two subsections.

7.1.2.1 Specifying the System

Since an Internet clone is a complex system involving many interacting components, its coordinated implementation will require the cooperation of many people. Each person involved will need to have a clear understanding of the system to be built and understand his or her role in the implementation project. This requires that your systems engineers specify and describe the system unambiguously and in sufficient detail. It is the purpose of the system detailed design document to capture these necessary details.

We recommend that you place the system specification under formal configuration control. This ensures that your implementation team will use only one authorized and released version of the document. You thus ensure that they will all be working from the same baseline. This requires that they understand, accept, and work according to an established configuration control process—i.e., a formal process for updating and re-releasing the document. For a large project, we recommend the establishment of a configuration control board (CCB) to oversee this process. Its members ought to be reasonably familiar with the project and represent all key stakeholder categories.

The system detailed design document specifies the exact network devices and software that will form part of the system. The system design document calls out all system components—servers, desktop machines, routers, and software. You should specify, for example, the exact configuration and version number of each software component, whether server or client software.

The system design document should also specify the physical interfaces between system components. This goes beyond the logical or functional interfaces illustrated previously. For example, if a router is to be connected to an Ethernet router at one port, and a PPP WAN connection at another, this fact should be called out in the document. **Error! Reference source not found.** presents a physical interface diagram depicting one Local Area Network interconnected with another (the details of the second LAN are not shown). It also shows the particular Network Interface Cards (NICs) that have to be installed to connect the Mac, the PC, and the VAX to the LAN. The Web software (both server and client) installations are also indicated. A router connects the two LANs.

All IP addresses assigned to individual devices on the internetwork should be included in the design document. In fact, many items specified in the URDB (user requirements database) can also be included in the system detailed design document. Before and after pictures depicting individual desktop configurations indicate how system components will meet the individual requirements specified in the URDB. (**Error! Reference source not found.** could serve as the “after” portion of such a diagram.) This information is valuable in helping to communicate to the intended users what tools they will receive and how these tools will satisfy their needs.

Although it may seem that this degree of detail, formality, and control in specifying the system may seem overly tedious and labor intensive, it need not be. By using Internet technologies themselves (a Web server, for example) to maintain the document electronically, you can keep all personnel associated with the project, both users and implementors, informed of the latest baseline configuration. The electronic document thus becomes a living document and provides just-in-time information to all interested parties. Project personnel can be notified of updates to the document—as well as project status—by e-mail messages. You can also obtain feedback from users via e-mail, and foster group discussions regarding implementation and project status by implementing dedicated USENET newsgroups. Using Internet methods themselves, all project planning and construction documents can be maintained in a virtually central location and disseminated immediately to all who have a need to know. In this way, you can minimize the labor normally associated with paper documents.

To elaborate, we note two key benefits of electronic documents. First, they eliminate delivery problems normally associated with paper documents. Usually delivered by interoffice mail and/or courier, traditional documents may sometimes fail to reach some of the intended recipients. The traditional delivery mechanisms also have built-in lag times of days, sometimes even weeks. Secondly, as indicated above, an electronic system ensures that project personnel are using the correct baseline. Relying on paper specs, a designer or builder may still use out-of-date material. With documents centrally controlled and electronically distributed, there is little danger of this (unless, of course, the recipients are downloading their own copies of the document). Thus, electronic documents help keep the project team current and working from the same set of specs.

It may appear that we are recommending a *Catch-22* situation: Build an Internet clone so that you can use it to document the specs you need to build an Internet clone! Naturally, a few traditional documents are needed in the beginning to get things started. But once a small prototype of the system is up and running, the designers and builders can use this prototype itself to maintain and deliver any further documentation. This also gives the designers and implementors an opportunity to personally interact with the system. In doing so, they will sharpen their insight into and appreciation for the strengths and weaknesses of the technology, and be in a better position later to train novices.

7.1.2.2 Setting Management Expectations

Detailed system design documentation can also serve to keep upper management informed of the system's evolving configuration. Management will know what to expect of the final system, and they will not be surprised at the time, labor, and financial resources required to complete the project.

The system detailed design document is an important information source for managing the project. Without a reasonable understanding of the system to be built, the project manager cannot produce a realistic project plan, and the system detailed design document provides a foundation for that understanding.

Thus, the project manager looks to the system detailed design document for information regarding the size and scope of the project he or she is to manage, and uses it to keep upper management informed of technical aspects of the system.

The project manager should schedule periodic meetings with management and other key stakeholders to review progress on the project. The exchange of information between management, stakeholders and the immediate project team will deepen the team's own understanding of the system they are trying to build. It will also help ensure a consistent level of stakeholder buy-in throughout the life of the system and keep your implementation focused on the high priority goals and tasks.

7.1.3 Selling the Solution

As an open and distributed system, the Internet clone will involve many different enterprise organizations. The number of served constituents and interested stakeholders is therefore potentially large. In an Internet clone, the traditional clear-cut distinction between the centralized MIS organization and the user community may become blurred. End users may help to build the system, and the principal MIS builders may also become intensive users. The glass house model, in which one organization builds and operates while another uses the system, may no longer be an accurate description in today's distributed, client/server computing environment, of which the Internet clone is but one example.

The project members may find themselves having to sell the design of the system to those who are supposed to benefit from it. Since there will be many departments involved in the construction and use of the Internet clone, the chief builders of the clone will find it necessary to expend some effort selling the system solution to all who will be involved, whether as builders or users. This is where all the documentation produced thus far will prove to be valuable. As mentioned above, the detailed system design document will serve to communicate the detailed system solution to management and the broader community of participants. Moreover, the previous design decisions, which finally culminated in the system detailed design document, will be documented in the system requirements specification. The top-level design documentation will show the trade-offs that yielded the final architecture. The system architect will need to call on this trail of decisions in order to answer the critics, who are guaranteed to be in abundant supply.

7.1.3.1 The MIS Role in an Open Systems Environment

In trying to build an Internet clone, the traditional MIS organization may find itself in an awkward position. Many MIS departments today are dominated by senior people whose roots trace back to the days of the mainframe glass house. It will be difficult for many of them to appreciate the apparent chaos and anarchy of the Internet. On the one hand, the client software tools seem to be the sole province of the users. Many users will want a certain degree of autonomy in choosing software for their desktop machines. On the other hand, these same users will probably expect the MIS organization to supply system administrators for servers and the network administrators for network connectivity and internetworking functionality.

Yet you may also have many less computer savvy users who will not want to install and configure their own client software. They may expect more service from the MIS organization. In defining their role in the building (and ultimately in maintaining) the Internet clone, MIS personnel will need to be sensitive to the diverse needs of the user population. In our experience, some MIS organizations provide excellent network and server expertise, but sometimes fail to fully satisfy the end user's needs. This is a genuine danger and can seriously impede the acceptance of the system by the end user.

7.1.3.2 Overcoming Political and Cultural Barriers

This blurring of distinctions between the end users and builders of the Internet clone is exacerbated by the "political"—i.e., departmental—barriers between these communities. MIS personnel, viewing the Internet clone as a grassroots movement of a few UNIX renegades and their co-conspirator users, may misinterpret the clone as an infringement of their territory. On the other hand, the more free-thinking users may view the efforts by the MIS organization to infuse order into the development as an attempt to impose a glass house mentality and style of control on an otherwise open and distributed system.

You can reduce the risk of such misperceptions by communicating appropriately. MIS personnel, assuming they have a lead role in designing and implementing the system, should make an extra effort to keep the targeted users informed of project progress and the rationale behind each major design decision. Regularly scheduled project reviews, attended by key user representatives, can pay big dividends by minimizing the mutual mistrust between the developers and users.

7.1.3.3 The Bootstrap Problem

As the system unfolds and begins to emerge as an operational network, some applications may suffer from what we call the Bootstrap Problem. This is a *Catch-22* situation affecting especially those applications that require, in order to be useful, extensive user participation. E-mail and USENET are prime examples. In particular, USENET newsgroups are often perceived merely as information repositories. However, during the initial phase of a newsgroup's life-cycle, there is little information of value in the newsgroup, since few users have discovered and deposited information in the newsgroup. Many users will scan the newsgroup, read what few postings are there, and decide not to ever visit the newsgroup again. Newsgroup traffic will then dwindle to nothing, and the newsgroup will die an untimely death. In other words, for a new newsgroup, the following dictum is true: "People won't use it unless it's useful—yet it won't be useful unless people use it." This we call the bootstrap problem.

Later in this chapter we will revisit this problem and give some pointers on what to do about it when it crops up. For now, we simply forewarn the reader about the potential problem and give some tips about preventing it from occurring in the first place. At this stage in the development of the system—the stage of specifying and selling the solution— the architect should start asking potential users for suggestions on the kinds of newsgroups they would find interesting. It is also useful to forewarn the users about the potential for the bootstrap problem and ask them to consider what commitments they would make to using the newsgroup they've suggested. At least some awareness of the dynamics involved in newsgroups can be created at this stage and the users won't be so quick later to condemn the newsgroup concept altogether simply because they are never used.

Another tactic that might help avoid the bootstrap problem later is for the system developers to actively promote the suggested newsgroups prior to their existence. Traditional means of communicating—memos, meetings, paper announcements on pin-up bulletin boards, articles in company newsletters—can serve to pave the way for the newsgroups that will soon become available to users of the system.

Such promotional efforts can help draw potential users to the information services that your clone will provide. This can help not only to avoid the bootstrap problem, but also to make prospective users aware of the potential benefits of the system. We recommend that you use traditional communications vehicles to internally advertise your clone's information resources.

7.2 Implementing the Solution

After you've specified the system down to the last detail and obtained stakeholder buy-in, you should commence construction of the system. Depending on the initial projected size of your clone, implementation can range anywhere from a quick installation project lasting a few weeks to a massive construction project spanning several months or years. For illustration purposes, we distinguish these two kinds of projects as the pilot project and the full-scale deployment.

The pilot project, which we have advocated strongly all along and which is detailed in Appendix B, is motivated by a try-before-you-fly/fly-before-you-buy attitude. In other words, it represents a cost-effective experiment on a small scale. With a pilot project, you can explore the principles and implications of corporate internetworking long before you make serious commitments of expensive resources to build a full-scale system. Because of the extra resource required for full-scale deployment, your management will probably require a more reliable prediction of return on investment. It is no wonder that many managers favor the pilot project approach in order to test the waters before spending lots of money.

7.2.1 Eating the Elephant One Bite at a Time

Of course, there is no reason why you can't have both: a grand scheme for full-scale deployment prudently preceded, however, by a conservative pilot project. In fact, the ramp-up to full-scale deployment can be a series of pilot projects, each pilot becoming more serious than its predecessor in terms of commitment of resources. This incremental approach allows the developing organization to stop, catch its breath, and replan future increments in accordance with the lessons learned from previous ones.

7.2.1.1 The Pilot Project

Our primary experience with Internet clones pilot project stems from our involvement with the Lockheed (now Lockheed Martin) Technology Broker System (TBS). The TBS project began in 1991 with the goal of providing scientists and research engineers across the Lockheed Corporation with access to an electronic database containing key research information. It sought to coordinate the numerous research activities dispersed across the U.S. at several of the Lockheed operating companies. TBS was the brainchild of Dr. R. P. Caren, the Lockheed Corporate Vice President of Science and Engineering.

The requirements for TBS were developed by a steering committee of representatives from each of the major Lockheed companies. From the beginning there was a desire to pursue a small, affordable pilot project. The committee first considered developing a relational database. In 1991, however, most relational database systems that could function in a heterogeneous computing environment had to run on a centralized machine and required terminal emulation at the user end. Corporate licenses for such database software were expensive, as was the data entry required to populate the database.

Fortunately, two Internet technologies, WAIS and USENET news, seemed to offer the required functionality and were available from the Internet at no cost. WAIS could make use of existing documents and thus avoid the expensive data entry process. USENET news, along with e-mail, could facilitate dialogue and collaboration among researchers. The price was certainly right for an experimental system. So a pilot project was conceived.

The TBS pilot was moderately successful in demonstrating the potential of Internet technology. By early 1993, researchers from around the U.S. at the major Lockheed facilities were using WAIS clients on Macintosh, PC, UNIX workstation and VAX/VMS platforms to access each other's research reports. By late 1993, Lockheed engineer Bob Kaehms added a version of the gopher server in Perl. In February of 1994, we held a conference at the Lockheed headquarters in Calabasas to bring together key representatives of the user community, (research directors), with those of the implementation team (mostly MIS system administrators and networking professionals. At this conference, we unveiled the World Wide Web and Mosaic technologies that, not surprisingly, subsequently proceeded to occupy center stage for all further developments. In late 1994, Lockheed announced its intention to merge with Martin Marietta and further development of TBS began to take a back seat to other more pressing consolidation issues.

7.2.1.1.1 Project Size

To demonstrate and explore the basic of Internet technology, you only have to execute a very small pilot project. One server with only a handful of client users is adequate for you to become acquainted with the technology and its potential.

Within limits, Internet technologies are inherently scaleable. This means that, as the number of users grows, the technical infrastructure can expand gracefully to meet the growing demand. New servers and clients can be added almost without limit. As we have discussed already, the primary performance consideration is bandwidth—you will probably have to upgrade your bandwidth as your clone grows.

7.2.1.1.2 Documenting Lessons Learned

It is important that you document your lessons learned during the pilot project. What works? What doesn't? As each new scaled-up increment emerges, the lessons learned from the previous increment can be incorporated.

An important lesson we learned from our Lockheed experience is that central coordination is necessary to keep the project moving in a single direction. The technology—especially WWW technology—caught on quickly, but each separate Lockheed company tended to go its own way in deploying infobases with several different presentation styles. Each company tended to organize its content differently from the rest giving the system as a whole a look and feel that was less than unified.

In this regard, corporate web construction is very similar to software development. As the number of interacting components and hyperdocument complexity grows, a top-down approach to designing the web's architectural framework will help ensure that the whole is consistent and complete. As in software development, we prefer a top-down approach to design but a bottom-up approach to actual construction.

By bottom-up construction we mean the building of subordinate, back pages prior to building the higher-level home pages. One advantage of this approach is that you can minimize the number of dead hyperlinks and pages under construction encountered by the user. If, on the other hand, you build the home page first and make it available to users on your web before building the subordinate pages hyperlinked to the home page, your users will attempt to take the links to the subordinate pages but will get error messages instead. This is what we mean by a dead hyperlink. Even if you put in pages labeled "under construction" as stubs, users will still be disappointed. It is best, we think, to first conceive the architecture and then build the lower-level modules. When you finally unveil the home page, your piece of the corporate web will be complete. This is just common sense. It says, in effect, that you should first stock your shelves with inventory before you have the grand opening and open your doors!

7.2.1.2 Full-Scale Deployment

Full-scale deployment usually means extending the infrastructure and applications to nearly every desktop in the enterprise. To bring this about requires considerable expenditure of funds and allocation of resources. It means going beyond the grassroots nature of the pilot project. It also means that you should take account of the lessons learned from the pilot project when planning your full-scale implementation.

7.2.2 Initiating and Managing the Project

Whether you pursue a pilot or full-scale Internet clone, you should kick off and manage your project in an orderly way. This means, first of all, that you should clearly define and assign someone the role of project manager. You should also make sure everyone involved understands and acknowledges that role. You should empower your project manager with the budget and authority necessary to be held accountable for the project. Our experience with pilot projects suggests that when nobody is in charge, nothing is accomplished. A grassroots pilot project may enjoy only minimal success unless someone is held accountable who can in turn hold others accountable.

Next, it is important that there be a written project plan indicating all the tasks to be accomplished, when they are due, and who is responsible for accomplishing them. At the project kick-off meeting, your project manager should brief the project plan to the key project participants. Notice of the assignments should also be sent to the participants' managers as well. Finally, periodic status reviews and walkthroughs are crucial to keeping the project on track.

7.2.3 What If Something Goes Wrong?

Even the best laid plans of mice and men can go awry. Indeed, Murphy's Law says you can count on it. This brings us to the crucial area of contingency planning. The technical aspects of contingency planning have already been touched upon in connection with risk management. Here the emphasis is on contingency planning from a project management point of view. The project manager needs to be aware of the potential points of failure in executing the project. The project manager should ask questions like: "What can possibly go wrong? What if this task is not accomplished on time? What will be the impact on project success? How do we recover from this kind of setback?" In short, your project manager should be proactive and look for ways to fail, building in mechanisms not only to avoid failures, but also to recover from them when they occur. All of this is just plain common sense and well-known management wisdom. We don't need to elaborate any further here. We simply wish to emphasize that contingency planning, far from being a reactive afterthought, is important up front in the early stages of planning the project.

7.2.4 Preparing the Users

In addition to briefing project participants and sponsors at the beginning and during the course of the project, it is also crucial to keep the user population informed of the tools and resources you are trying to put into their hands. A well thought out education program can go a long way to prepare your users to be effective in navigating your Internet clone.

One useful technique is to ask potential users to tell you what kinds of information they would like to see hosted on the clone. We discussed this already in connection with the User Requirements Database. It is a good idea to find out what kinds of documents to which the users wished they had central and shared electronic access. For example, we have found that department memos and activity reports are items for which departments wished they had electronic archives. Often these documents are already in electronic form and only need to be converted to a standard format and perhaps indexed into a full-text database like WAIS. This can be accomplished with a few simple shell scripts. There are also many custom tools and filters already available on the Internet that will convert documents from one word processing format to another.

As promised earlier, we now give some suggestions on how the bootstrap problem associated with newsgroups can be avoided and handled.

7.2.4.1 The Bootstrap Problem Revisited

The following three approaches are helpful in dealing with the USENET news bootstrap problem:

- Training
- Seeding
- Moderating

We now consider each of these approaches in turn.

7.2.4.1.1 Training

Training your users how to create newsgroups helps ensure that they will use the ones they create. The Internet has evolved a widely accepted process for newsgroup creation. This process is based on user consensus. Prospective users of your system should know how to follow this process. This will have the double effect of institutionalizing the process within your own organization and preparing your users for responsible Internet citizenship—i.e., netizenship.

In the next few paragraphs, we provide an overview of the USENET newsgroup creation process. However, since this process has it own terminology, we first review some of the key terms and acronyms it uses.

The acronym "CFV" stands for "Call for Votes." This is an official action that takes place after those interested have discussed the proposal for a new newsgroup.

The term "news admin" is short for "news administrator." This is the person in charge of keeping USENET news running at a site. Such sites are referred to as news sites. They consist of a news server. The news admin is often, but does not have to be, the sys admin for the machine that hosts the news server software. News admins decide which newsgroups to host on their server.

The person advocating the creation of a new newsgroup is usually referred to as the "proponent." The proponent usually sends out an "RFD," or "request for discussion," and sets up the CFV. Another key person is the "votetaker," who actually posts the CFVs and counts the votes. For obvious reasons, it is not a good idea to have the proponent and the votetaker be the same person!

Relying on this terminology, we now turn to the voting process itself, which occurs in five steps.

1. *Discussion of the idea.* If you have a good idea for a new newsgroup, you should first propose the idea to existing but related newsgroups. This makes you the proponent. USENET users are not known for their bashfulness, and they will quickly tell you what they think of your idea. Do not be surprised if you get some rather blunt or biting responses!

2. *Request for Discussion (RFD).* Assuming that you survived your initial query/response session in a few sample newsgroups, it is necessary to proceed to a more formal discussion of your proposal. There are specific newsgroups for this. In addition to posting to the ones that are somehow related to your proposed group, you should be sure to include the groups *news.announce.newgroups* and *news.groups.* The former especially is required in an official RFD. The official RFD should include the proposed title and purpose of the new newsgroup.

3. *Discussion in news.groups.* You should now monitor the reactive discussions taking place in each of the groups to which you posted the RFD. Again, do not be surprised at the wide range of responses, even hostile ones, that you might get in some of these groups. Should it become clear that modifications to your proposal are necessary to garner support, then you should change the RFD, return to step 2, and re-issue the changed RFD as a new one.
4. *Voting.* You need to identify someone who will set up an electronic polling place for the actual voting and be the votetaker. Voting is accomplished by means of e-mail messages sent to the votetaker. The vote usually starts around 30 days after the first RFD, but no earlier than 21 days after. The voting runs from 22 to 30 days, usually around 22, and the votetaker handles the official CFV.
5. *Results.* After the voting has ended, the votetaker tabulates the results and posts them to the appropriate newsgroups. If your proposal succeeds, the new group will start propagating within five days. During the five days, anyone can change their vote or challenge the voting procedure. If the proposal fails, however, you are not allowed to generate the same RFD for at least six months.

Success in creating a newsgroup usually requires two things. First, the proposed newsgroup must be approved by at least a two thirds majority. Second, the "yes" votes must exceed the "no" votes by at least 100.

In your clone of the Internet , you can streamline this process somewhat. Fewer users need to participate in the voting, and so you can shorten the voting timeline. Also, you can change the required margin of "yes" to "no" votes. We advise, however, that you make your internal process mirror roughly the USENET scheme for the simple reason that users within your enterprise will need to become familiar with and eventually participate in the USENET process as they venture out onto the Internet.

7.2.4.1.2 Seeding

Another technique aimed at bootstrapping new internal newsgroups is called seeding. Here, those interested in the newsgroup post relevant articles to create a small nucleus of information. This nucleus will at least attract some readers. In addition, it will be helpful for the proponents to post some genuine queries that can be answered by newsgroup visitors. This will also encourage lurkers to join the discussion.

7.2.4.1.3 Conducting Effective Electronic Meetings: Newsgroup Moderation

Finally, it is advisable to recruit volunteers to be newsgroup moderators. Moderators intercept and review postings headed for newsgroups. In this way, they can supply some quality control. A moderator is much like a facilitator or moderator at a face-to-face meeting. He or she makes sure that the meeting attendees stick to the theme of the meeting. A newsgroup moderator also posts periodic lists of answers to frequently asked questions (FAQs).

Although the participation of a moderator does not guarantee that anyone will be interested in posting to the newsgroup, it does help ensure that the information posted will be of reasonably high-quality and relevant. This adds value to the newsgroup as a whole and makes it a more attractive meeting room in which to conduct virtual conferences.

Chapter 8

OPERATING AND MAINTAINING THE SYSTEM

8.1 Overview

Whether you are operating internal servers to disseminate information company-wide or offering external servers to people on the Internet, the issues of operations and maintenance are central. To ensure maximum availability, consistent data quality, and data integrity, you must develop and implement a comprehensive plan for managing the day-to-day operations of your information servers.

In this chapter, we examine some broad maintenance issues like data dependency, cost, and the need for cooperation between distant and sometimes unrelated enterprise organizations. We also address day-to-day operational concerns from both administrative and end user perspectives. Finally, we conclude with a look at some methods for managing upgrades in the fast-paced world of Internet technologies.

Operating an Internet-based information system involves the management of systems and networks that support the flow of information to the end user. In a decentralized environment, this effort demands coordinated and reliable procedures for running the underlying systems and network infrastructure. Operational efforts must center on the availability and integrity of resources and connectivity.

Maintaining a distributed but interlinked system information resources requires recurring data preparation, formatting, and upkeep. In addition, design and construction efforts are needed for new interfaces and glueware that will adapt information to the needs of users. As you replace hardware and software components, you must also modify glueware to keep the system functioning as a whole. Thus, your efforts should focus on maintaining the integrity of the whole complex of hardware, software and data. They should facilitate the graceful and gradual insertion of each newly acquired functional capability.

8.2 Operating the System

Operating an Internet-based information system involves the ongoing support necessary to maintain systems that feed data to the end user. If the information is unavailable because of system failures and network outages, the result may be strain on enterprise-wide business processes—potentially compromising productive efforts in many areas.

Companies create new data and information sources everyday. The distribution of this information over a network depends on a well-managed and operationally sound infrastructure. The servers that act as distribution points and the network links that act as distribution channels are like the circulatory and central nervous systems of the enterprise organism; they perform vital enterprise functions.

Maintaining a competitive advantage with information systems doesn't simply mean that you can set up an Internet-based system and let it run itself. You should operate the system in a way that is consistent with your business goals and objectives. The effectiveness of an information system will translate directly into time and money.

The real danger here lies in the fact that in a distributed information system with distributed ownership of information assets, there is a strong tendency toward parochialism. Disintegration and chaos can set in unless you make a conscious effort to maintain system integrity at the enterprise level. Keeping the whole greater than the sum of its parts requires a coordinated effort. Operational efforts should also focus on end user assistance and support.

System operation can be expensive. The long-term maintenance costs of a distributed system can be many times its original purchase price. You should keep this in mind when you build an Internet clone, because many of the individual software components may come with seductively low price tags. You can obtain public domain freeware or shareware at little or no cost. Grassroots movements initiated among end users can develop tremendous momentum yet lack the vision and resources required to provide for a coherent and maintainable system on a large scale. Therefore, we advise you to give serious consideration to the complete life cycle cost of the system as a whole. You should do this in light of the business goals you intend your system to support. Maintenance and support are major cost drivers in the full system life cycle. By acquiring inexpensive or free software, you can avoid certain procurement costs. You should try to redirect these cost savings toward maintenance efforts.

While you can automate many processes required to put information on-line, you should also try to automate your procedures for maintaining this information once the data begins to change.

Operational concerns are everybody's business. Those who need information must ask for it. Those who have useful information should seek out news ways of making it available to others. Incentivized sharing is the key to keeping maintenance efforts on track.

8.2.1 Operational Issues

Different departments have different goals. Despite central policy mandates, they will manage their systems according to slightly different standards. In effect, decentralization puts information content and control back in the hands of users—many of whom have little or no formal training in system management.

Complications can arise due to overlapping responsibilities. For example, some Web browsers currently support only the HTML 2.0 standard while others fully support HTML 3.0. If the users in one organization all have the 3.0 version, they will naturally come to expect that their servers should supply HTML documents according to the 3.0 specification. However, another organization at the other end of a WAN link may have browsers only capable of HTML 2.0. When they access the first organization's Web server, they may see unintelligible data on their displays.

8.2.1.1 Decentralization

Decentralization is not an end in itself. It is important to understand the implications of decentralization of information in order to make the best possible use of resources.

The idea behind decentralizing information is to empower users to create and disseminate information as well as to consume it. Regardless, there is still a need for centralized information services for resources needed by more than one department. We're not talking about eliminating centralized functions, only about how we can make the most efficient use of all information resources. In the last analysis, it may be just as bad—perhaps worse—to decentralize all information activity as it is to centralize it.

Organizations. The decentralization of information creates concerns over the roles and responsibilities for operating a system. From an organizational perspective, there may be many different departments providing data with many more departments using that data. In order to prevent problems in data distribution, you should strive to clearly define the relationships and interfaces between these internal organizations.

Decentralized groups define their functional responsibilities much more narrowly than the centralized IS organization. These groups are often accountable for their own processes and budget—perhaps even their own profit and loss. In order to avoid parochialism, therefore, you should seek to create incentives that motivate individual organizations to cooperate with each other and with the central organization. These incentives should motivate them to spend an appropriate amount of time and effort on developing systems that serve not only their own needs but the needs of the larger organization.

Management teams must embrace these efforts in order to maintain continued information sharing throughout the re-engineering process. They must renew their commitment to making the network a valuable corporate resource.

In an era of cutbacks and layoffs, the problems of incentivized sharing become even more entangled. Competing departments are much less willing to cooperate with one another—especially if budget cuts and head count reductions are imminent. Departments are reluctant to relinquish control of information assets for the common good if the end result is a reduction in power and authority.

Since internal data recipients do not necessarily pay for the information they use, it becomes necessary to incentivize sharing at even lower levels in the organization. It is sometimes necessary to barter or arrange for reciprocation. Otherwise, some sort of chargeback or more formal financial arrangement may be necessary to offset the costs incurred by the information provider.

Systems and applications support is a good example of an operational concern that crosses organizational boundaries in a decentralized environment. Martin C. Clague, general manager of IBM's Worldwide Client/Server Computing unit, says "The real challenge, however, for IT managers who wish to deliver strategic value to their companies, is to create the right support structure for end-user applications that enables freedom and teamwork without forsaking discipline."[1] Herein lies the key to a successful distributed support structure. You must prioritize your goals not only with a local agenda, but with an enterprise-wide perspective. The bumper sticker that reminds us to "think globally and act locally" (a phrase borrowed from the political agenda of environmentalists) is a good policy for information providers as well.

Why should one division benefit from the fruits of another's labor? The answer, though simple, is all too easily sometimes forgotten in environments where layoffs and cutbacks are increasingly a fact of life. In larger, more complex organizations, it is sometimes difficult to foster a spirit of cooperation.

Discipline is necessary to maintain systems and networks with the highest possible availability. Everyday tasks like backups are necessary to ensure that data is available even after a system or disk failure.

Internally, cost issues seem to strain relationships between information providers and users. Users who benefit from the information provided may not be charged for it.

Computing. Distributed computing environments empower workers to manipulate information at their desktops. The power and flexibility of such systems make data more readily accessible to the end user. Information consumption is more efficient and less fatiguing in a graphical, user-friendly environment.

On the other hand, these environments generally demand more of administrative personnel. They often have to conduct system and software upgrades, training, maintenance,

---

[1] *HPCWire* (1994).

and troubleshooting on a one-on-one and host-by-host basis. In this regard, the role of the IS administrator should gradually migrate from one of being a central maintainer of data to that of a trainer, facilitator, or coach.

It seems that the pendulum of computing paradigms that was once moving rapidly away from mainframe environments toward networks of personal computers is now swinging back toward the center. Information technology organizations are realizing the best of both environments by implementing systems like UNIX workstations (which can be both servers and clients) coupled with X-terminals (generally clients only).[2] These have the same benefits as distributed assets without the additional maintenance and administrative burdens. For example, diskless workstations like X-terminals do not require backups. In this situation, you can minimize the backup burden. Since the data reside on relatively centralized servers, fewer computers need backup support.

The problem with distributed computing is not so much a technical problem as a managerial one. While costs of managing and operating these assets have skyrocketed, many end users feel that direct support for their concerns has deteriorated. The root cause, we believe, is over-reliance on technology. For years, we have been throwing information technology at end users and they are now becoming overloaded. We have spent millions within our organizations to supply users with the latest and greatest computing technology, but we have spent very little comparatively on training and support. At the risk of sounding like we are trying to dehumanize the end user, we claim that you must "program" end users no less than the hardware they use. By "programmed" we really mean "empowered"—empowered with knowledge and skills appropriate to the technology and the tasks demanded. Knowledge workers now have superior decision support tools, but do they know how to formulate and make good decisions?

You should clarify the roles and responsibilities of the end users and those of the system and network administrator. One approach is to allocate decision authority for user interface functionality to the end user. This assumes, of course, that the user understands the issues of interfacing with servers on the back end. You should leave data management, however, to system administrators.

This solution is too simplistic, however, for user workstations are rapidly approaching an era in which they too will be able to run server software and make information available to the whole enterprise. You can already acquire Web server software for an MS-Windows platform. You don't have to run UNIX to be a server. With Windows 95 this will become even more apparent. It is probably also too much to expect of X-terminal users that they do nothing more than consume information. They will no doubt want to

---

[2] Purists will be quick to point out, no doubt, that in the X-Windows system the typical roles of client and server are reversed. In our present discussion, we can safely ignore this distinction.

launch servers on the shared server platforms—servers that will provide information to the larger enterprise audience.

Data. Decentralization raises concerns about data ownership, security, and the interdependencies that often affect the relationships between data providers and end users. When you centralize the responsibilities for data organization and maintenance, the procedures and points of contacts are usually clear. As you distribute these responsibilities, however, the procedures and points of contact become less obvious.

In a centralized environment, you can control and distribute information; you can coordinate data dependencies and change control with the end users. Centralized data providers already have chargeback mechanisms in place and can coordinate content changes to suit a variety of different needs. However, because your enterprise generates much of its useful data at the department level, centralizing data distribution can add unnecessary delays to the information dissemination process.

Crucial to defining roles and responsibilities for maintaining data is the notion of data ownership. Who owns the information? How do data in one organization relate to or depend on data in others?

Small teams working on specific research projects or on the development of new systems often generate valuable data. Sharing this information means making it available so that others within the enterprise can also make effective use of it.

When you distribute the responsibility for data distribution, you can deliver data more quickly. Increased availability of information like financial reports, test results, product research, and late-breaking news assists managers in making decisions more rapidly. Interdependent systems can benefit from the availability of just-in-time information.

In environments promoting distributed information sharing, data providers are commonly separated physically and organizationally from data consumers. In this scenario, information dependencies may develop that stretch cooperation and internal collaboration efforts to their limits. Spontaneous data dependencies often surface in a distributed information web. Changes in a single information source may result in a chain reaction that affects interrelated processes and resources throughout an organization.

In some cases, information owners may not share information simply because they do not believe the effort is in their own best interest. Sometimes they are unfamiliar with the information-sharing technologies and sometimes they are simply unconcerned with the big picture of their enterprise.

External data dependencies evolve differently. Providing customers and suppliers with information seeks to fulfill several objectives. For example, an external information system may target new customers by providing sales and marketing information. Existing customers may find the availability of on-line support services easier and more effective. On the supplier side, information exchanges can bring about more coordinated intercompany processes that result in cost savings on both sides.

8.2.1.2 Roles

In the Internet clone, the key discernible operational roles are those of the network manager or administrator, the system manager or administrator, and the data owner. Network administrators are concerned with the operational integrity and availability of the underlying networking infrastructure. They make sure the internal LANs are operational by monitoring the cable plants and patching hubs, the routers and bridges, and perhaps some of the shared resources like file and print servers. They monitor network performance parameters such as packet traffic patterns and collisions, throughput, response time, and bandwidth utilization. They may also be responsible for the network interface cards resident in each host machine, whether workstation or server. Network administrators are also concerned with the wide area links connecting distant operating units and connecting to the Internet. Firewall system management often falls within their domain.

System administrators usually manage individual computing systems or groups of systems. For example, a single system administrator might have responsibility for a set of three UNIX workstations on a given LAN. Another system administrator might have another three workstations of his or her own. These administrators would be responsible for periodically backing up the data, configuring system parameters, performing periodic maintenance diagnostics, and installing hardware and software upgrades. They focus less on the operational integrity and availability of the network than on the integrity and availability of their assigned hosts.

Data owners are responsible for the generation and maintenance of source data. Ultimately, an information server make these data available to the whole enterprise. But the data owners maintain the original source data. Many data owners are also users of the networked system. As a builder of an Internet clone, you should strive to clearly define the obligations of data owners toward those who use the data.

8.2.1.3 Investment in People, Processes, and Technology

Investment in people, processes, and technology can ease considerably the operational burden of a system. We have mentioned already our belief that an enterprise should make serious investments in imparting to its workers the knowledge and skills demanded by the kind of empowerment implicit in distributed information technology. We have also stressed that highly empowered knowledge workers without processes to coordinate and guide them are ineffective. Similarly, network administrators, system administrators, and data owners need to have proper tools with which to accomplish their respective functions.

Tools like Hewlett-Packard's OpenView Network Node Manager, OperationsCenter, and Resource and Performance Management software can enable a small number of network and system administrators to manage a relatively large array of networked computing resources.

The vision called "Solution Partners," developed by HP and shared by many third-party vendors, recognizes that no single vendor can supply an all-encompassing enterprise-wide solution to the problem of managing information technology. Therefore, HP's OpenView software framework together with the tools and support of its Solution Partners combine to integrate network and system management functionality. The goal is to simplify planning, operations, and expansion of distributed computing systems across entire enterprises.

The Network Node Manager component of HP OpenView supports fault management, configuration management, and performance management tasks. It provides a color-coded graphical map of your entire TCP/IP network. This allows help desk personnel, for example, to monitor the status of each device connected to the network. If a device goes down, the corresponding symbol on the map changes color. Help desk personnel are then able to answer calls from network users who want to know what is going on with the network. Network managers can set thresholds for critical system resource parameters. The Network Node Manager software then automatically reports an alarm whenever a parameter exceeds one of these thresholds. Troubleshooters can use the Network Node Manager tools to isolate and diagnose problem.

You can also use the Network Node Manager to determine optimal routing paths throughout your network. This facilitates a more balanced distribution of packet traffic between network nodes. It also incorporates the *ping* command to verify physical and network layer reachability, and it can determine if an SNMP agent is executing on any given node.

Another convenient feature of HP OpenView's Network Node Manager is its ability to graphically baseline your network's normal performance profile and compare this in real-time with current operation. This feature helps you see at a glance whether or not your networked system is performing as expected.

Investment in tools like HP's OpenView may be necessary if you don't want to dissipate your time operating in continual crisis mode. In planning your Internet clone, you should give serious consideration to allocating budget to the purchase of a set of robust, commercial grade tools like HP OpenView. To our knowledge, there is no comparable network management software in the public domain.

Given that you have the knowledgeable people and adequate technology to operate your Internet clone, you still need policies and procedures to implement the processes that will take advantage of the people and the technology. Policies and procedures help ensure that diverse workgroups with different agendas cooperate and collaborate to build a seamlessly integrated TCP/IP network.

Cooperation is one primary difference between conducting business on the Internet and sharing information within an internal Internet clone. On the Internet, for example, there is no policy mandating that servers be free of disconnected information resources and dead links. On an Internet clone, style and document management guidelines can help standardize information presentation features, content coordination, information provider identification, and data effectivity and criticality. On the Internet, such coordination is usually lacking; within the corporate Internet clone, you can mandate and enforce it. You need adequate incentives, however, in order to institutionalize this sort of cooperation.

Operating and maintaining an information system in an Internet clone can often be a cooperative "team" effort between geographically separated sites. Local ownership naturally tends to distribute information.

Internally, an Internet clone can benefit from guidelines designed to enhance the delivery and presentation of information resources (a luxury not afforded to those seeking information on public networks). These guidelines need not be extensive, but they should contain a good description of what you expect from corporate information resources. In multi-subdomained environments often found in large corporations, for example, it is essential that hyperlinks contain full URL specifications. Users in *domain1.largecorp.com* will have no trouble accessing a local URL like *http://mysys/filename*, but users in *domain2.largecorp.com* will find a dead link because they were unable to resolve "mysys." The correct way to specify this link would be to use it's full domain path.[3] In this way, everyone on the internal internetwork can access the information resource easily without having to make local adjustments.

8.3 Maintaining the System

Operating the system is only half the battle. That is the job primarily of the system and network managers. Maintaining the information content in the proper format rests mostly with information owners who are typically also users of the system. They should constantly compile, revise, and update their source data. For end users to make the most of available information, it must be both accessible and meaningful. Accessibility falls to the system and network managers. Meaningfulness falls to the data owners. Both are crucial functions. Information that is not available is useless as is information whose content is not relevant to ongoing business concerns.

In the last section we considered the operational side of the Internet clone. In this section we look at the information maintenance side.

---

[3] For example, *http://mysys.domain1.larecorp.com/filename.*

8.3.1 Infobase Maintenance

To frame our discussion of infobase maintenance, we consider six key questions:

- What information should you maintain?
- Why should you maintain it?
- When or how often should you update it?
- How should you update it?
- What kinds of skills do you need to maintain this data?
- Who should maintain it?

8.3.1.1 What Information Should You Maintain?

Before proceeding headlong to slay the infobase maintenance dragon, you should take a step back and survey the situation. Take stock of your repositories with a view to determining which ones are the most critical for your enterprise. Simply listing these infobases in order of priority can go a long way in ensuring that your personnel will apply the right amount of resources and energy at the right places. But you have to know what the candidates are before you rank them. So your first task is simply to take inventory of your existing infobases.

8.3.1.2 Why Should You Maintain It?

Once you've determined the full suite of candidate infobases throughout your system, you can proceed to prioritizing them. The goal here is to determine which of these data stores are most worthy of receiving the benefit of labor hours expended to maintain them.

Some key subquestions to ask of each information store and which should help you with this prioritization are the following:

- Who uses or depends on this information? Are they key players in my organization?
- How important is this information to overall goals of my organization? Is it essential or incidental?
- What would happen if you left this infobase unattended? Who would care?

By the answers to the above questions, you should be able to determine the relative centrality of each infobase with regards to your organizations charter.

8.3.1.3 When or How Often Should You Update It?

Some information changes rapidly, even in real-time; other information is fairly static. Answers to this question should set the stage for determining what kind of maintenance strategy you need. Frequently updated data used by many key people in your organization will probably receive high rankings. Daily electronic feeds containing important news items about your market segment, the economy, your stock prices, and your supplier industries will probably outrank weekly status reports produced by a small team of highly specialized engineers. On the other hand, yearly summaries of progress in areas of strategic research may come but once a year, yet their importance to the whole organization may be paramount. However, you have a longer period of time to prepare for their arrival. In the case of the daily news feeds, you must be able to react and disseminate the information very quickly.

8.3.1.4 How Should You Update It?

This question focuses on the issue of manual versus automatic update. Your answers to the previous sets of questions should guide you in answering this one. If you need to refresh the infobase daily or even hourly, you should probably consider developing scripts and/or custom software to handle the formatting and integration tasks.

Also pertinent is the question of how you generate this information in the first place. Does somebody generate it by typing a memo on an old fashioned typewriter or is it a periodic output of a database program? Perhaps it is nothing more than photocopies of recent news clippings. How do you propose to get that on-line? By OCR scanning?

8.3.1.5 What Kinds of Skills Are Required?

After you determine what you need to maintain, how often and by what method you should maintain it, you should consider the skills required to upkeep the information. Perhaps secretaries can perform this function by entering data into a database program. Perhaps they require some complicated programming to read in, filter, and reformat data. For example, an electronic news feed may arrive via electronic mail. Perhaps you wish to post it on a Web page. You might consider writing a script to strip off the electronic mail header information, which nobody on your internal web wants to see anyway, and wrap the text body in appropriate HTML tags. Further, you might want summary information from this feed inserted along with the appropriate hyperlink into a higher level home page. If that is the case, you might consider writing a script to read in the current home page's HTML file, strip out yesterday's summary item, insert today's summary pulled from the e-mail message, and then append the rest of the existing HTML file after the insertion.

It should be evident that determining the kind of skill sets required will help you answer the next question.

8.3.1.6 Who Should Maintain It?

Do your people have the desired skills to effect the updates according to your requirements? If not, you may want to consider hiring a contractor or permanent employee who does have the required skills.

8.3.1.7 Specific Kinds of Infobases

E-Mail. Aside from the ongoing setup of new SMTP clients and the maintenance of e-mail lists, e-mail systems require very little recurring maintenance. Some of the maintenance tasks include the administration of e-mail aliases, postmaster functions, and ongoing troubleshooting of remote client applications.

E-mail aliases serve an important role in companies that have many distributed resources. Users that move from system to system need to have consistent e-mail addresses so that they do not have to notify senders of a change. If a user moves from one machine to another, he or she should not have to notify the entire world of his or her new e-mail destination. Aliases provide a convenient method for eliminating this problem. When a user moves, the alias pointer moves with him.

Aliases provide a consistent method of delivering e-mail to an intended recipient regardless of the actual mail destination. Since an alias is just a pointer, you can redirect when a user moves to a new system or decides simply to read mail on a different platform. Imagine the complexities of moving and then having to tell everyone who used your old address to now use the new one.

You can also use alias records to maintain mailing lists. For example, you may have a mailing list for quality engineers called *quality@widgets.com*. The e-mail user named *quality* is actually just an alias for the list of recipients. Whenever someone sends e-mail to *quality@widgets.com*, all recipients on the lists receive a copy of the message. Then you maintain another alias, *quality-request*, which redirects any messages coming to *quality-request@widget.com* to the owner of the mailing list. This might be a person, say, *joe@widget.com*. Presumably, Joe can add or delete e-mail addresses from the mailing list. The upshot of all this is that there is some overhead in maintaining such a list. It is best to delegate the maintenance function in this instance to someone like Joe, who presumably has an abiding interest in the ongoing discussions taking place by way of the list.

USENET. On the external Internet there is a widely accepted procedure for the creation of new newsgroups. The bottom line is that there has to be a large enough consensus to ratify the creation of a new group. For the internal corporate clone of the Internet, the process should be no less stringent. Proliferation of inactive, barren newsgroups makes it harder for users to find those groups in which active discussions are indeed taking place. There is usually no way to tell by looking at the title or name of a newsgroup whether or not it is active. You have to open it up and scan the posted articles to see if there is any recent activity. This takes time and may discourage people from putting any credence at all in the newsgroup concept. Thus, it is imperative that internal system managers not be allowed to proliferate newsgroups without first going through the process of achieving consensus on their potential value.

Even once active newsgroups can become inactive. Like all things, newsgroups have a life cycle of birth, maturation, and death. It is important to dispose of dead newsgroups by notifying users on the system of impending disposal, archiving the unproductive groups, and finally deleting them for good. You should also make the archives available via some other means like FTP for those users out there who are still interested in reviewing old discussions.

As mentioned above, it is important to prune your system of unproductive newsgroups, since they tend to clutter and discredit the newsgroup system as a whole.

Popular newsgroups tend to grow without bounds, and unless you have unlimited disk space at your disposal, you should consider archiving and purging some of the older articles from these lengthier groups. Again, you should notify the newsgroup participants of the location and retrieval method for the archive.

For further information on the operation and maintenance of USENET newsgroups, check the USENET FAQs at *ftp://rtfm.mit.edu*.

FTP. FTP requires very little maintenance. Functions that may require automation include archive organization and redistribution, building README files, and other data description files. FTP servers that maintain a public area for data exchange (usually an /incoming directory) will need periodic review and purging of unneeded files. It is a good idea to inform users who deposit files that you will delete their files after a certain time period, say, a month. You can then automate the deletion process by creating a script that checks the creation date and time of each deposited file, deleting those older than the allotted time. Such a script is trivial to build in the UNIX environment.

WWW. The vast and rapidly growing corporate Web can become a configuration management nightmare, unless you have well-defined processes for updating your HTML documents. These processes should ensure that you integrate important hyperlinks into each new added document and that you endow each new added document with hyperlink pointers back to preexisting documents in your Web.

Access logs can grow rapidly and require purging and archival. If your Web pages contain *mailto* hyperlinks[4] back to their webmasters, these webmasters can find themselves busy answering questions and suggestions from the user community. For example, one user running one browser may view a page differently than another running a different browser. In fact, one might not see all the intended information due to less capability in his or her browser. Your webmasters may get advice from users about how to change this or that page to accommodate the less capable browser.

---

[4] A *mailto* hyperlink in an HTML document tells the Web browser to display a standard screen to help the user create an e-mail message. The "To" field in the message is preloaded with the recipient's e-mail address. The message is sent by the user's ordinary mail server, not the Web server.

Webmasters may also find themselves deluged by constant change requests from the data owners, especially if these data owners did not create the original HTML files. They will hand information to the Webmaster, who will create the HTML file, integrate it with various graphics files, and post it on the server for general viewing. Quite often the data owner, once he or she views the page with a browser, will want to tweak the page in various ways. They will want to move graphics around, change some font characteristics, or request hyperlinks to various external pages. This can be a never-ending saga for the Webmaster.

The solution to this is to empower data owners to author their own Web documents, which requires investment in training. With the standard word processing software like MS Word and WordPerfect now supporting the generation of HTML files, we expect that some of the Web authoring responsibilities will migrate to the data owners themselves. Regardless, Webmasters can expect to invest considerable time in integrating pages produced by others who will probably not be aware of the relative directory structures employed by the Webmaster on the server itself. The Webmaster can expect to modify some of the hyperlinks the authors created to link their pages with others.

8.3.2 Maintaining Information Discovery Tools

Not only must information resources be up-to-date, but they must be easy to find and access. The use of standards and guidelines for implementing a system will help somewhat, but it may prove even more useful to establish common repositories containing pointers to information resources throughout an internetwork. These pointers or "Meta-Indexes" provide a common starting point for users to find information.

While Internet meta-indexes are sometimes out-of-date and may contain "dead links," an internal information system need not have this deficiency. Coordinating the flow and mapping of information resources to a common centralized directory database will help everyone be more productive.

Using smart directories to facilitate the rapid discovery of internal information resources is an important cyberstrategy. Whether internal or external, rapid acquisition and effective use of information is what gives managers better decision-making criteria, programmers more reference tools, and researchers the ability to collaborate. But it is senseless to build a vast conglomeration of information dumpsters without providing centralized tools like directories that serve as signposts and switchboards for rapidly locating the right information.

Browsing is a time-consuming way to find information. It involves a lot of backtracking over ground already covered. Not knowing exactly where to find the information you need, you can spend a lot of time following Web hyperlinks or Gopher menus down blind alleys in cyberspace. Not finding the information you need, you find yourself retracing your steps, sometimes even going in circles. All of this consumes valuable time and expensive labor resources—the time it takes to find the information diminishes its value.

Let's face it, browsing is slow! Looking for information in a complex enterprise internetwork is comparable to looking for paper documents in somebody else's office. You are not sure what organizing principle—assuming there is one at all—governs the unfamiliar workspace. So you just aimlessly plow your way through the stacks and stacks of papers until you happen to stumble across the desired document. Sometimes you make a mess of things along the way, losing your place and having to start over, or, worse yet, you fail to find the document at all.

Although browsing is inefficient, you can supplement it with some basic tools like meta-indexes and some solid style guidelines for information organization and presentation. In this way, well-organized virtual libraries facilitate users in their relentless search for appropriate information.

Meta-indexes are repositories of data locations on an internetwork (public or private). Some rely on owner or publisher registration, others simply roam the Web like a hungry worm looking for Web pages. The (benign) worm variety relentlessly searches the Web for documents. Inside each document it finds links to further documents. The worm then compares the thus discovered links with links it already knows about in its own database. If the worm finds a match for this link, it discards it. Otherwise, it adds the newly discovered link to its database and continues the search anew with the document pointed to by the newly discovered link, and so on ad infinitum.

Worms can catalog the discovered information according to the various HTML tags it finds in the document. For example, most Web documents have a pair of HTML tags that specify the title of the document. This pair of tags look like this: <TITLE> and </TITLE>. Often, the worm grabs the text enclosed by these tags and store it in its database. Thus, users can search through the entire database looking at keywords that may occur in the titles of HTML documents. The database returns to the user the entire record of information for every match in the database. Included in this record is the URL of the matching documents. The user can then point at and click on the hyperlink to go directly to the original HTML document (provided it still exists).

It is a good idea to set up a such a worm in the internal corporate web. It is even better to have a directory based on a registration scheme. Such directories provide on-line Web forms that users fill out to register their Web pages. It allows the author to categorize the registered Web page and supply various keywords to help users later in their searches.

One of most popular, registration-oriented meta-indexes on the external Internet is the Yahoo server at *http://www.yahoo.com*. Created by Stanford graduate students David Philo and Jerry Yang, Yahoo maintains a massive hierarchical directory of thousands of Web pages. Owners or publishers register Web pages by filling out an on-line form. The Yahoo Web server administrators then process the registration. In a few weeks, a hyperlink and description of the page in an appropriate category shows up on the Yahoo Web server. Yahoo also provides a search engine for those who want to skip climbing the hierarchical tree and go straight to their target by means of specific keywords.

Like the card catalog at your local library, a meta-index provides a good starting point for internetwork navigation. Unlike a card catalog, however, a single meta-index is incapable of logging all the rapidly changing information resources on the Internet. The "holdings" of the worldwide Internet, as well as those of your own Internet clone, are far too numerous and volatile.

There are many different indexes and virtual libraries available on the Internet. They work in different ways and contain different information. Some, like Carnegie Mellon University's Lycos server, have search engines that actively build information catalogs using the results of automated queries to web servers around the world. For each document fetched, Lycos keeps the title, headings, subheadings, and links, plus the 100 highest weighted words plus the first twenty lines.[5]

To use a meta-index like Lycos effectively sometimes requires repetitive searching. Like a card catalog, Lycos provides several good resources of information, but you often have to still further refine your search.

While Lycos attempts to make the results of automated searching coherent to the end user, it is still often necessary to supplement its findings with those provided by a registration-oriented information directory like Yahoo. Another registration-oriented service is the W3 Catalog at CERN, which does a good job of presenting "provider-prepared" resources for the information seeker. The W3 Catalog, however, relies on information providers to register their information in order to make it useful to end users. CERN makes no attempts to keep the information current, so you often find "dead links" to information resources that may no longer exist. The W3 Catalog offers this disclaimer:

> DISCLAIMER: We have no control over the contents of the consulted documents. If you find dead links in the catalog, you should notify the maintainer of the source document, not us.

Meta-indexes are important, not only for information seekers, but also for information providers. Providers can utilize these indexes to increase visibility and encourage traffic to their servers. Indexes can also help users of a corporate Internet clone to locate internal information quickly and efficiently. Like a FAQ (Frequently Asked Questions), a meta-index provides a resource for answering day-to-day questions and eliminating the overhead associated with bootstrapping new users. Chapter 9 contains more

---

[5] See Lycos at *http://lycos.cs.cmu.edu*

about the future directions of these indexes, their underlying search engines, and their impact on the Internet community.

Information gatherers sometimes use multiple indexes to help narrow a search. All too often, however, users will either find too much information (an infoglut—making it difficult to assimilate) or too little information (making it difficult to get the needed answers)

Repetitive searches place an unwelcome burden on the information seeker. As we indicated above, searching for information is less productive when it takes too long. That is why new search engines using artificial intelligence are being developed. This new generation of search engines, sometimes called autonomous agents (knowbots or simply "bots"), help you locate and extract information according to previously given specifications. They usually operate autonomously as a background process, freeing the user to work on other things. We will have more to say about autonomous agents in Chapter 9.

8.4 User Support / Customer Support

For several reasons, the user- and customer-support roles in developing and maintaining an Internet-based information system are critical to the success of your project. First, some users may be unfamiliar with Internet tools and unable to use them effectively. They will need a helping hand. If you don't help them, they may withhold their support for your project. Second, if your system provides information to your external customers, the situation is even more critical. Your organization's effectiveness as an enterprise is dependent on how well you serve your customer's information needs. If you provide your customers with poorly organized, poorly presented, inaccurate or stale information, their opinion of your organization is likely to be low. You cannot afford to neglect the important twin areas of user and customer support.

8.4.1 User and Customer Feedback Systems

Many major computer vendors strive to improve customer support in addition to providing sales and other reference information. Since the Internet and its information dissemination tools are a relatively inexpensive means to distribute product information to customers and prospects, the combination of reduced costs and improved support for customers is powerful.

Only a few years ago, a typical customer support scenario for resolving a computer-related problem or bug might have lasted several days. After logging a trouble call to a vendor, for example, subsequent diagnostic processes might take hours. In most cases, this involved repeating error messages (sometimes letter by letter) over a telephone to a remote support representative. Sometimes it became necessary to print and fax memory dumps to a remote trouble desk for review. If the problem turned out to be software-related (either operating system or application), the vendor would mail a patch on tape to your site. After several days, the tape would arrive and you could apply the patch to the troubled system.

Today, you can solve many problems end-to-end without ever initiating a support call. Companies like Hewlett-Packard, IBM, and DEC provide on-line databases of information on known problems. In most cases, a trouble fix is only a file transfer away. Should you have to log a trouble call, you will greatly improve your diagnostic process with the use of Internet tools. You can use e-mail and FTP, for example, to transmit error information and receive potential fixes.

It is not a bad idea to model your own support systems on those that have made successful use of the Internet. This applies to both internal user support systems as well as external customer support systems. You can use this to log problems, distribute patches, provide remote support, and gather customer feedback information. Archives of related solutions to similar problems provide a library of resources to be reused each time a new but related problem crops up.

A very important and growing application area for the use of Internet technologies—especially World Wide Web technology—is in customer communications and feedback. With the help of a simple question and answer survey, filled out on-line by the customer using an HTML forms page, companies can stay in touch with their customers' ever-changing needs. Such data can provide concrete measures to help determine how well your company's products and services are meeting your customers' needs.

Back-end programming to process customer feedback may require more sophistication, however, than that required to simply build HTML or even forms pages. Mailbots, survey tabulation, and SQL database interfaces generally require investment in staff hours to produce meaningful architectures and designs. Here you should think through the whole process before you jump in and start churning out forms pages. It pays to spend a reasonable amount of time deciding what you are going to do with the data once you capture it. Capturing it is easy. Processing it so that it adds value to your relationship with your customers is more difficult.

8.4.2 Help Desk and Training Facilities

In building a help desk facility to benefit your in-house users, you should give some thought to modeling it after one of the more popular Internet-base customer support systems. The Help Desk at NCSA (The National Center for Supercomputing Applications at the University of Illinois), for example, supplements their primary help desk functions with World Wide Web pages. Users can log problems, browse FAQs (both locally and remotely), and find out about upcoming maintenance and downtime. With carefully crafted Web pages and on-line forms, you can guide your users through the troubleshooting process without human intervention prior to allocating expensive staff hours to assist the user. Sometimes, the discipline of having to articulate a problem description in writing will help users to discover solutions for themselves.

System and network updates are good candidates for information sharing on an Internet clone. Just like HP, IBM and other companies field product releases from their Internet home pages, internal service departments can utilize this medium for service announcements, news, and other system information.

You can also use Internet-based systems for training. More and more often organizations are putting their documentation and data on-line. Netscape Communications, for example, sends out very little paper documentation with the shrinkwrap version of their *Netscape Navigator*. They don't even embed the help files on the distribution disks; instead, they make the help files available over the Internet. This keeps everyone in synch with the latest and greatest version of on-line help. The help facility is thus an electronic, living document. As soon as bug reports or productivity tips are available, Netscape publishes them on the Web. The documentation thus never goes out of date and there is no need to thumb through tomes of heavy user manuals.

8.5 Managing Upgrades

It is natural that the evolution of the Internet should affect the evolution of your Internet clone. Through your interaction with the Internet, you will learn of new developments in hardware and software; you will probably want to take advantage of these developments. In this subsection, we discuss how to manage upgrades to your system as new developments in Internet technology unfold.

8.5.1 Keeping Up with the Internet

Each layer of the Internet architecture evolves at its own pace. The lower layers in the OSI network model evolve more slowly than the higher ones. For example, the underlying infrastructure of the Internet, consisting of the physical, datalink, and network layers, are evolving steadily but much more slowly than the higher, application layers. You can probably get along just fine for years with 10 Mbps Ethernet technology in your LANs, but unless you upgrade your Web browsers bimonthly, you may be missing out on some important new features.

Changing even more rapidly than applications software are the information repositories they use. Hundreds of new Web sites crop up every day. Some of these may contain valuable information for your enterprise. How do you ensure that your users become aware and can take advantage of these resources?

Keeping up with the Internet can be very time-consuming. You could employ several people to just surf the Net looking for and digesting relevant developments in technology and information. Most enterprises cannot afford this luxury, however, unless they can justify the allocation of such resources in terms of the strategic interest these developments have for your business. If your enterprise is a software manufacturer, for example, you probably need to pay close attention to how your competition is using the Internet to market their software products to customers. But you may need to know much more. You may need to know about the rapidly changing demographics of certain regions of the world, for example, in order to determine if new market opportunities are opening up.

One way to keep up with net happenings is to read e-zines like WEBster and the Netsurfer Digest. Netsurfer Digest distributes an HTML Web page weekly via e-mail. A subscriber can save the message to a local file and then access the on-line magazine with virtually any Web browser. A key feature of this newsletter is that it contains hyperlinks to the sites being discussed. In effect, this sort of distribution is like receiving a journal complete with all of the source material referenced in the footnotes. You are receiving not only somebody's digest of the source material, but a whole virtual library which includes the source material.

8.5.2 Network Infrastructure Upgrades

Swapping out the physical cable plant can be a major undertaking. It is a good idea in the beginning of your project, therefore, to lay down the most capable—i.e., highest throughput—cabling system you can afford. A high capacity cable plant may provide sufficient bandwidth to last for years.

Changing the datalink layer may present more headaches. If you need to go from token ring to Ethernet, for example, you will probably have to upgrade your network interface cards (NICs) as well as the packet driver software that makes the translation from IP to the datalink layer protocol. The NIC manufacturer, however, usually provides such software, and you can accomplish the software upgrade at the same time as the card upgrade. Nonetheless, this kind of upgrade can be labor-intensive if you have many machines to upgrade. Once you have a TCP/IP network running, you should have little reason to upgrade the network and transport layers.

The main challenge in upgrading your network infrastructure is essentially managerial. You want to make the cutover process to the new infrastructure as painless as possible for end users. This means that you want to minimize any required downtime. Sometimes this requires that you run parallel networks in order to facilitate a smooth and uneventful transition.

8.5.3 Application Installation

There are ways to install and upgrade applications over your network. For a minimal, experimental configuration, application installation is not a problem. However, as soon as your Internet clone grows beyond this initial configuration, installation can become a real headache. Although the Internet provides facilities like FTP archives from which you can download software and install it on end user machines, many users are not able or willing to retrieve and install their own software. The burden falls on the network administrator.

There are three approaches to installation. First, you could walk around and install all the software yourself. Not only could this become a full-time (and thankless) job, it may well become impossible, once your network springs the boundaries of your local network. In other words, it may soon become a WAN. It is not cost-effective (nor fun) to travel around large geographic areas just to install software.

The second approach is to train the users to install the software themselves. You can accomplish this by providing them with a basic, generic understanding of how installation proceeds, or providing them with on-line instructions on how to do it. This former approach involves formal training which can be very costly. The latter method, as we saw above in the case of *Netscape Navigator*, seems to work quite well. Netcom has made it very easy, for example, to download and install upgrades to their popular *Netcruiser* navigation software.

The third method involves remote installation. A number of tools are beginning to emerge that handle the remote installation problem. They all require, however, that certain loader or cooperating agent software already be installed on the end users' machines. You need this loader software to bootstrap the loading process. You then maintain a centralized archive of applications on a distribution server.

One of the most robust tools for accomplishing remote file management—and hence remote installation—is NetManage's *NEWTwatch*. Based on the standard Internet Simple Network Management Protocol (SNMP), NEWTwatch is a desktop management application for users of Microsoft Windows. This tool can discover and monitor hosts on the network and support configuration of desktop parameters and files.

Another recent entry into this category is *Remotely Possible/Sockets* from Avalan Technology, Inc. Like *NEWTwatch*, this remote control software also works in the MS-Windows environment and supports TCP/IP-based file transfer between PC desktops.

Many system vendors offer built-in or optional capabilities for managing software distribution over a network. Hewlett-Packard, for example, provides what they call a network distribution (*netdist*) product with the HP-UX operating system. *Netdist* allows centralized software distribution to remote nodes throughout an internetwork. When used in conjunction with HP's boot server, you can even perform a complete system install over your TCP/IP network. Similarly, Sun Microsystems provides *swmtool* with Solaris 2.x.

Chapter 9

PLANNING FOR THE FUTURE

The Internet and its underlying technologies are changing rapidly. They barely hold still long enough for us to digest their present state, much less to see their future form. Predicting how the Internet will evolve is therefore very difficult. Nonetheless, we will discuss in this chapter some of the broader trends we perceive and their implications for building an Internet-based information system today.

Internet trends fall into two broad categories: cultural and technological. The cultural trends have to do with the social makeup and economics of the Internet community. The technological trends indicate how the technologies underlying and enabling the Internet are changing. In this chapter, we devote more attention to the technological rather than on the cultural trends.

9.1 Cultural Trends

As the Internet grows, various subcultures have emerged. These correspond roughly to the main Internet domains: *.mil*, *.edu*, *.org*, *.net*, and *.com*. The commercial domain, *.com*, is by far the fastest-growing Internet segment today.

As more and more commercial organizations connect their own networks to the Internet, the opportunity and the demand for more secure electronic commerce have grown. Several regional subcommunities of the Internet have indeed organized themselves around the need for electronic commerce, and we will discuss some of these below.

A consequence of this rapid growth, however, is the specter of infoglut. As more and more information providers and consumers gather to share information, the sheer quantity of information becomes unwieldy. Naturally, new technologies involving knowbots and autonomous agents are emerging to help keep the tide of infoglut in check. We will now discuss these two topics, electronic commerce and infoglut, before turning our attention to the subject of trends in information technology.

9.1.1 Civilization Comes to the Internet: Electronic Commerce

Electronic commerce involves the electronic transfer of information between suppliers and customers in support of specific business transactions. Examples include the sending and receiving of product order information, requests for quotes, and electronic funds transfer. This kind of electronic interaction has taken place on private, value-added networks for a number of years and is really nothing new. However, with increased commercial use of the Internet, many companies are naturally wondering if they can use the Internet as an underlying information infrastructure for electronic commerce.

There are at least three reasons for desiring to use the Internet as a medium for electronic access. First, the Internet is a neutral system of bitways, not owned by any one agency. As such it appears to be as much in the public domain as the air we breath and the streets we travel. This is one reason perhaps why the Internet is referred to so often as an information highway.

The second reason regards the vast extent of the Internet. It is global, extending its reach to over 100 countries around the world. In a global economy, a global information infrastructure makes a lot of sense.

The third reason has to do with the population of the Internet. With nearly 25 million individual users today and rapidly growing at nearly 10 percent per month, the Internet is very attractive to businesses that sell to consumers. As thousands of corporations in search of consumers connect their internal networks to the Internet, significant opportunities also emerge for businesses to establish various electronic trading partnerships with each other.

9.1.1.1 CommerceNet

Located in the San Francisco Bay Area, CommerceNet is a consortium of companies and organizations whose common goal is to create an electronic marketplace on the Internet. The U.S. Department of Defense's Advanced Projects Research Agency (ARPA) funds CommerceNet as part of its Technology Reinvestment Program (TRP). The lead organization for CommerceNet is a young Bay Area company called Enterprise Integration Technologies.

The CommerceNet member companies hope that a variety of value-added information services will emerge using the CommerceNet infrastructure to bring buyers and sellers together. Some of the expected services are specialized directories, broker and referral services, vendor certification and credit reporting, network notaries and repositories, as well as financial and transportation services.

Participating companies receive Internet connectivity through CommerceNet participant BARRNet, a San Francisco Bay Area Internet access provider.

CommerceNet was one of the first initiatives to adopt World Wide Web technology to enable electronic commerce. Graphical Web browsers like *NCSA Mosaic* provide the user interface to CommerceNet's collection of interlinked Web pages. Consortium members also receive software tools to help them develop uniform Web pages.

A key feature of CommerceNet is the availability to its members of security mechanisms, including authentication and encryption, based on the RSA public/private key method. CommerceNet also provides its members with public-key certification services. Many people consider the lack of consistent security mechanisms as a primary obstacle to using the Internet as an electronic marketplace.

Buyers and sellers using CommerceNet's security mechanisms can safely exchange sensitive information like credit card numbers and bid amounts. They can also sign legally enforceable contracts, maintain audit trails, and make or receive network payments through cooperating financial institutions.

Within five years, the organizers of CommerceNet hope to achieve the following goals:

- 3,000 organizations using CommerceNet routinely for business transactions and technical collaboration
- 300 organizations providing information services through CommerceNet
- 30 local, state and federal projects in Northern California using CommerceNet as a common infrastructure
- 30 profitable local businesses providing the CommerceNet infrastructure with computer products, telecommunication services, software, and consulting

CommerceNet also has ties to a research program at Stanford University's Center for Information Technology (CIT). This program is currently exploring the following areas:

- Shopping agents capable of searching through catalogs and negotiating deals
- Real-time interaction and videomail collaboration tools for distributed workgroups
- Natural language search and retrieval techniques for large, distributed information bases
- Format translation services enabling the exchange of engineering product data

For more information concerning CommerceNet, access the CommerceNet home page at *http://www.commerce.net/*. You can also obtain information via e-mail at *info@commerce.net*.

9.1.1.2 EINet

Another regional initiative dedicated to providing electronic commerce services via the Internet is EINet, formerly part of the Microelectronics and Computer Technology Corporation (MCC) in Austin, Texas. Like CommerceNet, EINet is funded in part by ARPA TRP funds. EINet also strives to provide security services. EINet's approach to security relies on the MIT-developed Kerberos system.

9.1.1.3 The Microsoft Network (MSN)

Another major electronic marketplace, which appeared in August 1995, is the Microsoft Network, or MSN. Created by software giant Microsoft in conjunction with UUNET, a well-known Internet access provider and networking service company, MSN provides consumer on-line services, relying on a worldwide system of X.25 networks. In some respects, this makes MSN similar to Compuserve or America On-Line. MSN also provides on-line services for businesses.

One of the goals of the Microsoft Network is to provide a secure electronic environment for business transactions. Microsoft expects to offer businesses a whole range of software to support their inter-business transactions, as well as a cost-effective distribution mechanism for Microsoft and other third-party software.

9.1.2 Inundation: The Infoglut

The Internet as a whole already has more information than any one person can master. The number of Internet information resources is well over 100,000. Similarly, many Internet clones within large organizations already house more information than any one person can fully digest.

Even if the quantity of information available via the Internet were manageable, the rate at which that quantity is currently changing rapidly renders it unmanageable. Similar growth trends are evident within corporate internetworks.

Further compounding the rapid growth of hyperlinked information resources on the Web is a similarly rapid increase in the number of links or paths leading to each single resource. Redundant paths (not to mention blind alleys) can reduce the effectiveness of browsing based searches. An information seeker may mistake a previously unexplored path of hyperlinks as a trail to a previously unexplored information resource, only to find that it leads to a resource already visited.

The upshot of this information explosion is an increase in entropy—a term used by physicists to measure the amount of disorder in a system. As the number of repositories and repository builders within your enterprise increases, the amount of information irrelevant to your purposes—i.e., the amount of noninformation—increases proportionately. The result is an increase in info-entropy. Another term used by scientists and engineers to describe this kind of phenomenon is "signal-to-noise ratio." This refers to the numeric ratio of signal strength to background noise. A low signal-to-noise ratio means that it is difficult to distinguish the desired signal from the background noise. Of course, when applied to the Internet, this concept of background noise is relative. What may be a signal to one person, may be just noise to another. Yet, on the whole across the Internet, and probably within your Internet clone as well, this relative signal-to-noise ratio may be decreasing. The info-signal may be growing more slowly than the info-noise, hence, an increase in info-entropy.

This is naturally of considerable concern to businesses because it can directly affect their return on investment for time spent acquiring information. If it takes more sophistication, more training, more time, and more expensive software to separate the wheat from the chaff and make your corporate information hunters more effective, your costs will go up.

9.1.2.1 Navigating the Information Ocean

Navigating this rising tide of infoglut requires tools, techniques, and expertise. We'll discuss some of the emerging tools later. Here we'll mention some of the techniques you can use and the type of experts you'll need to effectively surf internetworked resources.

The seven major Internet information resources are WWW, Gopher, FTP, WAIS, USENET News, listserv, e-mail. Each of these information spaces has developed some tools and techniques for planning and executing searches for information.

One of the best ways to begin a new search for information is to use one of the many electronic directories associated with each of the seven major information spaces. On the WWW, there are several directories containing hierarchically organized subject catalogues of hyperlinks. One of the best known is the previously mentioned Yahoo directory at *http://www.yahoo.com*. Another is the EINet Galaxy at *http://www.einet.net.* From these directories you can easily link to others such as CUI's WWW Virtual Library.

The remaining information spaces have search facilities as well. For gopherspace, we have the search engines jughead and veronica. Similarly, for FTP archives there are archie servers. For WAIS sources there is the directory of servers at *quake.think.com*. There are many USENET archives of newsgroups in searchable form. In addition to being a means of communication with other users, USENET News is also a valuable information resource. You should not overlook its numerous FAQ postings and WAIS-indexed archives; they are a source of valuable information, especially for newcomers to newsgroups.

9.1.2.2 Role of the Information Specialist

Although not difficult in principle, mastering all of these information spaces and their central directory and searching structures is probably unreasonable to expect of every knowledge worker. The problem is not one of difficulty but of time available to master each scheme.

In Chapter 3, we discussed the role of the corporate library and the need for a whole new generation of cybrarians. These information specialists have mastered the art of navigating the information spaces both inside and outside your organization. They have developed and perfected processes necessary for enterprise-wide information distribution. Cybrarians should also act as coaches who empower knowledge workers through training to become more effective information seekers in their own narrowly-defined domains. We see cybrarians as becoming more and more important in tomorrow's information-dominated world of business.

9.1.3 The Impact of Internet Economics

The economics of the Internet will exert, we believe, a profound impact on business. Just as the price-to-performance ratio of information technologies continues to drop steadily and thus fuel the information revolution, so the relatively inexpensive communications technologies associated with the Internet will continue to revolutionize business and personal communications.

Some examples will help illuminate this assertion.

Current Internet access generally uses a flat-rate pricing scheme. You pay a flat rate to a local Internet access provider. Often this involves nothing more than a local telephone call for individuals or a dedicated line for businesses. Because of the packet switching scheme of the Internet data communications, however, all connections between computers, no matter how far apart they are, are ***virtual***. This is vastly different from how a normal long distance phone call works. During a phone call, the participating telephone companies dedicate circuit connections. The call ties up a physical complex of switches between the call's two endpoints. Thus, it stands to reason that you should pay for the length of time that you use that physical circuit. Internet connections, however, are virtual; they do not require an allocation of extra physical resources. The switching circuitry is already in place before the packets are sent. Thus, there is no need to allocate extra cost for dedicated circuit resources.

There is another price paid by Internet users, however, and that is the price of congestion. With long distance telephone calls, you can nearly always rely on a minimum quality of service. With the Internet, however, you cannot count on a guaranteed quality of service. Congestion somewhere in the intervening networks may delay your packets. In this regard, the Internet can resemble a traffic jam on the highway at rush hour.

When the intervening networks are relatively free of congestion, however, the Internet offers communication across the world for the price of a local telephone call. Recently, one of us used Vocaltec's Internet phone (I-phone) to place a 1/2 hour voice conversation from Atlanta, GA to Sydney, Australia. The only charge for this was the usual local telephone call by each party in order to gain access to the Internet.

Similarly, it is now possible to send a FAX to many parts of the world via an e-mail-to-FAX gateway and not pay any extra charge! With MIME e-mail attachments and anonymous FTP, it is also possible to eliminate in many cases the cost of sending a large document through the mail or via an overnight delivery service.

We think that economic trends like these are going to revolutionize business communications. As encryption becomes more widespread and easier to use, companies will no longer need dedicated WAN links for ordinary private business communications. Asynchronous communications like e-mail, newsgroups, and static Web pages will use encryption to guarantee privacy. Dedicated links may still be necessary to ensure minimum bandwidth, but they will no longer be necessary to ensure business privacy. This will offer significant savings opportunities for businesses. It may also present significant challenges to long-distance telecommunications companies.

9.2 Information Technology Trends

This section deals with some of the trends we see affecting the further evolution of Internet technology. In particular, we discuss the following topics:

- Commercial-Grade Tools
- Multimedia
- Object Technology
- Network Technology
- Intelligent Information Technology

9.2.1 Commercial-Grade Tools

One trend already evident and previously noted is the evolution of Internet applications and tools toward greater functionality and commercial-grade robustness. This also includes a higher degree of functional integration. Many commercial Web browsers are becoming all-purpose navigation and communications tools. They provide access on the back end to numerous Internet applications protocols, including NNTP, SMTP, WAIS, Gopher, and FTP, not to mention the standard HTTP Web protocol. The latest version of NetManage Chameleon, for example, includes calendaring and scheduling functionality. The evolution of

Netscape's Web browser shows a similar trend toward incorporating additional functionality not traditionally associated with Web browsers. Likewise, groupware applications like Lotus Notes are beginning to incorporate Web browsing functionality. We can also expect Microsoft's TCP/IP support applications in Windows 95 to become more integrated with other Microsoft office applications.

These evolving environments will integrate local desktop applications and data resources with those of the local and wide area networks. Indeed, the distinction between desktop and networked resources will continue to blur and become transparent to the end user. (See the discussion below on Asynchronous Transfer Mode.)

With this blurring of the distinction between local and wide area networks will come an ever more pressing need for software-based security mechanisms. In former times, it was possible to rely on the physical isolation of networks to provide security. With increasing interconnectivity and seamless point-and-click access to information resources both inside and outside the corporation, however, security features like encryption and authentication will become more pervasive in commercial-grade Internet navigation applications.

Indeed, it appears that the commercial Web browser is heading toward becoming to the networked world what the GUI operating system (like MS Windows) is to the standalone desktop PC world.

9.2.2 Multimedia

The World Wide Web is already multimedia. It can support many applications protocols and presentation formats. The next phase of evolution will surely include the integration of real-time multimedia applications like video conferencing and animation. Indeed, the HTML 3.0 standard and certain Web browsers like *Netscape Navigator* today already support animation and other more dynamic interaction protocols.

9.2.2.1 Video Conferencing

Video teleconferencing with PCs has already made its debut on the Internet. Cornell University's CU-SeeMe program for Macintosh and PCs enables long-distance video conferencing over any TCP/IP internetwork. On the Internet, where bandwidth and thus response time are currently unpredictable, the quality of such videos can be lacking. The frame rate can be slow, yielding video reminiscent of the television pictures from space of the early astronauts.

On high-speed corporate backbones with more predictable bandwidth capacity at T-1 speeds or greater, however, the CU-SeeMe software provides quite adequate capability. CU-SeeMe conferences can go beyond point-to-point communications. They can also involve several dispersed sites in a single conference.

What is really attractive to businesses here is the affordability of this approach. With leased-lines already paid for at flat rates, companies stand to save in the ballpark of $300/hour, a nominal hourly rate for a multipoint video teleconference provided by a commercial telecommunications company. Naturally, the more a company relies on its leased line backbone to support video teleconferencing, the less available bandwidth will become, and it will have to invest in more leased lines. But the savings should be significant.

For more information on video conferencing products available on and for the Internet, check out the following Web site:

http://www2.ncsu.edu/eos/service/ece/project/succeed_info/dtvc_survey/products.html.

9.2.2.2 Audio

One of the more exciting applications to appear on the Internet recently is the Internet Phone (TM) made by VocalTec. The Internet Phone is a software product that enables Internet users to converse in half-duplex audio for the price of a local phone call.

With a 486 PC, a sound card, a microphone, and the Internet Phone software, you can engage in real-time voice conversations with people all over the world. To minimize the demands on the available bandwidth, VocalTec has employed voice compression and transfer technology.

Like video teleconferencing, real-time audio conversations will become more prevalent in the future. Together with software to enable the synchronous sharing of desktop applications, these two applications will make desktop collaboration and tele-collaboration an everyday occurrence in the work place.

9.2.3 Object Technology

Object technology relies on the paradigm of object-oriented design and programming. Central to this technology is the idea that data and closely-related functions are naturally "encapsulated" together in an object class. Also central is the notion of inheritance, which lets you derive new classes from old ones, inheriting all of the data and function properties and adding new ones. Objects are instances of classes. The result is a hierarchy of classes from which you can rapidly draw reusable objects to build new software applications.

On TCP/IP internetworks, most of the information exchanged comes in the form of specialized kinds of data files, such as text and HTML files. What object technology offers is the prospect of being able to exchange not just data, but objects, which encapsulate both data and functions.

A number of organizations are working on the problem of exchanging objects between heterogeneous platforms in a networked environment. Most notable among these is the Object Management Group (OMG), a consortium of independent software vendors (ISVs) and end users interested in the development and promotion of object technology. One of the key products of the OMG consortium is the Common Object Request Broker Architecture (CORBA). CORBA enables the exchange of object information in a heterogeneous networked environment. A number of companies have already implemented experimental software wrappers and agents which are CORBA-compliant. Software agents adhering to the CORBA standard are capable of interacting at a very high level, transferring not only data, but the knowledge of how to manipulate that data as well. What we are beginning to see here is exchange at the knowledge level.

The fundamental problem as seen by the OMG is that of application integration. At the applications level, we find software and data that are heterogeneous, networked, physically separated, and produced by multiple vendors. The CORBA approach to solving this problem goes beyond the Open Software Foundation's DCE (Distributed Computing Environment), because DCE operates a component level (remote procedure calls) below the application level. By providing a single view of a distributed, heterogeneous system, object technology offers reusability of components, interoperability, and portability. The goal is to achieve commercially available plug-and-play software components. Toward this end, the OMG has proposed a single set of terminology for object orientation, a common abstract framework, and common reference model, and common interfaces and protocols. To achieve its goals, the OMG seeks consensus among its members, who are largely third-party software vendors.

9.2.4 Network Technology

Network technology will continue to improve and the Internet will continue to take advantage of it. Further growth of the Internet requires improvements at all levels of the network hierarchy. We discuss in this subsection some of the evolutionary paths we see at the physical, datalink, network, and applications layers.

9.2.4.1 ATM and Sonet

ATM stands for Asynchronous Transfer Mode and is for many the packet switching network technology of tomorrow. Unlike Ethernet and the Internet Protocol, ATM uses fixed-length packets, known as "cells." Each cell is 53 bytes in length, 48 of which are actual payload data bytes, while the remaining 5 are overhead and control bytes. A key advantage of this fixed cell length is predictability—and hence control—of the quality of service.

Today's WAN technology uses the legacy of voice-oriented circuits. Ordinarily, a single voice channel can carry data at a rate of no more than 56 Kbps.[1] In order to achieve

---

[1] Although you can actually achieve 64 Kbps with ISDN, the T-carrier system reserves 8 bits for control purposes yielding an *effective* data rate of 56 Kbps.

higher speeds, the Bell T-carrier system multiplexes several channels together. For example, a T-1 line at 1.544 Mbps is really a collection of 24 of these 56 Kbps voice grade lines multiplexed together. A T-3 line multiplexes 28 T-1 lines together to produce a bandwidth of 45 Mbps. Thus, the T-carrier system ultimately relies on the underlying 56 Kbps constraints of the voice-grade system.

ATM, however, does limit data rates to multiples of 56 Kbps. A more continuous range of data rates are achievable and controllable. This makes ATM technology attractive for a wide range of multimedia applications. It also reduces the distinction between LAN and WAN.

In contrast with today's Internet protocols, ATM technology enables a more controlled allocation of bandwidth. With ATM, you can prioritize bandwidth allocation depending on need. For example, e-mail and newsgroup packets are not very time-critical; they are asynchronous, non-real-time communications. Using ATM, you could send these packets at a lower priority, only consuming bandwidth not consumed by higher priority, time-critical applications like video teleconferencing.

ATM also enables better control and accounting of data traffic. This may ultimately change the economics enjoyed by today's Internet users. With ATM, network providers may be able to implement more accurate chargeback schemes for network traffic.

Evolving hand-in-hand with ATM and in some ways providing an underlying enabling technology is the Synchronous Optical Network, or SONET standard. SONET is an international standard governing the transmission of optically encoded data over fiber optic lines. ATM technology integrates well with the SONET standard. Both will figure prominently in the future. Indeed there are many network providers today, especially the so-called Competitive Access Providers or CAPs, who have built their backbones on SONET and ATM.

9.2.4.2 IPng—Internet Protocol next generation

The lowest layer of networking infrastructure peculiar to the Internet is the Internet Protocol itself, generally referred to simply as IP. In the OSI hierarchy, IP resides at the network layer. Originally designed in the 1970s and modified up through version 4 in the 1980s, IP is not robust enough to handle the increasing demands on the Internet. It is incapable of handling the large numbers of hosts that will soon connect to the Internet. To meet the expanding requirements imposed by the explosive growth of the Internet, network scientists have submitted a number of proposals to the Internet Engineering Task Force (IETF). One such proposal is the IP version 6 (IPv6), sometimes referred to as IPng, for IP next generation.

As of this writing there is an Internet Draft outlining the proposed changes to be effected by IPv6. This draft proposes to improve upon IPv4 through introduction of the following changes:

- Expanded Address Space—IPv6 increases the IP address size from 4 to 16 bytes. This will support additional layers in the addressing hierarchy, greatly increasing the number of addressable hosts. It also introduces the concept of "anycast" addressing, which will allow you to send packets to a group of hosts.
- Header Simplification—IPv6 eliminates or makes optional some header fields seldom used in IPv4. This reduces the processing and bandwidth burdens associated with packet handling.
- Improved Support for Extensions and Options—IPv6 encoding of IP header options will enable more efficient forwarding of packets. They will also place fewer restrictions on the length of option fields and make it easier to extend IP options.
- Flow Control Labeling—This capability allows the user to specify minimal quality of service. IPv6 will label packets to identify them with specific traffic flows. With this enhancement, IPv6 should be able to handle real-time interaction across the Internet (assuming the intervening networks have the capacity required for this).
- Authentication and Privacy—IPv6 will support authentication, data integrity, and data confidentiality.

9.2.4.3 Application Protocols—Security

Security continues to be of vital concern to those who want to use the Internet for electronic commerce. In safe transactions, both the client and server must be able to authenticate each other. However, most current implementations of HTTP, the World Wide Web's HyperText Transfer Protocol, provide only modest support for the encryption required of secure transactions. One of the most promising recent developments, however, toward making the Internet safe for electronic commerce is the emergence of S-HTTP, a secure extension of HTTP.

Developed jointly by Enterprise Integration Technologies and the National Center for Supercomputing Applications, S-HTTP provides security services to ensure the confidentiality of Web transactions. It also ensures the authenticity, integrity, and non-repudiability of origin. In facilitating the negotiation of options among transacting parties, S-HTTP allows multiple key management schemes, security policies, and cryptographic algorithms.

The S-HTTP protocol is an add-on or extension to the underlying HTTP and treats clients and servers equally. The one exception to this has to do with public encryption key certification. Servers need public key certificates; clients do not.

Server implementations of S-HTTP are already in operation. One example is Secure NCSA *httpd*, developed by Enterprise Integration Technologies together with RSA Data Security and the National Center for Supercomputing Applications (NCSA) at the University of Illinois, Urbana-Champaign. You can find the draft protocol specification for S-HTTP at *http://www.eit.com/projects/s-http/shttp.txt*.

Secure Sockets Layer, or SSL, is another approach to Web security. The chief advantage of SSL is that it is independent of the applications protocol. This means that a higher level application protocol like HTTP, FTP, or TELNET can layer on top of the SSL protocol. Thus, unlike S-HTTP, SSL is not merely an extension of S-HTTP. Before the application protocol transmits or receives data, the SSL protocol negotiates the encryption algorithm, the session key, and authenticates the server.

The primary reference implementation of SSL is the commercial Netscape Commerce Server and is already in widespread use. For more information, consult Netscape at *http://www.netscape.com*.

9.2.5 Intelligent Information Technology—Tools to Help Master the Infoglut

We've mentioned already several times throughout the book that the growth of the Internet and, in particular, the World Wide Web, is exacerbating the problem of information overload. We believe this problem will give rise to some powerful, innovative technology to help users master the tide of infoglut. Whether designed for the large inland seas of internal corporate information or the vast outer oceans of the Internet, new tools will assist cyber-travelers on their voyages. In this section, we highlight some information technologies offering ways to manage, navigate, and tame this glut of information.

The following four areas show considerable promise:

- Intelligent Agents
- Data Mining
- Smart Bookmarking
- Intelligent Data Warehouses

The following four subsections deal with each of these topics in turn.

9.2.5.1 Intelligent Agents: Knowbots

Intelligent agents—also known as knowbots—are systems designed to ease the time-consuming and repetitive search and retrieval tasks associated with the Internet today. These agents are initialized by the user in an interactive session, but otherwise execute in the background and notify the user only if they find information items matching the user's previously given search directions. Theoretically, this frees up the user to devote attention to other matters besides searching for information.

The user endows an agent with "intelligence" by imparting knowledge of networked resources and characteristics of the desired information items. The agent then successively accesses the indicated resources through the internetwork independently of the user, collecting all relevant information items for later viewing by the user. In theory, this method of traversing the internetwork reduces workload and frees the user for other tasks. For repetitive searching tasks this approach works well. However, such agents sometimes dig up more information than is required, and the user is still faced with the task of sifting through piles of irrelevant information retrieved by the agent.

Nonetheless, the basic idea behind intelligent agents is praiseworthy, and as the worldwide collection of interlinked networks continues to grow exponentially, the need and demand for more capable agents will continue to grow as well. While the interactivity of Web browsers is currently still a novelty, to serious business users faced with the task of gathering key business data, this interactivity will lose its novelty and become tedious. Moreover, the number of distractions out on the Net can adversely affect the productivity of workers. Intelligent agents, on the other hand, are not tempted to surf the net for frivolous entertainment. Intelligent agent technology shows some promise, therefore, of being able to assist business users in the automation of otherwise very tedious and time-consuming searches.

We expect a new breed of intelligent agents to appear that will be able to "observe" and record the information search activities of users much in the same way that macro recorders work in spreadsheet programs.

9.2.5.2 Data Mining

Like intelligent agents, data mining springs from the research labs of artificial intelligence. It relies on both inductive and deductive reasoning techniques to unearth information patterns in large collections of information sources. Like agents, data-mining tools must first be initialized with a representation of the knowledge space to be built by the analyst. This includes *a priori* specification of relationships among data items. Data-mining engines are especially good at finding patterns in highly structured databases, such as relational databases.

One approach to data mining involves the formulation by the data analyst of an hypothesis concerning relationships purported to exist among the data. The data mining tool then examines the data and either supports or rejects the hypothesis. Based on this support or rejection, the analyst refines the original hypothesis, and the cycle of analysis begins anew.

We expect that data mining technologies will eventually find their way into search and retrieval engines handling less well-structured information repositories like full-text infobases. Today's full-text search and retrieval methods like WAIS, for example, are a good start toward making full-text information repositories searchable and accessible within a wide area environment. In most implementations, however, they still lack anything closely resembling data mining capabilities.

9.2.5.3 Smart Bookmarking—Local URL Databases

A common approach today to managing the infoglut on the Web is to ***bookmark*** the locations of interesting sites. This facilitates a rapid return to the site later. The result is a list of bookmarks or hotlists of favorite sites. However, as the number of Web sites continues to increase exponentially, even these bookmark lists can become unmanageable. We anticipate that Web browsers in the future will incorporate local search engines to hierarchically organize, index, and save URLs. In fact, we expect such local URL databases to include much more than just URLs. We expect they will include summary information as well. Perhaps the user will be able to highlight certain subsections of a Web page and tell the browser to store the URL along with the selected text in the local database. The user might also be able to add keywords and other annotations that will be stored alongside the URLs and copied text. This will provide more fields and keys with which to sort and retrieve URL records later. Such local URL databases may also be accessible to intelligent agents, which will automatically roam the Net looking for updates and the appearance of new sites similar to those contained in the local database.

9.2.5.4 Intelligent Data Warehouses or Virtual Knowledge Bases

TCP/IP internetworks, both inside and outside the corporate walls, support inherently distributed and decentralized collections of information resources. Although these internetworks provide users a low-level means to access information on a resource-by-resource basis, the resources often stand alone without any appreciable integration except as provided by hyperlinks on the front end at the user-interface level. Otherwise, the information servers are often not coupled in any significant fashion.

On the worldwide Internet with so many players and different charters and agendas, it is difficult to achieve a high-level of back-end integration. Interoperability of data communications and protocols is one thing, but integration of content is another. Within the corporate Internet clone, however, such integration is achievable because the owners of information are ostensibly subordinate to the single purpose of the single enterprise to which they belong. Thus, given the appropriate amount of authorization and incentive, information owners and server operators within the corporate environment can be enticed to cooperate and collaborate in building a cohesive and coherent information infrastructure with a unified look and feel.

Still, it would be desirable to have the back-end servers of information be capable of automatically updating each other and overarching directory services as new information is added to the system. This is where intelligent data warehouses and virtual knowledge bases come in.

Intelligent data warehouses and virtual knowledge bases provide users with access to largely heterogeneous information resources, yet give the look and feel of an integrated, centralized database. To some extent, World Wide Web technology is already an initial example of this. In the corporate environment, however, an overarching superstructure of value-added information and hyperlinks are needed in order for the information resource as a whole to be more than just a collection of loosely coupled repositories. Effective directories and search engines able to survey and scan all of the distributed repositories are needed. When endowed with inference engines, these overarching applications transform the distributed database or warehouse into a virtual knowledge base.

We see virtual knowledge bases as part of the next wave of development in internal distributed information systems. The current wave involves the development of corporate internal Webs of information employing World Wide Web technology for ease of integration and access. As more and more companies pass beyond this exploration phase, however, they will begin to realize the need to endow the interlinked whole with a more intelligent superstructure.

Chapter 10

WHEN ALL IS SAID AND DONE

We have discussed the process and technology for developing an Internet-based information system, an internal clone of Internet. We have noted the need to align that development with the enterprise mission and to comply with the constraints inherent in both the enterprise and the currently available Internet technologies. We have stressed the importance of integrating the Internet-based information system with existing legacy systems and the need to incorporate adequate security. We have presented some of the nuts and bolts of synthesizing the Internet clone, evaluating alternative designs, specifying and implementing the system, and handling day-to-day operations. Finally, we have glimpsed the future and speculated regarding technology changes likely to affect the evolution of both the Internet and its underlying technologies.

At this point you should be probably somewhat acquainted with the technologies, issues, and tasks associated with building an Internet clone. Now you must decide if developing such a system makes sense for you. This chapter should help you with that decision.

Admittedly, an Internet clone may be currently inappropriate for some enterprises, or perhaps inappropriate for some organizations within an enterprise. Smaller enterprises, for example, may have little present need for any kind of internal networking. Nevertheless, it is safe to conjecture that the trend toward interconnectivity with external trading partners and customers will continue to exert pressures on even small enterprises to establish external network connections. Moreover, small enterprises wanting to become large ones will inevitably recognize the need for implementing internal networks as well.

At this point, you should ask yourself some fundamental questions regarding your perceived need for an Internet-based information system. To assist you, we revisit some of the questions raised at the beginning of the book and which you can now probably better appreciate in light of the deeper understanding you have gained from reading the foregoing chapters. The following question is fundamental:

10.1 Is It Worth It?

Naturally, we think the answer to this question for many organizations is a resounding "yes!" Otherwise, we wouldn't have written the book! But we acknowledge that an Internet clone may not be appropriate for every organization, and that you might still be hesitant to build such a system.

One reason for being hesitant is that the Internet and its technologies are fast-moving targets. Their pace of evolution seems to indicate an underlying instability. You might argue that because of this explosive growth, it is too soon to cast your lot with any of the Internet technologies; they might become obsolete before you can install them in your system.

We respond to this exception by asserting that in today's Information Age, change is a fact of life. By adopting specific Internet technologies today, you are adopting not so much the specific technologies themselves, but the directions and trends they indicate. You are betting not so much on the tools, but on the methods and paradigms underlying these tools. In so doing you are advancing along the experience curve and putting yourself in a better position to adapt to each new generation of technology as it becomes available.

Naturally, there is every reason to be prudent when it comes to expending valuable resources. When Netscape Communications' Netsite Webserver software was first announced, it sold for over $20K a license. Within a few months of the original announcement, however, the price dropped by nearly an order of magnitude! So there is plenty of room for a wait-and-see attitude. But the time constants are now shorter than they used to be. Whereas traditional IS managers might be inclined to wait years before making new technology commitments, today's managers may be able to wait only a few months.

Apart from the value of advancing along the experience curve, the key issue revolves around your anticipated use of these technologies. The technologies are merely a means to an end. It is now time to focus once more on those ends. So the question of whether or not it is worth it for you to build an Internet clone translates into the following question:

10.1.1 Does an Internet Clone Make Sense for Your Organization?

To fully answer this question you should review your enterprise's mission and goals, bearing in mind the financial resources (i.e., the constraints) at your disposal. Will Internet technologies help your enterprise achieve its mission and goals? Or will their contributions be only marginal? In other words, will their benefits far outweigh their costs? We have already indicated that the direct, tangible costs of acquiring these technologies can be extremely low. But you may also incur substantial indirect, intangible costs for documentation, training, and maintenance not normally associated with turnkey commercial solutions. So what's the bang for the buck?

In order to adopt Internet technologies, you may have to make substantial investments in training your IS personnel. You have to ask yourself, then, if developing this expertise is consistent with your core competencies. Perhaps it makes more sense to outsource your pilot project to a competent team of information technologists and management professionals who can take an independent look at your organization, its mission and goals, and determine the mix of infrastructure, tools, and processes that is best for your enterprise.

10.1.2 Alternatives to Internet Technologies

There are plenty of alternatives to Internet technologies. Any number of large information technology companies will gladly sell you a turnkey, proprietary network solution complete with a vast array of routers, hosts, and applications software custom tailored for your organization—all for a price, of course! And that price may not just be up-front dollars. You may end up paying in the form of a long-term dependence on the vendor, and that long-term dependence may in turn translate into long-term costs.

Even if you hire external consultants to introduce open standards and TCP/IP internetworking into your organization, they may retain key knowledge and understanding of the as-built system. They may then be the only ones who can extend and maintain your system. This too may result in a dependency, perhaps not as detrimental as the single-vendor proprietary dependency mentioned in the previous paragraph, but nonetheless undesirable. Fortunately, you can mitigate the risk of such dependency by embracing open standards like TCP/IP. In principle, open standards allow you to operate and maintain your system while you draw on the resources of many independent, competing vendors.

Nevertheless, when it comes to documenting your system, whether built in-house or by external contractors, you should ensure that the documentation is complete, up-to-date, and in your possession. This will also reduce the risk of being held hostage by a single vendor.

10.2 Closing Remarks

Before closing we would like to review the important points made in the previous chapters.

The first point relates to acquiring and maintaining an organic and comprehensive view of designing and building an Internet clone. By this we mean simply that you should retain a broad perspective and approach an Internet-based information system well equipped with sound principles of systems engineering. Otherwise, you can become easily fascinated with the Internet and its technologies and lose sight of how you should integrate these tools into a whole system. The trees are indeed interesting, but they are not the forest.

We urge you to keep the strategic perspective in mind. Whatever you decide to do, you should align your goals with those of your enterprise. You should be aware of your constraints, whether technological, financial, or cultural. You should develop your system in an orderly way if you wish to retain the support of your key stakeholders, whether direct beneficiaries like end users, or ultimate beneficiaries like customers and owners.

It is also important to keep in mind some of the real challenges facing the builder of an Internet clone. We have stressed repeatedly the importance of implementing adequate security controls. We have also discussed at length the difficulties in building and maintaining an information system that is dependent on the collaborative efforts of many individual users and information providers. It is especially important and challenging to keep everybody synchronized and committed to keeping their information current. Unlike most traditional central databases, an Internet clone is not a centrally controlled information system. It is distributed, decentralized, and highly dependent on collaboration. It takes a continuous infusion of labor and oversight to ensure the coherence and reliability of both information content and delivery.

Finally, we recommend—even if you do not plan to build an Internet clone soon—that you keep your eye on the Internet, its underlying technologies and principles, and its evolution. The Internet represents the new frontier, the frontier of cyberspace; successful enterprises tomorrow will successfully establish a presence in and conduct commerce in this frontier. The principles of open networking, as illustrated by the TCP/IP protocol suite, form the bulwark of a new information paradigm that is radically transforming enterprises of all kinds. Enterprises need to stand up and take note.

We now conclude the book with a few paragraphs that underscore the importance of watching the development of the Internet.

10.2.1 The Internet

While there has been much ballyhoo and hype in the media surrounding the Information Superhighway and the National Information Infrastructure (NII), many have failed to realize that the Internet already ***is*** these things. Although some might argue that the Internet today is more like a collection of country roads than an interstate highway system, few would dispute that the so-called Information Superhighway or National Information Infrastructure of tomorrow will evolve out of today's Internet.

The following final paragraphs discuss this aspect of the Internet, namely that it is the de facto International Information Infrastructure (III), the forerunner of the Information Superhighway. We also discuss two other aspects of the Internet that we feel are important for enterprises of all kinds, especially businesses. These aspects are the Internet as a business resource and the Internet as a key enabler of virtual corporations.

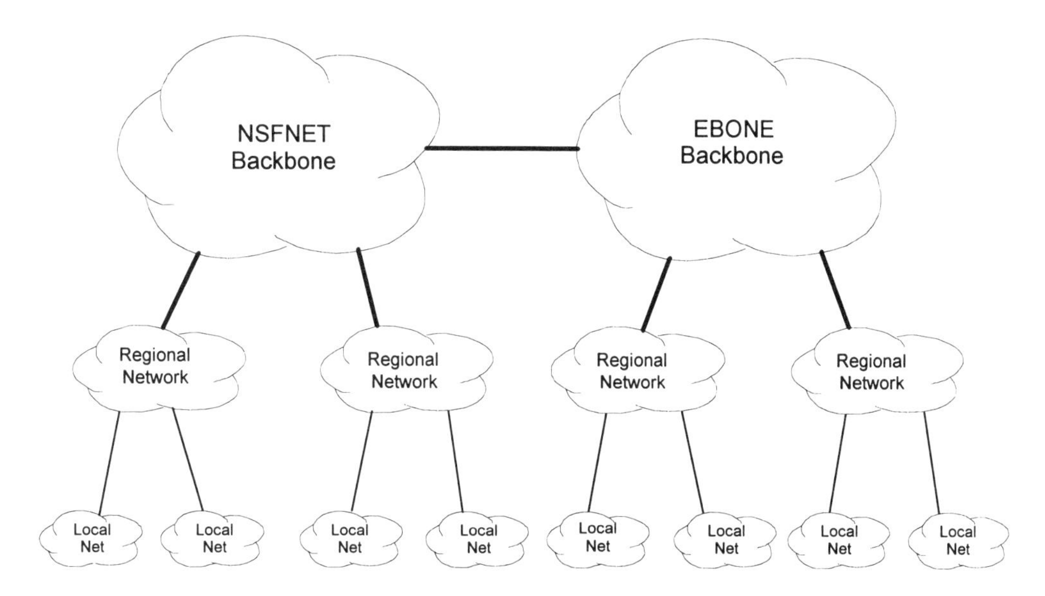

Figure 10-1. *NSFNET and EBONE: Similar Three-Level Hierarchies*

10.2.1.1 The De facto International Information Infrastructure

We previously alluded to the Internet as the de facto International Information Infrastructure. We will now explore this concept a little more fully and place emphasis on the word "International."

Many people not intimately familiar with its inner workings mistakenly identify the Internet with the government-subsidized NSFNET. While the NSFNET backbone is indeed a major system of high-speed links connecting several major regional networks, the Internet is much broader than the NSFNET and its associated feeder networks. There are important links, for example, between the NSFNET and the major European backbone known as the EBONE. In many ways, the EBONE is to the Internet in Europe what the NSFNET is to the Internet in the United States. For example, the EBONE, like the NSFNET, is at the top of a three-level hierarchical arrangement of networks, the lower two levels consisting of regional and local networks. The NSFNET connects to EBONE across the Atlantic by several T-1 wide area links. Figure 10-1 shows the relationship between the NSFNET and the EBONE.

Structurally similar to the NSFNET, the EBONE backbone is as much an integral part of the Internet as the NSFNET. Similarly, most major regional backbones throughout Europe and the United States connect either to the EBONE or the NSFNET. Thus the

Internet, made up of many networks located throughout the world, is a truly international information infrastructure.

Given the international nature of both the Internet and the world economy—and especially the openness of the TCP/IP protocol suite—it is difficult to see how a "National" Information Infrastructure can be patterned after the Internet without automatically becoming an "International" Information Infrastructure. To limit this infrastructure to the United States alone would require that firewalls be placed at the "borders," i.e., at the points of interconnection between the major American and foreign networks. Because it represents a step backwards in terms of openness, this approach, though technically feasible, is likely to fail. At best, certain individual networks and computational resources could be limited to promote the national economy. However, the open and convenient access it offers to international trading partners is for many businesses one of the Internet's main attractions. When given the option of trading in an open manner as they do today over the Internet, versus trading amongst themselves via a closed network to which only American companies have direct access, most businesses would opt for the Internet.

The Internet is already an international marketplace; you can't turn back the clock. With the horses already out of the barn, there is little value in closing the barn door! Or, to use another rural metaphor, "How ya gonna keep 'em down on the farm, once they've see Paree?"

Thus it appears unlikely that any attempt to build a closed *National* Information Infrastructure separate from the Internet will garner much support. And if it isn't separate from the Internet, it will be by definition a part of the Internet! That is why we maintain that the Internet is and will remain—perhaps in altered form—the de facto *International* Information Infrastructure.

10.2.1.2 A Business Resource

While infrastructure is nice, content is even nicer. Businesses today are flocking to the Internet not only because they can use it to interact with trading partners, but also because they can find on the Internet a wealth of useful resources. Besides valuable repositories like FTP archives of reusable freeware components, businesses have also discovered that they now have access to otherwise unaffordable computational resources like supercomputers. General purpose supercomputers can cost millions of dollars and are often too expensive for most small businesses, yet timeshare access to these gigaflop machines via the Internet is now an affordable option.

Since the end of the cold war, many high performance computing assets originally funded by the U.S. government have become available to commercial enterprises on a pay-per-use basis. Many Department of Energy laboratories like Argonne, Los Alamos, and the Idaho National Engineering Laboratory have supercomputers available for commercial use. Companies wishing to buy time on these large computers can connect to them through the

Internet. Indeed, one of the main functions of the NSFNET backbone is to connect the major U.S. supercomputing centers. Several prototype gigabit-per-second links connect these centers.[1]

Companies in the market to buy supercomputers can use the Internet to try before they buy. Many manufacturers like Cray Research, Convex, and Intel encourage prospective buyers to upload their codes via the Internet for trial benchmarking runs. The prospective buyers can then download the results for analysis and comparative evaluation.

10.2.1.3 Key Enabler of Virtual Enterprises

As the number of enterprises connecting to the Internet increases, we will see tighter coupling between partners' information systems. There will be more backward integration from major integrators toward their suppliers. We are already seeing this in the retail industry. Major department stores like Kmart and Wal-Mart have integrated portions of their inventory control systems with those of their major suppliers. Although most companies today conduct this sort of EDI primarily over private dedicated lines using proprietary protocols, the Internet will soon catch up and become the primary marketplace for electronic commerce.

Regardless of the trends toward forming virtual enterprises with external enterprises, you can still use Internet technologies like the World Wide Web to virtualize your internal organization. With these tools, you can enable and support customer/supplier relationships among departments, project teams, and functional organizations.

In conclusion, we would like to recommend that you give these technologies a try by initiating at least a small-scale pilot project. We think the experience you will gain from first-hand exposure to Internet technologies will spark your imagination and help you discover which applications are best for you and your organization.

---

[1] In contrast to the proposed National Information Infrastructure, this collection of high performance computing and communications assets could well serve as a national computational infrastructure available only to American firms.

REFERENCES

Elmer-Dewitt, Philip, 1994. "Battle for the Soul of the Internet." *Time*, 25 July , 50–56.

Estrada, Susan, 1993. *Connecting to the Internet.* O'Reilly & Associates.

Davenport, Thomas H., 1993. *Process Innovation: Reengineering Work through Information Technology*. Harvard Business School Press.

Davenport, Thomas H., 1994. "Saving IT's Soul: Human-Centered Information Management." *Harvard Business Review*, March-April, 23.

Dern, Daniel P., 1992. "Index Everything, Share it Company-Wide with WAIS." *MACWEEK*, October 26, 24.

Dern, Daniel P., 1994. *The Internet Guide for New Users*. McGraw-Hill, 391.

Hammer, Michael and Champy, James, 1993. *Reengineering the Corporation: A Manifesto for Business Revolution.* Harper Business, 84-87.

HPCWire, 1994. "IBM Client/Server Study Shows Culture/Organization Key to Success." *HPCwire*, June 14.

Hughes, Kevin, 1994. *Entering the World-Wide Web: A Guide to Cyberspace*, May, 5.

Kline, David, "The Day the Web Exploded." *HotWired,* August 1995, *http:www.hotwired.com/market/.*

Lewis, Peter H., 1994. "Doubts are Raised on Actual Number of Internet's Users." *New York Times*, August, A1.

Novak, Jeannie and Markiewicz, Pete, 1995. "Setting Up Shop: The Kaleidospace Experience." *Internet World*, January.

Quittner, Joshua, 1994. "Cracks in the Net", *Time*, February 27, Volume 145, No. 9.

Rechtin, Eberhardt, 1991. *Systems Architecting: Creating and Building Complex Systems.* Prentice-Hall.

Sherizen, Sanford, 1995. "Power & Protection", *Beyond Computing*, January/February, 51.

Tapscott, Don and Carston, Art, 1993. *Paradigm Shift: The New Promise of Information Technology,* McGraw-Hill, 23-25.

Appendix A

THE CLIENT/SERVER PARADIGM

The Internet is arguably the world's largest collection of client/server systems. To fully appreciate that assertion, you must understand the client/server paradigm. In this appendix we provide a brief overview of this paradigm for the benefit of those readers who may be somewhat unfamiliar with its major features.

A.1 Evolutionary Trends in Information Technology

The client/server paradigm is an approach to computing that distributes the computational load across multiple computers. It is one form of distributed computing. It represents a major shift in the history of computing, as we shall describe below.

A.1.1 From Master/Slave to Client/Server

Since the invention of the computer, the dominant computational model has been that of the centralized computer surrounded by "peripherals." As their name suggests, peripherals originally occupied the periphery of the system, primarily as human interface and data storage devices. They lacked computational capability and provided highly specialized functions. An appropriate description of this model would be "master/slave," the central computer being the master, the peripherals the slaves.

As computational components like microprocessors became less expensive, they began to proliferate. It became possible to distribute them across the whole computing system until the peripherals became more complex and more highly endowed with computational capability. Also, even in the early days of computing, researchers began experimenting with ways of making computers communicate and share data. By the time microprocessors became ubiquitous, sophisticated mechanisms like the Internet Protocol were already available for enabling data communication among computers. This hand-shaking between peer computers is at the heart of the "client/server" paradigm. In particular, one of the computers in a client/server interaction, the server, is passive in the sense that it waits for other computers, the clients, to issue processing requests. Quite often, though not exclusively, the client computers run human interface software, while the servers perform computational or data-fetching requests. Servers, of course, can behave like clients. They can issue requests to other servers in order to retrieve data or request computational services.

You should also recognize that the client and server programs do not have to execute on separate computers. You can separate them virtually by separate processes executing on the same multi-tasking operating system like UNIX or VAX/VMS.

A.1.2 Decoupling Data and Applications

Quite often the strategy for allocating functions between the client and the server involves the separation of the applications functions from the data storage and retrieval functions. The server in such cases becomes little more than a data server. The client, on the other hand, manages the user interface and often much of the required computation. This is typical of client/server implementations of database engines and file servers. The primary purpose of such servers is to provide data on demand. They do not manipulate or process the data in any significant way. The HTTP (HyperText Transfer Protocol) or Web server on the Internet is a prime example. It responds to client requests by reading an HTML (HyperText Markup Language) file and transmitting across a network to the client. Client software handles the processing required to format and present the data to the user.

A.1.3 Infrastructure Requirements

Although the client/server model does not require the use of a network, it is well matched for it. The evolution toward network-based computing reinforces the evolution of computing away from centralized mainframes toward distributed systems as exhibited in the client/server paradigm.

A.1.3.1 The Network is the System

Today the phrase "the network is the system" has become a rallying cry of network enthusiasts and proponents of open systems. Although we have heard this slogan often, some of us are slow to realize what it really means. Whereas in the past whole support organizations grew up around a mainframe computing center, today the focus is on the network. Unfortunately, for many companies this focus only translates into the addition of a few network specialists. Often these specialists understand only the lower levels of the layered network architecture and provide mostly hardware-oriented network troubleshooting support. You can call upon these professionals to install new versions of networked applications and configure each desktop machine accordingly, but you can seldom expect them to integrate applications at the higher levels of the layered architecture. Thus, applications tend to stand alone with little interaction.

What you need are system architects who can ensure that the network-as-system evolves in a cohesive fashion. Since many networks have come into being by piecing together formerly isolated platforms, they host very little truly integrated functionality. System architects, however, can supply the missing top-down, functional cohesion that we nearly always took for granted in the mainframe environment.

Like the heterogeneous platform legacy, the network legacy in many companies consists of several heterogeneous network islands with a great variety of incompatible data communications protocols, as we have discussed in the last section. The solution is not simply to continue piecing together a system out of these isolated networks, but to step back and perceive the network as a whole. However, at the level of infrastructure (i.e., those layers of the OSI—Open Systems Interconnect—network reference model below the application layer), there is one family of protocols in existence today that spans the OSI reference model from the applications to the transport layer and *has widespread implementation and third-party support*—and that is TCP/IP.

Therefore, any system architect who would achieve a high degree of integration across diverse platforms and applications and also achieve compatibility with the Internet, should give serious consideration to building a networked system on a foundation of TCP/IP.

A.1.3.2 The Layers of Infrastructure

To install Internet software tools like WAIS, USENET News, and *NCSA Mosaic*, certain layers of infrastructure must be in place. It is helpful to consider these infrastructure requirements in the context of the OSI reference model:

- Physical
- Datalink
- Network
- Transport
- Session
- Presentation
- Application

While the Internet tools we deal with in this book represent the upper application layer, the first four layers are the most important from the point of view of infrastructure.

A.1.3.2.1 The Physical Layer

This layer deals with the physical media used to transmit signals between network devices. For local area networks the most common media are twisted pair, coaxial, and fiber optic cables. For wide area networks, fiber optic media are the most common, although wireless media like satellite communications are becoming more common. Chances are your business already has some form of cable infrastructure, probably coaxial.

Coaxial cables consist of two layers of conductors separated by insulation and shielding. There are two types of coax cables for networks: baseband and broadband. Baseband coax uses a thinner inner core conductor and thinner shielding and insulation than broadband, resulting in higher sensitivity to noise. Baseband coax is also less capable in terms of maximum bandwidth achievable and number of devices it can support. It can support up to 100 devices at a bandwidth up to 50 Mbps, while broadband can support more than 1500 devices at a bandwidth up to 140 Mbps. Baseband cable is also more limited in length. Networks using baseband cabling are limited to less than 2 km, while those using broadband cabling can be as long as 15 km. Naturally, baseband is less expensive than broadband, earning itself the name "cheapernet." Many older Ethernet installations use a variety of coax called 10BaseT, or Thinwire coax.

Most LANs built using coax use one of two signaling protocols: token passing or carrier sense multiple access/collision detection (CSMA/CD). A token passing network is often built as a ring of devices. Each devices passes a token to the next adjacent device in a consistent direction. Each device, upon receiving the token, has the opportunity to append a message and retransmit the token plus message in the predefined direction. When the message finally arrives at its destination, the destination device reads and processes the data contained in the message. The token passes in this manner around the network and returns to the original device, which then strips off its message and begins the process anew.

CSMA/CD is called a contention-based protocol, because devices contend for control of the network by sensing the carrier signal and modulating it in amplitude, frequency or phase, and listening for contention from other devices. Most networks using this protocol are organized in a bus or passive star topology. Ethernet networks, based on the IEEE 802.3 standard, use CSMA/CD control protocol.

A.1.3.2.2 The Datalink Layer

This layer deals with communication between physically adjacent devices on a network. The collections of 1s and 0s transmitted from one device to its neighbor are called frames. Ethernet is the most common Datalink layer protocol. To install Internet tools on hosts connected by an Ethernet network, each host must have a Network Interface Unit (NIU) or Interface Message Processor (IMP). These are typically cards (sometimes called Network Interface Cards or NICs) installed in the computer's expansion slots. Thus, communication at the Datalink layer is essentially communication between these cards. The host computer, in turn, communicates with its own card.

Most companies build TCP/IP networking on a datalink layer of Ethernet. This protocol is almost always limited to a bandwidth of 10 Mbps. This is not a serious constraint for most current Internet-based applications. FTP and TELNET, for example, were designed with Ethernet in mind and function well within the Ethernet bandwidth regime.

Many emerging applications, however, have more voracious bandwidth appetites. Mosaic, the popular multimedia browser for the World Wide Web, can be very bandwidth-hungry, depending on the size of the information resources being accessed. Many World Wide Web hypertext documents incorporate graphics files, which can run easily into the megabyte region, depending on resolution and color. Accessing these files remotely can often take several seconds. Although this may not appear to be a problem now, it may become more of a problem once networks themselves become more congested with such traffic; what now takes only a few seconds may soon take a few minutes.

Worse still, in terms of bandwidth requirements, are video clips and interactive video teleconferencing sessions. To download a video clip that takes only a few seconds to play can take several minutes. That is an overhead factor that may be unacceptable to many business users.

Of course, we expect the general bandwidth situation to improve with time. Bandwidth supply will undoubtedly follow demand. The point we are making, however, is that current bandwidth limitations, both internal and external to your system, constitute an important consideration in designing an Internet-based information system. If you happen to be fortunate enough to have the opportunity to lay out a whole new network infrastructure based on tomorrow's needs, the constraints of yesteryear's networks will not present any problem; but if you are not so fortunate, you may have to employ network management policies and controls to keep your network traffic flowing at a rate equitable for most of your users. The bandwidth constraints are real and you should face them.

A.1.3.2.3 The Network Layer

At this layer we begin to talk about peer-to-peer communication between hosts, albeit at a low level. Software running on each host computer accomplishes this communication. This software translates network layer protocols into Datalink layer frames and vice versa. In the Internet or TCP/IP family of protocols, this is where the Internet Protocol, or IP, comes in. IP stands for "Internet Protocol" and is responsible for routing of data among hosts. IP organizes data into "packets," and software operating at this layer is sometimes referred to as "packet driver software."

A.1.3.2.4 The Transport Layer

The transport layer deals with reliable, end-to-end transport between user processes running on host machines. For Internet software this is TCP, the Transmission Control Protocol. Other protocols are UDP (User Datagram Protocol—also in the Internet family) and PEX (Packet Exchange Protocol from Xerox). On most UNIX machines, both TCP and IP communications software are standard. On PCs, some packet drivers implement both TCP and IP; the applications program needs only to communicate with this packet driver software.

These first four layers of the OSI reference model are essential aspects of the underlying infrastructure. To execute a pilot project aimed at exploring Internet tools and methods, you must examine your current infrastructure to determine compatibility with TCP/IP, the heart of the Internet infrastructure. You must also take into account the hardware platforms and operating systems you plan to use. You may have to lay cable, purchase and install Ethernet cards and driver software, and finally install the relevant applications. For a minimal system, you could try connecting two 486 PCs, one running as a server using Linux, a public domain version of UNIX, the other running as a client under DOS or MS-Windows. Of course, it will be helpful to have at least dial-up access to the Internet, in order download the appropriate software. This minimal client/server configuration is very inexpensive and offers a good first introduction to TCP/IP client/server computing and Internet applications. It provides a good testbed for evaluating which applications are of value to you and your enterprise. With Linux, you can also gain some experience with UNIX without investing in a new workstation. Figure A-1 provides a block diagram of such a minimal system.

A.1.3.3 The Need for Tools

Frequently, one hears network designers and managers complain about the lack of good tools for designing, managing, and monitoring the performance of their networks.

Client/server networks are inherently complex systems. They have many interacting pieces, many single points of failure, and can have many potential bottlenecks. Because of this, we advise serious network builders to acquire adequate network design and performance simulation tools. For a small pilot project this may not be necessary, but for large-scale deployment it is a must. Such tools provide visibility into expected availability and reliability, and identify chokepoints. They can also alert you regarding potential over- and under-capacity in the system.

Whether you are building a full-scale or just a pilot system, you should monitor the performance of your system. In the former case, performance modeling is necessary to keep

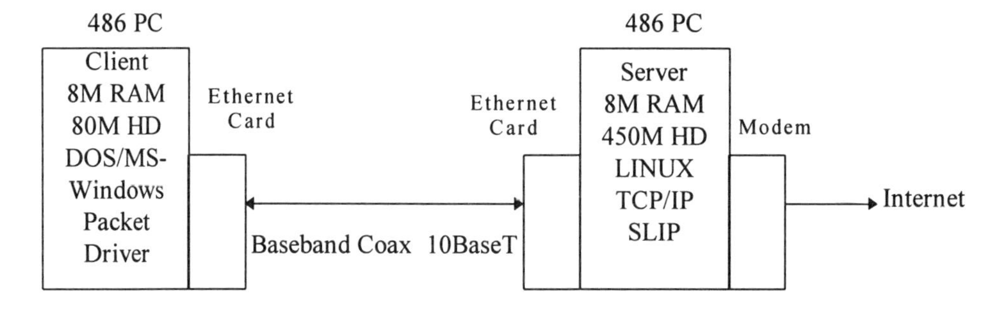

***Figure A-1**. Minimal TCP/IP System Configuration*

your system running. In the latter, it can provide valuable data to guide you during full-scale implementation. Utilization trends are especially helpful in selling the Internet-based concepts to upper management. By showing executives that there is growing user interest in the tools and information sources, you can help justify the added expense in going to a full-scale system. On the other hand, underutilized tools and sources will tell you what not to waste your money and time on.

A.1.4 Typical Client/Server Flow of Communication

Figure A-2 on the next page shows a typical flow of communication between the client and server processes. It uses the terminology of the Berkeley Standard Distribution version of UNIX. The term "socket," for example, means a logical endpoint for network communications. A socket is created at the client endpoint and also at the server endpoint. In the flow depicted in Figure A-2, the server process must first create a socket to which the client process will attach through its socket. Thus, the server socket must exist before the client socket. After the initial handshaking required to establish communication, the two programs communicate through their respective sockets using read and write calls much as they would to local files.

A.2 Organizational Trends—From Individuals to Workgroups

Coinciding with and to some extent enabled by the trend toward client/server computing is the trend toward workgroup computing. This is already fairly obvious to those who have experienced workplaces using local area networks. With the rise in the deployment and use of wide area networks, however, new vistas for virtual collocation have opened up.

A.2.1 Integrated Product Development

Integrated product development and concurrent engineering are fairly recent attempts to integrate functional disciplines involved in the development of products. The emphasis here is to avoid the traditional approach to development which involves passing work products down a pipeline from one functional discipline to another. To shorten development cycle times and hence time to market, many forward-thinking companies are using integrated product development techniques. These techniques bring together several disciplines during the early stages of product development. Naturally, when you have many players involved in the development of anything, you need reliable and complete communications. And since the required experts may work in different parts of the world, it is natural to look to wide area networks as a means to foster communications between such widely dispersed resources.

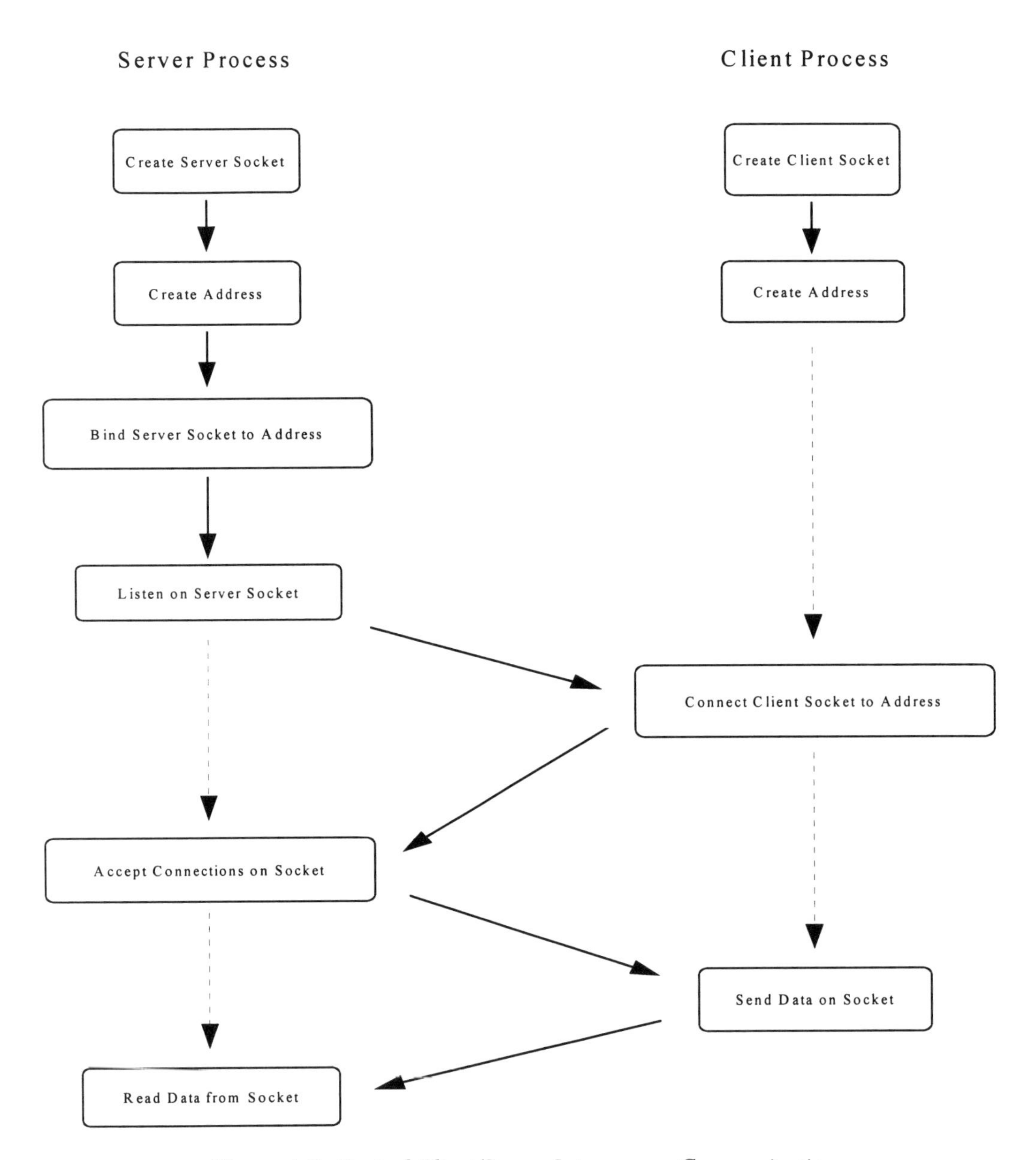

Figure A-2. *Typical Client/Server Interprocess Communication*

Client/server technology is a good match for integrated product development teams because the functional allocation—like the expertise—is distributed. Mechanical engineers can have their own specialized, high-end graphics workstations and yet share their computer-aided design information with manufacturing engineers who work thousands of miles away near the machinery on the shop floor. High-speed wide area networks make this kind of data sharing possible. Publicly accessible networks like the Internet make such sharing possible not only between teammates working for the same company, but also between teammates working at completely different companies.

A.2.2 The Key Role of Process

In order to effectively use client/server technology to help enable integrated product development, it is crucial that effective processes be designed to facilitate the communication and flow of information between IPD team members. Technology by itself will accomplish nothing. Without adequate processes to integrate the operations of diverse functional disciplines and take advantage of network-based computing assets, those assets will remain islands of information.

A.2.3 Empowering End Users

The whole idea behind effective implementation of client/server technology is the productive empowerment of end users. Empowerment, however, involves more than just handing individual users powerful information technology. It involves extensive training so that end users are aware of their capabilities and responsibilities.

In a year-long study of corporate client/server projects, IBM concluded that the success of client/server implementations hinges on the proper balance of organizational culture and process. According to Mike Sinneck, vice-president, Application Solutions Consulting, IBM Consulting Group, "There is nothing magical about client/server. Its ultimate appeal lies in increased user involvement and more adaptive solutions which facilitate rapid business changes and enable business reengineering processes. The key is to turn this appeal into real measurable business value."[1]

---

[1] "IBM Client/Server Study Shows Culture/Organization Key to Success," News Brief, HPCwire, 14 June 1995.

Appendix B

PLANNING AND EXECUTING AN INTERNET PILOT PROJECT

B.1 Planning the Pilot Project: Preliminary Considerations

The first step in planning a pilot project is determining whether one is even necessary. The criticality of this preliminary go/no-go decision increases with the size of the proposed project. To determine if a pilot project is even necessary, you should analyze your current enterprise situation in light of your business objectives. If you have valid concerns about how well your present information systems support your objectives, then we recommend you consider embarking on a pilot project.

This appendix should acquaint you with some of the primary considerations and steps in planning an Internet pilot project. While much of the advice here is generally applicable to any kind of project, we apply it to the specifics of building an Internet-based information system. We lean heavily on the tried and tested principles of systems engineering and project management.

B.1.1 Introduction: Requirements Analysis and Specification

This section provides a brief introduction to the systems engineering methodology. We do not pretend to cover all tasks and methods used in systems engineering. This methodology has provided the organizing principle for the book. The remainder of this appendix deals with the most important aspects of systems engineering: determining what problems your system will help solve. In other words, before you gallop off into the sunset ready to build the world's greatest clone of the Internet, you should ask yourself how, or even if, such a beast will help solve some of the information-related problems hindering your enterprise from being the best it can be in a competitive world. Naturally, to make that determination, you have to spend a considerable amount of time and effort in understanding the goals of your enterprise and how Internet technologies relate to these goals. Accordingly, the later sections of this appendix will focus on these issues.

B.1.1.1 Systems Engineering Methodology

The discipline of systems engineering grew up primarily during the 1950s and 1960s as a result of programs aimed at developing some of the most complex systems ever conceived. These included the ICBM (InterContinental Ballistic Missile), satellite, aircraft, and the Apollo lunar mission programs. Companies like Lockheed, TRW, Hughes, and Rockwell were pioneers in developing and applying systems engineering techniques to the development of these highly complex systems.

In the traditional systems engineering methodology, we focus on the following main activities:

- Developing and Analyzing Goals
- Discovering and Understanding Constraints
- Developing Alternatives
- Generating Representations
- Implementing the Solution

This represents the logical flow of systems engineering activities in developing a system. The goal phase considers the particular ends the system will serve. During this phase, the systems engineer tries to understand the problems to be remedied by the system, how those problems are currently solved, and what objective measures or metrics would be suitable for determining whether goals are met.

The second phase involves analysis of constraints. Constraints, unlike goals, are not desired for their own sake. They are facts of life that limit the means at your disposal for achieving your goals. They may be financial, technical, physical, cultural, political, or psychological. Constraints analysis flushes out the constraints affecting the design of the system. We can subsume both goals and constraints under the general heading of requirements.

An important part of the first two phases of requirements engineering is the specification of a functional architecture. It is here that you identify the major functions of the system. You then group these functions into logically related aggregates, and you analyze or decompose them into subfunctions. You should also identify, analyze, and document all logical or functional interfaces between functions and groups of functions. The resulting collection of functions and functional interfaces represents the functional architecture of the system. The functional architecture should be valid independent of any physical implementations. It forms the functional baseline or framework against which you should consider all candidate physical architectures.

The third phase involves the process of synthesizing alternative conceptual solutions to the problem defined by the goals and constraints. It takes into account available technologies and translates functional interfaces into physical ones. Here the constraints—especially budget and schedule constraints—play a significant role, as they determine to a large extent what is feasible.

An important part of the alternatives phase is the evaluation of various candidate physical architectures. It is desirable to select the architecture which optimizes the attainment of goals subject to all the constraints.

After selecting an optimal physical architecture, you must now specify the system in sufficient detail to allow its construction. This is the representations phase. For a vehicle, for example, this means turning loose the mechanical and electrical designers on their CAD workstations, so that they can produce detailed drawings of the system. This phase covers the translation of the functional and physical architecture into representations. Using these representations, the implementation team can actually construct the system.

The solutions phase is simply that in which the actual building takes place.

Though there are still other phases (business development, deployment, and disposal, for example) that are integral to the whole systems engineering methodology, the phases we mention here represent the heart of this methodology. We also note that this model does not imply a strict waterfall timeline of project phases. It represents techniques that are iteratively applicable in all phases. Thus, the evaluation of alternatives may well continue into the solutions or manufacturing phase. For example, you may discover during this phase previously unknown feasibility constraints impeding the original solution. New trade-offs may be necessary to resolve this situation. You perform these trade-offs using the techniques of the alternatives phase.

B.1.1.2 Analyzing Goals and Constraints

Perhaps the most important task of the systems engineer is to analyze and achieve an understanding of the goals and constraints affecting the system. It is here that you make the most serious blunders. Decisions made here have the greatest impact on the life-cycle cost and performance of the system.

You must thoroughly understand your system goals within the context of your overall business goals. It makes no sense to build an Internet clone, for example, without tracing its purpose to some clearly measurable enterprise objectives. We have personally experienced the evolution of an Internet-based information system that took on the character of a grassroots, bottom-up approach that sometimes lost sight of the overarching business objectives. The gap between clearly perceptible business objectives and the goals of the system was obvious. At one point, when we briefed the CEO on the status of the system and gave him a demonstration using *NCSA Mosaic* and other tools, he commented that, while the technology framework looked good, the information content was marginal and the organization of the information appeared haphazard. In our fascination with and effort to get the delivery mechanisms up and running, we failed to pay enough attention to content and organization. This is one of the potential weaknesses of an Internet clone, and it is directly related to the distributed, collaborative nature of the system. The data owners have to make firm commitments to imbue the system with quality information, to keep the information well organized and current.

Although this theme recurs throughout the book, it bears repeating. Content and organization comprise one of the primary issues of an Internet clone within a business enterprise. These two items, together with high quality, easy-to-use information access and delivery mechanisms, are pivotal.

B.1.1.3 Trading Off Requirements

Sometimes you simply cannot meet your goals. Sometimes new constraints surface which invalidate goals. As time marches on, budget, schedule, and technology constraints can change. Given this environment of change, the systems engineer must be constantly ready to trade off requirements. This means prioritizing goals, distinguishing between must-haves and nice-to-haves, and reworking both the functional and physical architectures as the situation changes.

B.1.1.4 Documenting the Requirements

Documenting the requirements is crucial in a complex project involving many people. Requirements documents express the goals and constraints of the project and help keep project personnel in synch regarding project objectives. Without adequate documentation in this area, the project is likely to fail. Without a consistent and well-documented set of requirements, it is very easy for designers, hardware and software engineers to get off track and go down blind alleys.

B.1.2 Goal Determination: Inductive and Deductive Approaches

A common criticism of the use of information technology in the business environment is that they represent technology push instead of market pull. This means that technically inclined persons might be prone to fall in love with the latest software, hardware tools, and gadgets, and look around for problems to solve with their pet solutions. This results in putting the cart before the horse, and is one of the major reasons why one tends to hear from upper management the rhetorical question, “If it’s not broken, why fix it?”

While managers have a right to ask this question, they should also realize that new technologies, especially information technologies, have a way of making us aware of "problems" we never knew we had before. Sometimes they stimulate the imagination into discovering new opportunities. The fixation on problems to be solved can be the result of a reactive management attitude. The willingness to be open to new opportunities represents a proactive attitude. Many management theorists today recognize that you should supplement problem solving skills with skills for discovering and taking proactive advantage of opportunities.

Hammer and Champy (1993) distinguish two approaches to using information technology: inductive and deductive. The inductive approach is associated with the proactive attitude we have just mentioned, because it is concerned with discovering how information technology can help us to break traditional rules of business and solve previously unperceived problems. In fact, many previously "unperceived" problems may well have been perceived, but not as problems! The inductive approach thus helps us to seize opportunities.

The deductive approach, by contrast, focuses on first identifying problems. This approach is implicit in the systems engineering methodology we have advocated and followed throughout the book. That does not mean that we are not in favor of the inductive approach. On the contrary, we believe that the inductive approach is highly applicable to discovering new uses for Internet technologies. That is precisely why we advocate them, even at the risk of looking like we are proposing a solution before knowing what the problem is!

What you need, of course, is a balanced approach that leaves room for both deductive/reactive and inductive/proactive attitudes. Another way of looking at this is to say that you need a balance between top-down and bottom-up perspectives. We are convinced that the systems engineering methodology represents not only a discipline for pursuing a top-down development, but also a discipline for stimulating—yet channeling—bottom-up, inductive thinking. The discipline itself stimulates and harnesses creativity.

B.1.3 Business Environment

In order for the inductive approach to remain focused on and traceable back to the goals of the enterprise, it is important to consider the environment in which your enterprise finds itself. Although the techniques for so doing are little more than the application of standard principles of strategic management, we have found that many information technologists and lower level IS managers are not familiar with these principles. Therefore, we present some of them here for reference.

B.1.3.1 The Enterprise Mission

Most businesses today have mission statements emanating from the top. They are often broad statements of the vision the chief executive has for the enterprise. What is often missing, however, are subordinate mission statements from those reporting to the chief executive. In many U.S. firms there is a serious lack of alignment between top-level mission statements and subordinate ones. There is also often a lack of traceability from the objectives back to the mission statement.

Nevertheless, the builder of an Internet clone would do well to ponder his or her enterprise's mission statement and determine how to translate the corporate vision into clearly measurable objectives to be met in part by the Internet-based information system.

Usually, the mission statement includes some reference to the key stakeholders in the enterprise. We know of no mission statement that does not seek to maximize the benefits accruing to these stakeholders. Naturally, customers are preeminent among stakeholders, and we now turn to a consideration of them.

B.1.3.2 Customers and Suppliers Inside and Out

The external customers for your enterprise's products and services form the marketplace context or business environment surrounding your enterprise. Without external customers you don't have a business. Therefore, these customers are the ultimate beneficiaries of the Internet clone you intend to build. Therefore, you have to ask yourself: How will your customers benefit from this system? Will they be able to access important information about your products and services via the Internet? If so, you need to interface with the Internet and that means integrating Internet technologies with your existing information systems. It also means appropriate security, since you quite likely possess sensitive data that are inappropriate for outsiders. Through the Internet you will project an image to the Internet-using community. Will the message conveyed by that image imply that you are Internet savvy or total Internet oafs? What kinds of information do you want to make available? Are you going to make information available to outsiders but not to your own internal stakeholders?

This last question leads to a consideration of internal customers. Nearly every enterprise has multiple internal customer/supplier relationships. Management, for example, is a customer of the accounting department when it comes to "consuming" financial reports. Manufacturing "consumes" engineering drawings of products to be built. Marketing needs to receive engineering data in order to know when new features are likely to be available in products and services downstream. Engineering should be a customer of marketing for market intelligence data. You should strive to use information technology to support, strengthen, facilitate, and improve internal customer/supplier relationships. How do you disseminate information now? Can you improve such dissemination by using Internet technologies? If so, then how?

Returning to external relationships, let us look at how suppliers can benefit from Internet-based technologies. Are your suppliers using the Internet at all? If so, how can you integrate your information systems using Internet technologies to make relationships with suppliers more effective? Can you give your suppliers access to some of your internal inventory databases using Mosaic, or WAIS, for example?

B.1.3.3 Threats and Opportunities

Strategic planners know that they must continually assess their external environment. The analysis of current and potential customer and supplier relationships is part of that assessment. Given this backdrop of customers and suppliers, you should assess the environment in terms of specific threats and opportunities.

An external threat is any entity or collusion of events in the outside world that can have an adverse effect on your organization. The most obvious ones are economic. A business enterprise, for example, is an economic entity that lives or dies by its ability to transform external needs into economic gain. There are many potential economic threats. Competitors are one. Government regulators are another. Dwindling demand for one's products and services, regardless of competitors, is a serious threat.

To put the assessment of external threats in the context of building an Internet clone, you should consider how your competitors are using information technology. Are they using it more effectively than you are? Perhaps your customers are using costly proprietary systems to disseminate information internally. Can you achieve the same functionality as your competitors more inexpensively using Internet technologies? Or, thinking inductively, what problems are so ubiquitous that neither you nor your competitors are even aware of them?

Inductive thinking leads us to consider the other major category associated with external assessment: opportunities. Opportunities abound when it comes to linking up electronically with customers and suppliers, and the Internet itself offers the most obvious opportunity associated with Internet technologies.

The Internet is growing at roughly 10 percent a month, and some estimate its user population at 25 million. Although one can quibble over the exact figures, the trend is clear. The Internet is growing at an almost exponential rate. This trend indicates that the Internet is a fast accumulating collection of potential customers and a rapidly developing communications medium for trading partners. As such, it presents many opportunities for many kinds of enterprises.

Naturally, this growth cannot continue indefinitely. What we are seeing most likely is the sharp incline of an incipient S-curve. An S-curve is exponential in the beginning, more linear during midcourse, and then flattened out at saturation. Many innovative technologies and whole industries exhibit this kind of life-cycle growth and decay pattern. Strategic managers familiar with this pattern will be quick to recognize that the Internet and Internet technologies are near the beginning of an S-curve which marks the beginning of opportunity. Figure B-1 shows a sample S-curve.

Some predict that the Internet growth S-curve will taper off towards its asymptote during the next decade, as the number of Internet hosts approaches the number of people on the face of the earth. But it is misleading to identify IP addresses with people. Hosts are generally computers. Some hosts may support many interactive human users while some may be embedded computers not supporting any humans (not directly, at any rate). The time may come when computers managing vehicle maintenance data under the hood of your car are assigned IP addresses so that they can communicate via satellite links to service computers at your favorite service center. Indeed, there is reportedly already one coffee pot

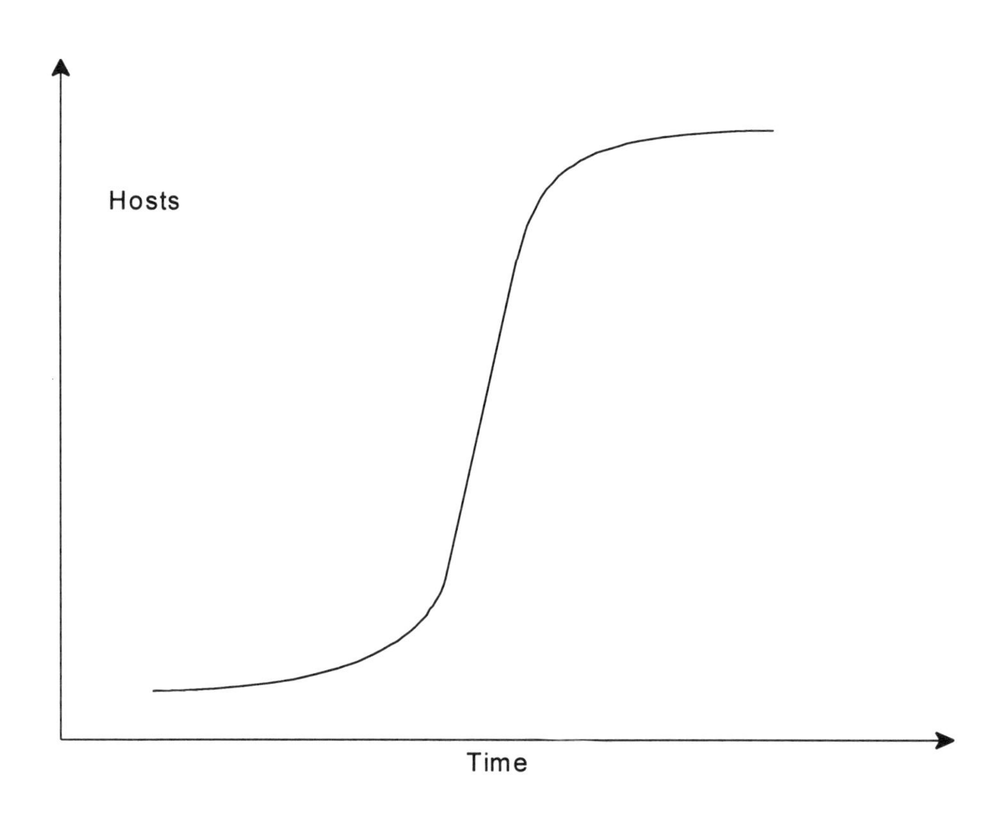

Figure B-1. *Notional S-Curve of Internet Growth*

on the Internet that has an IP address! This trend seems to be unbounded.

The opportunities of the Internet—to interact electronically with global trading partners, to access one-of-a-kind computational resources like supercomputers, to plumb the depths of huge information storehouses—should be prime motivators in building an Internet clone. Which of these opportunities are most important for your business depends on the particular nature of your enterprise. To determine your needs you should consider your core competencies.

B.1.3.4 Core Competencies (and Incompetencies)

Core competencies are those internal strengths that give your enterprise its distinctive competitive advantage over similar competing enterprises. They are what you know how to do well. They relate to your internal base of knowledge and skills. They provide your products and services with unique features not provided by your competitors, but they are not limited only to products and services. You might have particular competence in customer service or marketing or in strategic planning.

You should evaluate Internet technologies and information systems using these technologies in terms of how they contribute to strengthening your core competencies. You should also consider how they can help you develop new, previously unimagined competencies. This is the inductive approach we mentioned before. In Chapter 1, we discussed a hypothetical corporation using the World Wide Web paradigm to automate and better organize its weekly status reporting system. In so doing, this corporation discovered that it had developed a core competency in internal communications. It also discovered that it could save money by helping its offices to become more paperless. With rapid and effective internal communications, this corporation was better able to respond faster to both internal crises and external opportunities and gain market share over its competitors; it was able to respond faster to changing market conditions by quickly disseminating market-related information to all internal stakeholders.

Another key strategic consideration of interest to the builders of Internet clones is that of enterprise weaknesses, or what we like to call core incompetencies. We don't like to talk about weaknesses, probably because often our organizations reward us only for being strong, not for being weak. So we tend to disregard our weaknesses and sweep them under the rug. We also don't talk about them because it costs money, effort, and resources to remedy them—all scarce commodities in lean times.

Yet internal weaknesses are really opportunities. The forward-thinking CEO of our hypothetical corporation was motivated to consider using a GUI Web browser like *NCSA Mosaic* and the World Wide Web to improve internal communications, because she was fed up with the time lag in obtaining status and historical information. The previous, paper-dominated status reporting system was a real sore point, a real core incompetency. With the new system, the flow of information was now horizontal, not just up the chain. Employees at all ends of the hierarchy could access everyone else's status reports and keep abreast of the latest important happenings across the whole corporation. Morale improved as employees no longer felt they were in the dark.

Strengths and weaknesses bear fruit most conspicuously in the products and services produced by your organization. To determine if Internet technologies can assist in the delivery of quality products and services to your customers, you should analyze the flow of information that accompanies the development of those products or services. This focuses once again on the internal customer/supplier relationships, since there are usually producers and consumers of information at every step of product or service development. How can Internet technologies bolster the strengths and eliminate the weaknesses associated with this flow of information?

B.1.3.5 Processes and Process Re-Engineering

In analyzing the flow of information associated with the creation of products and services, we are considering just one aspect of the whole product or service creation process. This process will naturally reflect to some extent the information technology available when the process was designed. They may reflect information technology long since antiquated. Although there is some value (often only marginal) in inserting new information technology into an existing legacy process, you can achieve significant value when you conceive and enact new processes in light of new information technology. Process re-engineering goes hand in hand with new information technology.

B.1.3.5.1 Translating Mission into Day-to-Day Operations

The processes of an enterprise translate the enterprise mission into day-to-day operations. They combine supplies and knowledge into items of value for customers. Processes should be product-driven, products should be mission-driven, and missions should be customer-driven. Because of the key roles played by processes within the enterprise, Internet clone builders should give prime consideration to the potential enabling role to be played by the Internet technologies.

B.1.3.5.2 Information Technology: An Inductive Catalyst

Hammer and Champy have noted at length the enabling role played in process re-engineering by information technology. We noted above their distinction between inductive and deductive approaches to using information technology. Here we wish to dwell in particular on the inductive catalytic nature of Internet information technologies.

Collocation—Virtual and Otherwise. Many enterprises have discovered the virtues of integrated product developing involving multi-disciplinary teams. This means all disciplines—business development, engineering, purchasing, and manufacturing, for example—associated with the development of a given product are being collocated and integrated into product development teams. With the advent of information technology like groupware, these teams do not necessarily need to be physically collocated—they can be virtually collocated.

An ideal workstation for virtual collocation would include the capabilities for video teleconferencing, electronic whiteboarding and bulletinboarding, e-mail, and file sharing. You can now purchase such workstations for less than $5,000.

You can record video teleconferences and save them on HTTP file servers. You can make these conferences available to the whole team for later review. You can review the decisions and commitments made at virtual meetings at any time by pointing and clicking a mouse. Although the video-related technologies associated with the Internet are still fairly primitive, they are rapidly improving. Using an HTTP server, for example, you can not only make the VTC archives available to the whole team, but you can also annotate these virtual meetings with value-added comments, related files, document references, and so forth. Once again, a Web browser like *NCSA Mosaic* can serve as a significant integrator.

Organizational Memory. This is a term referring to the retention of information and knowledge specific to the organization's core competencies. It contains the trail of decisions associated with all aspects of the enterprise's operations.

There are two key issues associated with such memory: storage and retrieval. If the storage process for retaining corporate memory is cumbersome and a nuisance, people will ignore it and not use it—to the detriment of posterity. They will lose the trail of decisions.

The other issue is retrieval. If the retrieval process is time-consuming and inefficient, nobody will use it. Again, they will lose corporate memory.

Most paper-based records retention centers are inefficient in both storing and retrieving. Image processing systems are not much better, in our opinion, because they are wasteful of electronic storage, and the process of scanning documents is labor-intensive and slow. Furthermore, graphic images are not amenable to searching. On all of these scores, multimedia documents are superior. You can rapidly index and search the text components of multimedia documents. Provided you keep these documents on shared media like file servers, you can automate their indexing and archival.

In our hypothetical corporation, the CIO, not wanting to be upstaged by the CEO, decided that he would take steps to automate the corporate records retention system. To do this, he mandated that all authors store their internal memos on file servers and have them indexed by WAIS. Since there were multiple word processing formats, he had to have his programmers write scripts to recognize the various formats and prepare them, if necessary, for input to the WAIS indexer. He also mandated that authors of important documents like management policies generate them in HTML and make them available using the internal corporate web servers. When new versions of the documents superseded older ones, system administrators archived the older versions using WAIS. Both documents and memos were now retrievable using search terms and a WAIS client.

The previous process involved sending paper documents and memos to a central warehouse repository. The only items indexed were the title, author, and date. It was a very slow, manual process. Employees gave this central repository the nickname "the black hole," because few documents going into the repository ever came out. Searching was very slow and inefficient. Few people even bothered trying to retrieve records from the black hole.

With the new system, all documents and memos were just a few mouse clicks away. More importantly, the search engine helped employees find the right information without spending an inordinate amount of time wading through infoglut.

B.2 Executing the Pilot Project: A List of Tasks

This section contains a brief description of the major tasks required in building an Internet clone. The order in which we present them roughly matches the order in which we think you should execute them.

B.2.1 Assemble Project Management Team

The project should have at least one person designated as project manager. This person should be accountable for the success or failure of the project and be empowered to succeed with adequate budget and tasking authority. Depending on the size of the project, the project manager should engage a team consisting of a chief architect or chief systems engineer, and representatives from the major stakeholder groups. If the Internet clone is going to span multiple divisions separated geographically, it is a good idea to have a steering committee that meets every few months to review progress.

One of the team's first activities is a kick-off meeting. Here they present an overview of the project's scope and duration. Naturally, without first accomplishing the next task, requirements engineering, you will not be able to report much about the details of the proposed system.

B.2.2 Perform Requirements Engineering

This task encompasses all the issues and questions we discussed at length above. Here you should analyze in detail the goals and constraints in preparation for building the detailed project plan, briefing upper management, and synthesizing various candidate architectures. The system requirements at this stage should reflect inputs received from the intended users.

You should determine any network-specific building constraints affecting your system. You should survey the sites and consult the appropriate facilities personnel regarding the structure of the building, the location of wiring closets, existing conduits, fire protection partitioning, existing cable infrastructure, and telecommunications on-premise equipment. If you need permits for facility changes, it is a good idea to inquire at this time regarding the procedure and cost for doing so.

Also, at each site, you should take inventory of the hosts and existing interface equipment, if any, that you will have to connect to your system. You should also create the User Requirements Database and initialize it with the inventory data you gather. You should also interview prospective users in order to compile their functional wish list.

B.2.3 Develop Project Plan

Once you understand the goals and constraints and document them appropriately, you can plan the project. To facilitate this, you should create a work breakdown structure, determine your budget requirements, lay out a schedule of tasks, and estimate the kind and number of personnel resources you will need. We discuss these items in more detail below.

B.2.3.1 The WBS

Developers of large, complex systems often use a work breakdown structure, or WBS when planning the development project. The WBS helps you decompose the system, or product, into manageable units consisting of major subsystems and components. It facilitates the allocation of budget, personnel, and tasks to each of the major subsystems and helps ensure that you don't overlook anything. Figure B-2 illustrates a sample WBS that is tailored to the construction of an Internet clone.

B.2.3.2 Budget

As soon as you have a good overview of the size and complexity of the system to be built—based on the WBS—you are now in a position to estimate the total budget required. Most of

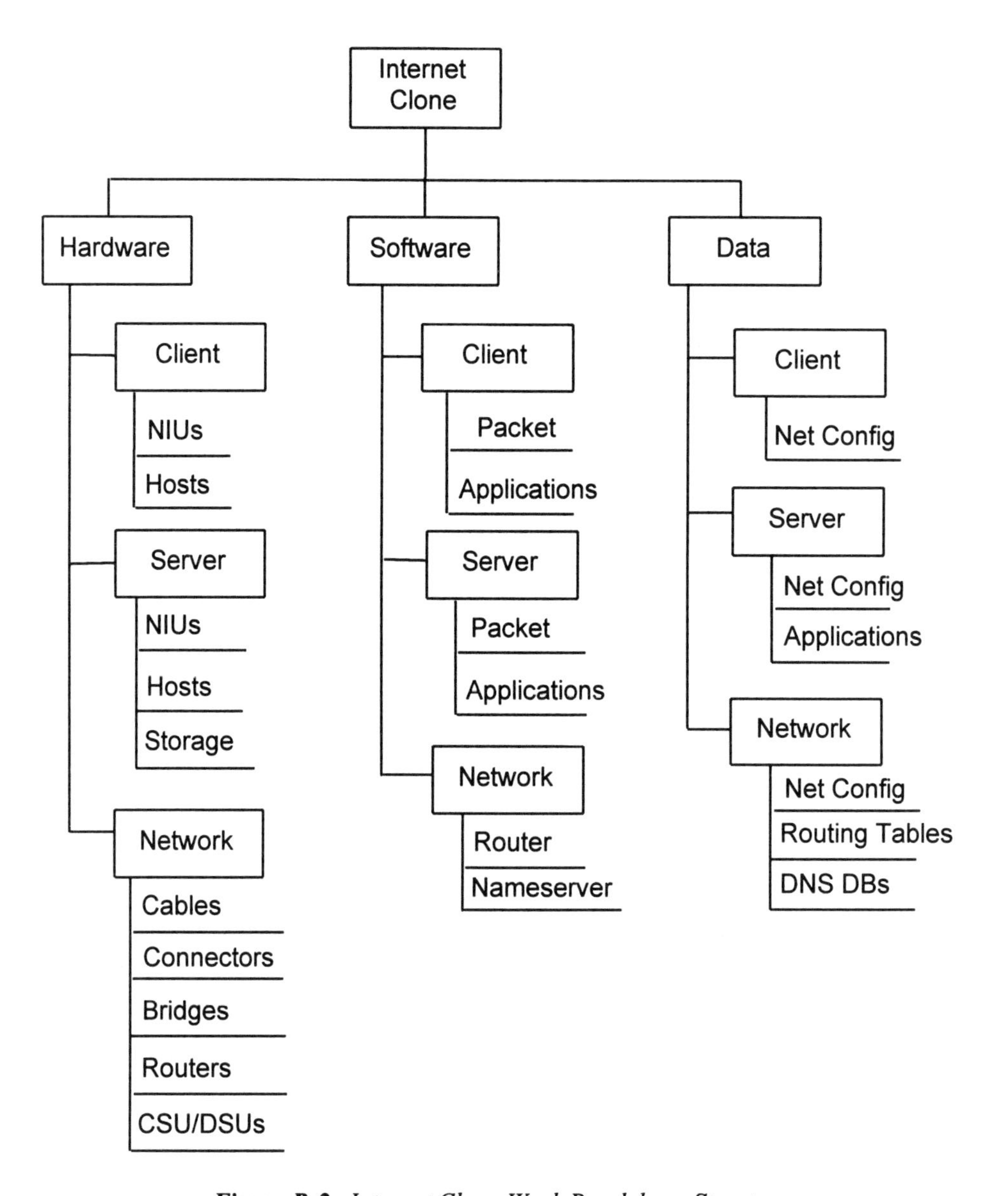

Figure B-2. *Internet Clone Work Breakdown Structure*

the budget will consist of the labor to develop and install the clone. Fortunately, you can realize major savings by using freeware available from the Internet for client, server, and network software. Otherwise, software development costs for custom software can contribute significantly to the overall cost of the system.

Be sure not to overlook the importance of the Data component of the system. (See the WBS in Figure B-2.) This is where the real content of the system resides. The rest of the system is for the most part a means to deliver the data to the user. The data is what the user is after. You should be sure to allocate an adequate number of budget hours to locating, compiling, indexing, and organizing the data.

Finally, you should be sure to remember that in addition to the nonrecurring engineering development of the system, there will be significant recurring costs as well. Internet access is one example, and it usually carries a fixed monthly cost. Managing the network and maintaining the data sources are important drivers of recurring cost. An inadequate budget allocated to keeping the information content up to date will result in users shunning your system as a repository of stale data.

B.2.3.3 Schedule

After identifying the components of your system and the tasks to build them, you need to schedule the project tasks. We advise that you use a robust project management software package for this. Claris's MacProject for the Macintosh, Microsoft's Project, and AMS's Schedule/Publisher are all adequate for this purpose. These tools can help you identify the critical path of tasks in your project. They can also help you determine when you will need key project personnel.

B.2.3.4 Resources

Using your project management software, you can identify the kinds and number of personnel needed by your project. The resource requirements can be rolled-up, summarized, and forwarded to your functional or personnel managers.

B.2.4 Brief to Management and Obtain Go-Ahead

At this point you should have a pretty good idea of the basic requirements of your project. It is now time to brief upper management on your project plan to secure sponsorship and buy-in. If you cannot meet your budget requirements, you may need to go back and revisit some of the previous tasks in order to downscope the system and the project.

B.2.5 Synthesize and Evaluate Alternative Solutions

We have already dealt with this subject in the first part of this appendix and in Chapter 6. To reiterate, the task here is to translate the functional architecture in several candidate physical architectures, evaluate the alternatives, and select the best one.

B.2.6 Develop Test Plans and Procedures

Once you know the physical architecture, you should commence the development of test plans and procedures. Again, your WBS should be your guide. You should plan to separately test each individual piece of hardware and software. You should test in depth the first article installations of representative configurations (e.g., client/server pairs), but subsequent repeat installations need less detailed testing.

You should test major subsystems as you integrate them. You need to plan for this incremental integration testing. Finally, you should plan for full system acceptance testing. Security systems, in particular, need extra special attention.

To facilitate the development of performance test data, use network simulation software.

At this point the emphasis is more on the plans than the procedures. Although some of the detailed procedural information will have to wait until vendor equipment shows up and you have downloaded software from the Internet, you can document at this time the initial procedural framework.

B.2.7 Develop Security Policies, Plans, and Procedures

It is a good time to begin developing and documenting the security policies that will govern the use and operation of your system. Feedback from the user community is helpful. Of crucial importance are contingency plans and procedures.

B.2.8 Develop Configuration Control Procedures

In building networks, it is easy to overlook the matter of configuration control. You need to identify and keep track of the system configuration, i.e., the version numbers of each major component in your system. You should establish procedures for updating both hardware and software. Also, you should develop procedures for troubleshooting the system.

B.2.9 Order Long-Lead Items

You should order early in the project some of the long-lead hardware, data, and service items, so that later tasks requiring these items can proceed on schedule.

B.2.9.1 Test Equipment

At this stage, you should order any specialized networking test equipment. These include multimeters, logic and protocol analyzers, and test equipment for cables and interface cards.

B.2.9.2 Internet Addresses

After determining the number of hosts that be part of your network, you need to contact the InterNIC to register your domain and reserve an adequate supply of IP addresses for the hosts on your system. This can take several weeks, so you need to initiate this well in advance of installing and deploying your system.

B.2.9.3 Telecom Access to Internet

You need to choose an Internet access provider and determine the kind of interface equipment you will need on your premises and at the provider's facilities. Working with your telecom provider, you should establish a dedicated tail circuit between your facility and that of your Internet access provider. Many Internet access providers find themselves swamped with requests for connections these days, and you will probably need to allow several weeks for installation and setup of your Internet connection.

B.2.9.4 Hardware and Software

You should order from your vendors any specialized hardware like CSU/DSUs, NIUs, routers, bridges, cables, connectors, workstations, and servers.

Likewise, you need to identify and purchase the appropriate software from vendors or download it from the Internet (in the case of freeware).

B.2.10 Generate Detailed Documentation

You should elaborate the details in system design documentation. Adequate diagrams need to be available to all those involved in helping you implement the system. Strict configuration control on this documentation will help ensure that everyone in "singing from the same sheet of music."

B.2.11 Train Network and System Managers

You should adequately train your network managers and system administrators. Many vendors offer training sessions at their facilities. For example, router manufacturer Cisco Systems has several training classes designed to familiarize network managers with the operation of their routers. Many consulting firms and Web software developers like Netscape Communications offer training in Web authoring.

If you plan to install some UNIX servers and you do not already have UNIX system administrators available, you should send prospective administrators for your system to a crash course in UNIX system administration. They should learn not only the basic UNIX commands but also the techniques of shell programming. We recommend that they learn to program in Perl, since there are many freeware Perl scripts available for interfacing Web servers with other programs like WAIS and relational database engines.

B.2.12 Install and Test Cable System

When the hardware and test equipment associated with the cable system shows up, you should begin wringing it out. This means end-to-end electrical testing of the cables to make sure there are no breaks anywhere along the line. You should also test all the connectors. Then you should install the cabling system and test it once more to make sure you haven't damaged cables and connectors in the process. Using protocol analyzers, you can send test messages (e.g., Ethernet frames) down the line to ensure that network devices can adequately receive and interpret messages. You can also measure collision and error rates and stress test the cabling with simulated high volume traffic.

B.2.13 Install and Test Telecom Links for Internet Access

Once the CSU/DSU and dedicated WAN routers arrive, you can install them and test the Internet connection. A simple client PC at your end is adequate to verify that you have full access to Internet servers. You can use test programs like *traceroute* and *ping* to verify the routing and bandwidth provided by your Internet access provider.

B.2.14 Install and Test Routers and Network Interface Hardware

Within your internal network you should now install both routers and network interface hardware. This requires that you install interface cards in all client and server hosts throughout your system. The time it takes to do this depends, naturally, on the number of network devices, so allow adequate time in your schedule.

B.2.15 Install and Test IP Packet Driver Software

After you install the cards, you should install and configure the IP driver software. This means initializing the underlying packet driver software and Winsock with IP addresses for the local host, nameservers, and router or gateways.

You can test these installations by using a small client program with a DNS nameserver.

B.2.16 Install and Test Server Applications Software

Before installing any applications servers, you should first install Domain Name System nameservers. You can then use these to test the client installations outlined in the previous task. After the nameservers, you should begin installing and testing the applications software for various services like WAIS, NNTP, HTTP, FTP, and gopher.

B.2.17 Populate Servers with Data

You should populate your applications servers with quality data soon after installing the server software itself. Failure do this will result in users forming a low opinion of your system, since they will inevitably try to connect to your servers and discover that "the lights are on, but nobody's home." To mitigate the risk of this happening, you can defer the installation of client software until the next task. However, there are always those savvy users out there who will be one step ahead of you and will install client software on their own and try out the system before you can "officially" install the software. Therefore, it is best to have your servers already populated with bona fide data.

B.2.18 Install and Test Client Applications Software

Install and test the client applications software. For one representative or first article installation, you should test very thoroughly, verifying that all features are indeed functioning correctly. Then you can proceed with the full production installation, verifying only briefly at each client station that you can connect to the appropriate server.

B.2.19 Perform System Acceptance Testing

The final step before turning users loose on your system is to perform a full system acceptance test. It is good here to select a random client from each of the subnets you've built and to verify that this sample client can connect to each of the servers you've made available internally, and a few external Internet servers, if you plan to have direct access to the Internet from the desktop.

B.2.20 Deploy and Operate the System

You should announce to users and upper management that they can now use your system. Throw a party for your project team, for they have achieved a major milestone. However, your work is not over, since now you have to make sure that your system continues to provide reliable service and make quality information available to users. Congratulations! You've have successfully built an Internet clone!

INDEX

—K—

—L—

—M—

—T—

—U—

—V—

—W—

—Y—